Dear Iletra

HOW IS MY DRIVING?
MOTIVATIONAL TIPS FOR SUCCESS IN BUSINESS AND LIFE

Enjoy

[signature]

Larry O'Sullivan

authorHOUSE®

AuthorHouse™ UK Ltd.
1663 Liberty Drive
Bloomington, IN 47403 USA
www.authorhouse.co.uk
Phone: 0800.197.4150

Published by AuthorHouse   06/12/2014

ISBN: 978-1-4918-9465-1 (sc)
ISBN: 978-1-4918-9468-2 (hc)
ISBN: 978-1-4918-9469-9 (e)

Library of Congress Control Number: 2014903059

CONTENTS

"Anytime a thought, sentence

or paragraph inspires you

or opens your thinking,

you need to capture it

like a butterfly in a net

and later release it into

your own field of consciousness."

—Steve Chandler

Introduction

Driving on the roads anywhere in the world these days can be quite an arduous experience, as one can encounter many challenges (such as potholes, unattended animals, cyclists, jaywalkers, traffic that comes to a standstill, and then those motorists who have no respect for the rules of the road or their fellow motorists).

It was during one of those gridlock traffic situations that I happened to find myself behind a vehicle with a rear-end bumper sticker that read, *"How is My Driving?"* The more I sat frustrated in the traffic, the more I realized the importance of these four words and what impact they have—not only in terms of our control of a motor vehicle but in our businesses and our personal lives—every day.

You see, everything you do in life gets measured in some way. If you go on a diet then you are quick to establish how many kilograms you are losing, or if you are an athlete, training for a specific event, then you monitor your times in order to determine whether you are improving or not. People will react in some way to how, why, and what you did or didn't do. You may be criticized, condemned, praised, or honoured. You could go from zero to hero in one day, so always be at your best, do your best, and watch your values, words, and actions.

How Is My Driving? is a wonderful concept that brings the responsibility back to you. Now it's time you stop and smell the roses and take stock on how you personally are faring and to either stop, start, add to, or change the way that you do things.

You can do this by substituting the word "driving" with the following words: "service", "listening", "communication", "leadership", "attitude", "goals", and "ambitions". This will give you a clue as to how you are performing in each category. You can continue substituting as many words as possible and continue to measure your capabilities in each area of your life or business career.

It was this concept that inspired me to take the "soft skills", experiences, and qualities required to achieve success in life, sport, sales, service, or business in general and weave these into a web of simple, tried and tested, success stories. This is what this book is all about. It's a combination of analogies, quotes, humorous tales, and largely true-life, inspirational stories that have a profound message and moral.

Most of these stories are already out there in the universe, recognized and told by fellow authors and motivational speakers. What I have done is to capture these wonderful insights into one all-inspiring book with various motivational themes. These themes, which hold the key to achieving success in business and life, are already part and parcel of your daily lives . . . but are you using the various attributes and concepts advocated in each chapter to your advantage?

The book is designed in such a way that you can merely open it at any page or select a specific topic that may interest you. It's my humble wish, however, that you do in fact read it from cover to cover. I am extremely excited about this book, and I hope you can identify with the array of stories presented; they have been included in the hope that they will speak directly to your heart and mind.

In conclusion, I would like to thank my wife, Kathy, for vetting and editing the material contained in this book and my colleague Razanne Kamaar for her support and help in preparing the groundwork for *How is My Driving?*

1   Attitude

1.1. Attitude is a choice

1.1.1. To have a positive or negative attitude? The choice is yours!

"A healthy attitude is contagious but don't wait to catch it from others. Be a carrier."

—anonymous

Author and keynote speaker Chick Mooran tells a story in one of his books about a teacher who got her fourth-grade students to write all the things they could not do on a piece of paper, for example, "I can't do ten press-ups."

The teacher then put all the lists in a shoebox and with a spade proceeded outside, dug a hole, and buried the "I can't lists" in this hole. She then proceeded to read a eulogy to the class:

> **Friends, we are gathered here today to honour the memory of "I Can't". While he was on Earth, he touched the lives of everyone, some more than others. His name, "I Can't", unfortunately has been spoken in every public place, school, office, hospital, and government building. We have provided "I Can't" with his final resting place and a headstone holding an epitaph:**
>
> *He is survived by his brothers and sisters,*
> *I Can, I Will, and I'm Going to Do That Right Away.*
> *They are not as well-known as their relative*
> *and are certainly not as strong and powerful yet.*

Attitude is a choice. Choose to be positive. It's got to come from within you. It must spurt forth from the core of you. It's got to be in your entire fibre, for it's not enough to only think positively; you need to act positively, and you need to speak positively. Your words and actions are just as important as your thoughts. Your actions and words must complement your thoughts.

You need to demonstrate to all and sundry that you are practising what you preach, that you are not just "all talk and no action", and that you are not just paying lip service to some ideal.

It is time to rise up and see and do things differently. It just takes a different, positive, and determined mindset or effort. Dr Wayne Dyer summed this up succinctly when he said, "Circumstances do not make a man, they reveal him." So have a positive attitude, but don't only think positively . . . speak and act positively.

1.1.2. Same circumstances—different attitude

"When attitude is right, there is no barrier too high, no valley too deep, no dream too extreme, and no challenge too great for you."

—Charles Swindoll

Two workers were approached by a TV reporter. In response to the reporter's question the first worker, a bricklayer, talked of himself in his role as, "An underpaid, bored, slave, spending my days wasting my time, placing one brick on top of another."

The second worker, also a bricklayer, gave the following answer to a similar question asked by the reporter. "I'm the luckiest person in the world. I get to be part of the beautiful pieces of architecture being built."*

What a different mindset between two parties in the same trade. The funny thing is that they are both being truthful in their answers—it's just attitude, passion for work, and outlook in life that separates each worker.

One of the truths in life is *that we see in life what we want to see.* If you look for faults in someone or the world—you will certainly find them. But the opposite is also true. If you look for the extraordinary in the ordinary you can train yourself to see it.

Take extraordinary care to cultivate your attitude. Make it a strong, positive, success-driven, and purpose-fulfilled attitude. Make it contagious, vibrant, and zealously sought after. You are the boss of your attitude. You hold all the power.

*Source: L. O'Sullivan, Client Service Excellence; The 10 commandments (Johannesburg: Knowledge Resources, 2010). (Page 145-146)

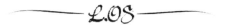

1.1.3. It's not what happens to you, it's what you do about it

"I am in charge of my own spaceship . . . it's my up, my down. I could choose to see this situation as a setback or a starting point."
—William ("Bill") Mitchell

By age forty-six Bill Mitchell, a former marine, was burned beyond recognition in a motorbike accident. In fact, he had sixteen surgeries where skin grafts were employed over approximately 65 per cent of his body. He couldn't eat with a fork, dial a telephone, or go to the bathroom without help.

Six months later he was piloting a plane again. Later, he bought a house, his own plane, and, with two friends, he co-founded a wood-burning stove company that grew to be Vermont's second largest private employer. Then, four years after the motorcycle accident, the plane he was piloting crashed back on to the runway, leaving him permanently paralyzed from the waist down.

Undaunted, Bill worked day and night in order to regain some independence. He went on to be elected mayor of Crested Butte, Colorado, got married, became a millionaire, a respected public speaker, did white water rafting, skydiving, and ran for political office.*

Bill Mitchell overcame severe adversity, not once but twice. After the first crash one could admire Bill Mitchell's attitude, determination, courage, and will to lead a near normal life. Then the second crash leaves him paralyzed. No one would blame Bill if he just gave up and felt sorry for himself. But, no, not Bill. What a remarkable story and testimony to his strength of character and an inspiration to us all.

To fully understand his powerful zest for life, take comfort from his message, and may his words live in your heart.

> *Before I was paralyzed there were 10 000 things I could do. Now there are 9000. I can either dwell on the 1000 I lost OR focus on the 9000 I have left. I tell people I had two big bumps in life. If I have chosen not to use them as an excuse to quit, then maybe some of the experiences you are having which are pulling you back can be put in a new perspective. You can step back, take a wider view and have a chance to say, "Maybe that isn't such a big deal after all."**

*Source: One of the Chicken Soup for the Soul books: M. V. Hansen and J. Canfield, Chicken Soup for the Soul (Florida; HCI, date unknown).

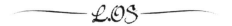

1.1.4. Are you a pessimist or an optimist?

"Nothing of any importance has ever been accomplished by a pessimist."
—Jack Welsh

There is a story about a set of identical twins who happened to be a pessimist and an optimist. The worried parents decided to take their children to a psychologist who gave them instructions to see, once and for all, their true nature, so they could decide which twin needed the most attention.

On their next birthday they put the twins in separate rooms to open their presents. The optimist was given a box full of manure. The pessimist was given the best toys and gifts—a computer, a toy car, and dozens of expensive items. When the pessimist opened his gifts he was crestfallen. His parents couldn't understand it, but when they asked him why, he explained that he felt sure he wouldn't understand all the functions of the computer and that his friend would have a better toy car than him.

The optimist child, on the other hand, was thrilled with his huge box of manure. His parents again couldn't

understand this emotion and asked him why the gift could possibly please him. He grinned from ear to ear, and he responded, "If there is this much manure, that must mean I have a pony."

Someone once said that our lives are not determined by what happens to us but by how we react to what happens. That is, our lives are not defined by what life brings to us but by the attitude we bring to life. It's certainly true in this message from Jack Welsh: "*Nothing of any importance has ever been accomplished by a pessimist.*"

A positive attitude causes a chain reaction of positive thoughts, events, and outcomes. It's a catalyst—a spark—that creates extraordinary results. What an outlook to have in life or in business. Be an optimist.

1.2. Attitude is contagious

1.2.1. Your attitude not only affects you . . . but everyone around you

"You cannot tailor make the situations in life but you can tailor make the attitudes to fit those situations."

—Zig Ziglar

Recently, I stopped by a convenience store to get a newspaper and a pack of gum. The young woman at the checkout counter said, "That'll be five dollars please," and as I reached into my wallet, the thought occurred to me that a newspaper and gum didn't quite make it to five dollars. When I looked up to get a "re-quote", she had a big smile on her face and said, "Gotcha! I got to get my tip in there somehow!" I laughed when I knew I'd been had.

She then glanced down at the paper I was buying and said, "I'm sick and tired of all this negative stuff on the front pages. I want to read some good news for a change." She then said, "In fact, I think someone should just publish a Good News newspaper—a paper with wonderful,

inspirational stories about people overcoming adversity and doing good things for others. I'd buy one every day!"

The following day after my business appointments, I dropped by the same store again to pick up bottled water, but a different young lady was behind the counter. As I checked out I said, "Good afternoon," and I handed her my money for the water. She said nothing—not a word, not a smile . . . nothing. She just handed me my change and in a negative tone, ordered, "Next!"*

This is a tale of two young ladies, probably about the same age, doing the same type of work but with completely different attitudes to their work and clients. One made this man feel great, and the other, that he had inconvenienced her by showing up.

One of the most wonderful things about having a positive attitude is the number of people it touches, many times in ways you'll never know. This point is so well illustrated in the above excerpt from the chapter entitled *"The Good News Girl"—from the book Power of Attitude by Mac Anderson.*

It's a wonderful illustration that the choices we make and the attitudes we exhibit have a huge impact on our outlook in life. But it doesn't end there; outlook also plays a massive role in influencing the lives and attitudes of the people around us, whether on a daily or an hourly basis, either in a positive or negative way.

Attitudes are contagious.

*Source: M. Anderson, The Power of Attitude (Edinburgh; Thomas Nelson, 2004).

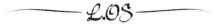

1.2.2. That what we sow, so shall we reap

"People are always blaming their circumstances for what they are. I don't believe in circumstances. The people who get on in this world are the people who get up and look for the circumstances they want, and if they can't find them, they make them."

—George Bernard Shaw

A parable of the farmer who has two seeds in his hand; one is a seed of corn, the other is nightshade, a deadly poison. He digs two little holes in the earth and he plants both seeds—one corn, the other nightshade. He covers up the holes, waters, and takes care of the land . . . and what do you think will happen?

Invariably, the land will return what was planted.

The land gives the farmer a choice; he may plant in that land whatever he chooses. The land doesn't care. It's up to the farmer to make the decision, and the land will return to the farmer what he has sown—what you sow, so shall you reap.

In the same manner, we can compare the human mind to that of the land, and just as the land doesn't care what you plant in it (for it will return what you plant) the mind will also manifest whatever thoughts, ideas, or knowledge it has been fed. It will not discriminate between race and gender, wealth or poverty, positive or negative, good or bad—but it will be concerned with whatever food it receives.

Think positively, act positively, and live positively. What you sow, so shall you reap.

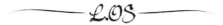

1.2.3. Change your woe to a wow!

"If you only walk on sunny days, you will never reach your destination."
—Paulo Coelho

Author Rob White has written an interesting article "Five Proven, Successful & Motivation Tips to Age Backwards" wherein he advocates that we change our WOE (that is an acronym standing for What on Earth), which consists of finding fault and passing blame, to a WOW (that means Wonderfully Obsessed with Winning).*

WOW is that frame of mind that motivates you to do your best. WOW is that comment that stops people in their tracks to hail something different, special, and unique.

While it's difficult to rid the WOE immediately, you can minimize the presence of WOE and focus more on the WOW. The trick is to consciously opt for WOW, so it will manifest as a positive WOW habit, a WOW way of life.

A person with a WOW attitude will see every day as sunny. They don't depend on the weather; they bring sunshine with them. They have the magnetism to chase those dark or stormy clouds away. A WOW attitude is contagious.

Source: Rob White, Five Proven, Successful and Motivational Tips to Age Backwards <http:// www.selfgrowth.com/ . . . /five-proven-successful-motivational-ways-to-age-backwards> date posted unknown, date last accessed 19 May 2014

1.3. Attitude—the way you look at things

1.3.1. Our perceptions define our attitude

"The doors we open and close each day decide the lives we live."

—Flora Whittemore

One day a father of a rich family took his son on a trip to the country with the firm purpose of showing him how poor people can be. They spent a day and a night on the farm of a very poor family. When they got back from their trip, the father asked his son, "How was the trip?"

"Very good, Dad!" was the son's retort.

"Did you see how poor people can be?" the father asked.

The son answered, "I saw that we have a dog at home, and they have four. We have a pool that reaches to the middle of the garden; they have a creek that has no end. We have imported lamps in the garden; they have the stars. Our patio reaches to the front yard; they have a whole horizon." When the little boy was finished, his father was speechless. His son added, "Thanks, Dad, for showing me how 'poor' we are!"*

The above story is a prime example of how perceptions and mindset affect a person's attitude to an event, circumstance, job, or adventure. Simply put, it all depends on the way you look at things.

So it's important to appreciate the bigger picture and finer things in life instead of having tunnel vision and being negative.

*Source:—"One day a father of a rich family took his son on a trip." <http://paulocoelhoblog.com/2014/02/28/how-poor-we-are/> date last accessed 13 May 2014

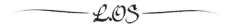

1.3.2. The 212 degrees concept

"There are two types of people that don't achieve much in their life time. One is the person who does not do what he/she is told to do, and the other is the person who does no more than he or she is told to do."

—Andrew Carnegie

At 211 degrees Fahrenheit (or 99 degrees Celsius) water is hot, hot hot . . . but not boiling. By increasing the temperature by 1 degree from 211 to 212 degrees, water boils, and with boiling water, comes steam.

And with steam one can power a locomotive. It's that one extra degree that . . . *makes all the difference.**

The 212 degrees concept is one of the most profound concepts for improving certain aspects of our life: our attitudes, leadership skills, respect for others, service ethos, communication abilities, and so forth. The idea, which originated with Sam Parker, is simple, versatile, and unforgettable and, yet, so important. It's easy and practical to understand. It doesn't ask for miracles or earth-shattering changes or commitment—just a small mindset change: just one degree.

And so many times it's that one extra degree of effort in business and in life that separates the good from the great and gets you from mediocre to successful.

*Source: S. L. Parker with M. Anderson, 212; The Extra Degree—Illinois; Simple Truths 2006.

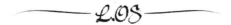

1.3.3. The computer concept

"All personal achievement starts in the mind of the individual. Your personal achievement starts in your mind. The first step is to know exactly what your problem, desire or goal is."

—W. Clement Stone

One day a young student was entering an enormous amount of data into his computer. He was working on a long and complicated question that required a great deal of concentration and input of numbers. He then hit the "enter" button and sat back to await the answer.

He was dumbfounded when the answer appeared within a second.*

The computer works much like a human brain; it takes every bit of data, gives it either a positive or negative electrical impulse, and then stores it away. In the same manner, before anything goes into our "mental" computer—before any sight, sound, taste, feel, or intuition gets stored in the brain—it's first stamped positively or negatively. That positive or negative sensation created is put away in our memory permanently.

All personal achievement starts in the mind, and so many experiences and perceptions are engraved in our memory banks. We are the programmers of our computer, and we alone can change the data or re-program the software. So pay attention to what you are feeding into your computer, as it will merely return what has been stored.

Train your mind to see the good and positive things in life and to get rid of those negative, conditioned responses.

*Source: Adapted from a similar story in: J. Osteen, Become a Better you—7 keys to improving your life every day (London; Simon & Schuster, 2007).

1.3.4. The very old lady

"If you don't like something, change it. If you can't change it, change your attitude."

—Maya Angelou

A very old lady looked in the mirror one morning. She had three remaining hairs on her head, and, being a positive soul, she said, "I think I'll braid my hair today." So she braided her three hairs, and she had a great day.

Some days later, looking in the mirror one morning, preparing for her day, the old lady saw that she had only two hairs remaining. "Hmm, two hairs . . . I fancy a centre parting today." She duly parted her two hairs, and, as ever, she had a great day.

A week or so later, she saw that she had just one hair left on her head. "One hair, huh," she mused. "I know: A ponytail will be perfect." And again she had a great day.

The next morning she looked in the mirror. She was completely bald.

"Finally bald, huh," she said to herself. "How wonderful! I won't have to waste time doing my hair any more . . ."*

Very often in life you may find that your situation has more to do with your outlook on it than the actual circumstances. Your perception or attitude of these particular circumstances plays mind games with you, so please ensure that your focus and thinking is not too narrow and that things are considered from all aspects.

Maya Angelou is correct: If you don't like it, change it. If you can't change it, change your attitude.

*Source:—Positive Attitude-CiteHr Community insights, CiteHr-CiteHr Human Resource Management <http://www.citehr.com/426051-positive-attitude.html> accessed 22 May 2014

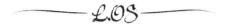

1.3.5. Are our perceptions our reality?

"The thoughts we choose to think are the tools we use to paint the canvas of our lives."

—Louise Hay

There is an opening scene in the movie **Love Hurts** where a widower and self-help author arrives in **Seattle** to talk to a "sold-out" seminar of people who have lost someone close to them. He then takes a group of them out on to a busy road, stopping traffic, and he asks the members of the group to take a moment, look around, and tell him what they see or hear.

The answers are varied and range from honking horns, sirens, cars, stop-lights, and homeless people to irate drivers.

He then takes them up on to the roof top of a high-rise building across the street from the earlier experiment and again asks them the same question, "What do you see or hear?" This time the answers are quite different—the ocean, skyscrapers, trees, the sun, and beautiful rivers.

He then addresses the group with the following quote:

"It's very different up here, isn't it? Yet it's the same. We haven't gone anywhere. We haven't left the city or the street to find these better sights, vision, or outcomes. We are just looking at things from a new perspective. Inside each of you there are sirens, honking horns, gridlock traffic, homeless people . . . but there is also all of this [pointing to the beautiful ocean, rivers, trees, the sun, and skyscrapers]. You just have to do the work and climb the stairs to find it."

What a profound message and way to express the concept of one's perception, mindset, and attitude to life. So often we react to our perception of things, events, or people that they become our reality.

The questions we now need to consider are the following: How accurate and reliable are our perceptions? What if we don't like the reality we have created? Don't let your thoughts or preconceived ideas become the tool with which you will paint the canvas of your life. Look for a fresh perspective.

Gaining a fresh perspective isn't easy—there are times when, no matter how hard you try, things don't go your way. This is when you need to stop, take a step back, and look at things from a different angle. In so doing, don't be too rigid in your pattern and don't be scared to network or talk to others. They may just have the right advice or guidance for you.

*Source: Adapted from Love Hurts, dir. Barra Grant (2009), starring Richard E Grant and Carrie Anne Moss.—Pageant Productions

1.4. A can-do attitude

1.4.1. Keep the balloons inflated

"Our attitude towards life determines life's attitude towards us."

—John N. Mitchell

A few years ago my son turned twenty-one, and I hired the hall at our local sports club to accommodate family and friends at this special occasion. Part of my responsibility was the decoration of the hall, and I had to oversee to the blowing up and arrangement of the balloons. I must say my team of volunteers did an excellent job, and the hall looked a real picture, as though done by professional organizers.

The next morning began the tedious task of cleaning up after the festivities. What really struck me was how the decor had changed in a period of less than a day. The balloons were already losing their shape, some sagging

more than others. They were looking tired and defeated, no more bobbing on their strings.

Yet, all one had to do was to blow into the balloons to re-inflate them, and they would look the same as the day before—fresh, radiant, and energized.

The same principle would apply to our attitude and passions in life. Every day we start with the best of intentions, but, similar to the balloons, we start to leak slowly. We start to run out of "gas", our enthusiasm wanders, and our attitudes tend to change, especially if we become tired and irritable.

All is not lost. Just as we can replenish those balloons to give them a fresh new appeal, so too can we breathe new life into our thought processes and actions; we can re-vitalize our attitude and re-flame our passions. Don't let your balloons leak for any length of time—keep your balloons inflated.

1.4.2. Word power—life power

"If an egg is broken by an outside force . . . life ends. If an egg breaks from within . . . life begins."

—anonymous

Vernon Howard tells in one of his books of a man who had fifteen steps leading to his garden. He walked up and down these steps many times during the day, but, instead of complaining, the man used his imagination to foster his self-development.

Each step was renamed after a "quality" to improve his life. Hence, as he ascended or descended the steps, he reflected on a specific quality within his life: patience, optimism, having a positive attitude, listening . . .

Perhaps we can learn from this man's mindset, attitude, and innovative process. We can even use this process in our workplace or life and substitute the "stairs" for the virtues within our business or personal world environment, for example, communication, leadership, mentoring, passion, trust, teamwork, and relationship-building.

So don't take the elevator—take the stairs and enhance the quality of your skills to face your daily chores.

1.4.3. The Bethany Hamilton story

"Life is like Facebook. People will like your problems and comment, but no one will solve them because everyone is busy updating their own."

—anonymous

Bethany Hamilton began her career as a surfer with her first competition at the age of eleven. By the age of thirteen, she was riding the waves at the top of her sport. Her lifelong dream was to become a professional surfer.

But on 31 October 2003 that dream was nearly shattered when she was attacked by a 14-foot tiger shark while surfing in Hawaii. Calmly, she pushed the pain aside and began to paddle with one arm. Getting to the beach was her only thought. She was rushed to hospital, and after surgery the first thing Bethany asked was, "When can I surf again?"*

The attack left Bethany with a severed arm but did not destroy her eagerness to keep riding the waves, and she continued to surf with one arm. The movie *Soul Surfer*, based on her ordeal and featuring Bethany in the water, is testimony to her courage, faith, and strength of character.

In fact, the shark attack just made her stronger and more competitive, and she is a fine example when it comes to a can-do attitude and being an inspiration to others. Bethany has chosen to use her experience to help others to overcome difficulties.

So when you are having a bad day reflect on the first thought Bethany had following her surgery—"When can I surf again?" Have a can-do attitude!

*Source: B. Hamilton, *Soul Surfer: A true story of faith, family and fighting to get back on the board* (New York; MTV books, 2004).

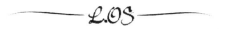

1.5. Death to negativity

1.5.1. My dog can walk on water

"The only disability in life is a bad attitude."

—Ewan Rob

There was a hunter who had a special breed of "bird dog". The dog was the only one of its kind, as it could walk on water. One day he invited a friend to go hunting with him so that he could show off his prized possession. After some time, they shot a few ducks, which fell into the river. The man ordered his dog to run and fetch the birds. The dog ran on water to fetch the birds. The man was expecting a compliment about the amazing dog, but he did not receive it.

Being curious, he asked his friend if the friend had noticed anything unusual about the dog. The friend replied, "Yes, I did see something unusual about your dog. Your dog can't swim!"*

Every day we have to face, work with, or even live with people who display more negative tendencies than positive ones. They are always complaining, criticizing, and dredging up all the negatives in life. They are the world champions in spreading fear, broadcasting gossip, or chasing people away; they choose to look at the hole in the middle rather than the whole doughnut.

One can't expect compliments or encouragement from them. These are the people who won't pull you out of your present situation but rather push you down or gossip about you. So be aware of them, spend less time with them, and do not let them steal your dreams away from you.

*Source: Inspirational Story-My Dog Can Walk On Water-CiteHR-CiteHr—(Citehr Community Insights), <http://www.citehr.com/31230-inspirational-story-my-dog-can-walk-water.html> accessed 20 May 2014

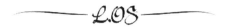

1.5.2. The frogs' story

"When everything seems to be going against you, remember that the airplane takes off against the wind, not with it."

—Henry Ford

Sometimes we can learn so much from fables, in particular the story below, which I have entitled "The Frogs' Story".

> Once upon a time there was a bunch of tiny frogs who arranged a running competition. The goal was to reach the top of a very high tower. A big crowd had gathered around the tower to see the race and cheer on the contestants.
>
> The race began, and, in all honesty, no one in the crowd really believed that any of the tiny frogs would reach the top of the tower. You heard statements like:
>
> "Oh, *way* too difficult!"
>
> "They will never make it to the top."
>
> "Not a chance that they will succeed. The tower is too high!"
>
> The tiny frogs began collapsing—one by one. That is, except for those frogs who, in a fresh tempo, were climbing higher and higher. The crowd continued to yell, "It is too difficult! No one will make it!"
>
> More tiny frogs got tired and gave up. However, one frog continued higher and higher and higher. This one wouldn't give up! At the end, every frog except for this one had given up climbing the tower, but this frog, after his big effort, reached the top!
>
> All of the other tiny frogs naturally wanted to know how this one frog had managed to do it.

A contestant asked the tiny frog how he had found the strength to succeed and reach the goal. It turned out . . . the winner was deaf!*

The wisdom this frog teaches us is to not to listen to people who have the tendency to be negative or pessimistic, as they can squash your most wonderful dreams. Their words have power, so everything you hear and read from these sources will affect your actions.

Be "deaf" to those who taunt and negatively goad you or your goals. Always remain positive and believe in yourself. Say to yourself, "I can do this!" And then go out and do it.

*Source: **Tiny Green Frogs Motivation Story—Global Home Exchange** <http://www.4homex.com/homeexchangemotivation.htm> accessed **15 May 2014**

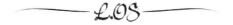

1.5.3. Regret City

"The difference between can and cannot is only 3 letters. Three letters that determine your life's direction."

—Remez Sasson

I had not really planned on taking a trip at this time of year, and yet I found myself packing rather hurriedly. This trip was going to be unpleasant, and I knew in advance that no real good would come of it. This is my annual "Guilt Trip".

I got tickets to fly there on "wish-I-had" airlines. It was an extremely short flight so I chose to carry my baggage with me all the way. It was loaded down with a thousand memories of "what may have been". No one greeted me as I entered the terminal to Regret City International Airport. I say "international" because people from all over the world come to this dismal town.

As I checked into Last Resort Hotel, I noticed that they would be hosting the year's most important event—the annual Pity Party. I wasn't going to miss that great social occasion. Many of the town's leading citizens would be there.

First, there would be the Done family—you know, Should Have, Would Have, and Could Have—and then would come the I Had family. You probably know old Wish and his clan. Of course, the Opportunities family would make an appearance; Missed and Lost would certainly be present. The biggest family there would be the Yesterdays.

There are far too many of them to count, but each one would have a very sad story to share. Of course, Shattered Dreams would surely make an appearance. Members of the It's Their Fault family would regale us with stories (excuses) about how things had failed in their life. Each story would be loudly applauded by the Don't Blame Me and I Couldn't Help It committees.

To cut a long story short, I went to this depressing party, knowing full well that there would be no real benefit in doing so. And, as usual, I became very depressed. But as I thought about all of the stories of failures brought back from the past, it occurred to me that this trip and subsequent "pity parties" *could* be cancelled by *me*!

I started to realize that I did not have to be there. And I didn't have to be depressed. One thing kept going through my mind: "I can't change yesterday, but I do have the power to make today a wonderful day." I can be happy, joyous, fulfilled, and encouraged, as well as being encouraging. Knowing this, I left Regret City immediately, and I didn't leave a forwarding address. Am I sorry for mistakes I've made in the past? *Yes*. But there is no way to undo them.

So, if you're planning a trip back to Regret City, please cancel all those reservations now. Instead, take a trip to a nice place called Starting Again. I like it so much that I made it my permanent residence. My neighbours, the Have Been Forgiven and the We're Saved are so very helpful. By the way, you don't have to carry around the heavy baggage anymore either. That load is lifted from your shoulders upon arrival. But don't take my word for it: Find out for yourself.*

*Source: Leaving the City of Regret-Inspirational Stories <http://www.inspirationalstories.com/3/314.html> accessed 19 May 2014

1.5.4. The burglar story

"You can conquer almost any fear, if you will only make up your mind to do so. For remember, fear only exists in the mind."

—Dale Carnegie

A wife always seemed to think that there were baddies prowling around the home. At least once a week she would wake her husband up, claiming that she was hearing the sounds of intruders downstairs. Time and time again the husband would get up, take his nine-iron golf club, and go hunt the ghost burglars down. This went on for months.

Finally, one night, she cried, "Get up . . . get up, there is somebody downstairs." The patient man got up and, as per his old routine, he took his golf club and proceeded to tread downstairs when suddenly he was confronted with a real burglar. A gun was pointed at his head.

"Don't make a sound," said the burglar. "Just give me all your money and valuables." The man handed over all his valuables, but just as the burglar was about to run off the patient man shouted, "No you can't go just yet. You have to come upstairs to meet my wife—she has been expecting you for months."

This amusing tale has a simple moral for us to consider. If we keep thinking negative thoughts or if our outlook is depressing and fearful then we are inviting trouble, and soon that spiral of "bad occurrences" will begin to manifest in our lives.

This is why the law of attraction and positivity is so powerful.

1.6. Overcoming adversity

1.6.1. Fences in the mind

"Men are not prisoners of fate, but prisoners of their own minds."

—Franklin D. Roosevelt

In the storyline of the movie Chicken Run there are a number of wonderful messages told through the eyes of a bunch of claymation chickens trying to break out of their chicken-wire world to escape their fate at the chopping block. Their freedom leader, a feisty little hen named Ginger, comments profoundly in one scene: "The fences are all in your mind."*

Ginger reminds her fellow chickens (and us) that a bigger obstacle than the physical fences they're surrounded by are the mental fences that hold them captive. The above message is a wonderful reminder for all of us that we have to face those invisible fences every day. Not only do we have to face these obstacles, but we have to master them; we have to be able to climb through them, over them, or even under them—it doesn't matter as long as we endure.

What are these "fences" of the mind? They are perhaps those thoughts that are created by self-doubt, uncertainty, fear, procrastination, or a bad habit. There are many variations of the things that hold us back, but the result is still the same: We stay stuck like the chickens in the movie.

Limitations live inside us, but the antidote to being trapped by our mental fences is to create a compelling enough vision to break out . . . and then to take action to the plan. These two ingredients—vision and action—will help eliminate those invisible fences in our minds.

Yes, it may take some bold, even outrageous, steps to break free, but it can be done. Ginger and her flock of chicken friends are willing to resort to amazing measures to break out. And it is good to remember that the mental fences are all in your mind! Change your mindset, and you will change your life.

*Source: Adapted from book: B Mahalik (2008) Living a five star Life: A path to greater joy and reaching your full potential. (Illinois, USA; Simple Truths, 2008)

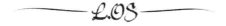

1.6.2. Broken or dislocated bones

"Everything can be taken from a man but one thing: the last of the human freedoms—to choose one's attitude in any given set of circumstances, to choose one's own way."

—Victor Frankl

Last year my niece Jenna ended up in hospital with a broken collarbone following a freak sporting accident. While she was undergoing corrective surgery to reset the fault, I sat in the waiting room with my sister. During that anxious time we witnessed quite a few patients being wheeled in and then out of theatre, some with visible casts or bandages to highlight the extent of their injuries. Others, the "walking wounded", hobbled around on crutches.

Sitting there with my sister got me thinking: If these people, all with broken or dislocated limbs, could be healed in a matter of weeks, then what about us—with our "broken spirits", disappointing events, or problems in our life, job, and/or family?

Those casts, slings, bandages, or even crutches are a physical sign of hope to take us from a "broken" or "dislocated" state to one of healing—from negativity and depression and feelings of being bored and uninspired to positivity, joy, peace, happiness, greater ambition, and passion.

Those casts, slings, bandages, and crutches are also a mental or emotional reminder to us that we have two choices—to remain "broken" and hurting or to take action and set goals and change one's beliefs and overcome those obstacles.

Aren't you tired of going through work or life with "broken bones or dislocated limbs"? If so, take some "X-rays", and see what's really broken or dislocated inside you. Remember that if one can fix broken bones or dislocated limbs in just a few weeks, surely one can change their outlook, thoughts, and beliefs in their life or work ethic in the same manner.

The mind is so powerful, so if we channel all our energy and faith in a positive direction, it can be done. Healings do occur and so do miracles—so don't give up. They may take a bit of time but they do happen. Life is too short to go around with "broken bones".

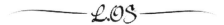

1.6.3. Stay positive—bloom among the weeds!

"When your desires are strong enough you will appear to possess superhuman powers to achieve."

—Napoleon Hill

Recently, my gardener, Washington, had to go back home to Zimbabwe to get his passport and papers sorted out. The process turned into weeks and, unfortunately, his timing coincided with the period that we received more than our average rainfall. Needless to say, our garden, including my wife's much loved rose bed, was soon overrun with weeds.

But despite the massive scale of weeds, the odd flower and rose stood tall, proudly, in full bloom, for all to see and admire.

The odd flower and rose stood there defiantly, colourfully, and majestically for all to see. Even though it was surrounded by weeds and overgrown vegetation, it did not succumb to its surroundings.

In like manner, you may be surrounded by problems, negativity, stress, and conflict, but that doesn't mean that you have accepted them into your life. You don't need to sink to that level. You may not be able to change people, events, or circumstances, but that doesn't mean you must change who you are or what you stand for. Don't give your power away. Don't let others drag you down, but rather see if you can lift them up.

Stay positive. As difficult as it may seem, you can bloom just where you are—even in a bed of weeds.

1.6.4. Your background need not determine who you become

"We are not creatures of circumstance; we are creators of circumstance."
—Benjamin Disraeli

Twin boys spent the first few years of their lives in an abusive household where their father drank and beat them often and generally kept them in a state of neglect. Eventually they were taken away and separately adopted and grew up to adulthood without meeting each other until they were in their thirties.

When they were united one had himself become an alcoholic who was abusive towards his family, but the other was a successful surgeon and a respected leader in the community with a healthy family who adored him.

When the boys were asked separately what it was that had pushed them to become the men they were, they both answered the same: "With my background, how else could I have turned out?"

The world is full of examples where people have overcome great adversity, bad childhood circumstances, and financial hardships, serving to prove that your background or underprivileged circumstances need not hold you ransom.

There is a world of opportunity out there waiting for you, so take your old negative surroundings by the throat and throttle those hang-ups to a proverbial death. Then breathe in new life, embrace new beginnings, and become a better you. Your background or handicaps need not determine who you are or what you become.

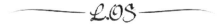

1.7. Attitude in the workplace

1.7.1. Are you proud of your job?

"Anyone who is in business is in show business."

—Robin Sharma

As I walked into the washroom, I was greeted by a young man with a 1,000 watt smile. His job was clearly to keep the place clean. Some would call him a janitor. But to me, he viewed himself as an inventor—innovating and iterating within his sphere of responsibility.

"Welcome to my office," he said with a sparkle in his eyes. "It's nice to have you visit." His uniform was impeccable. His counters were immaculate. His manners were superb. He could have made excuses to deny his enthusiasm. He could have complained about the base position, the lack of authority, and the limited power. But he didn't.

Instead, he assumed his power to influence all those he met, to have an impact on others by his excellent example, and to inspire all by transcending his conditions. This young man did his work like Rembrandt painted, Beckham bends the ball, and Columbus explored."*

The above is a true-life experience and conversation as witnessed by Robin Sharma during a speaking tour at a venue in Nelson Mandela Square, Sandton, Johannesburg.

Here is a living, real, and refreshing mindset that a job is not just a job unless viewed as just a job. There are no mundane jobs, only our perceptions of such functions. We have the choice; we can be proud of our job, or we can be ashamed of our daily work. We can see the benefits, add value, and make a unique contribution to the community or the business . . . or play the victim and wallow in the mire of job insecurity and unhappiness.

*Source: Adapted from: Lead where you are planted | Robin Sharma Blog <http://www.robinsharma.com/blog/06/lead-where-you-are-planted-2/> posted 20 January 2011, accessed 18 May 2014

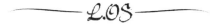

1.7.2. Hire attitude—then train them

"Attitude determines Altitude."

—Zig Ziglar

A senior executive of a very successful organization was once asked the following question, "With the service your people give, you must have a training manual 2 inches thick?" In response, he said, "We don't have a training manual. What we do is find the best people we can find, and we empower them to do whatever it takes to satisfy the customer."*

The above excerpt is based on the book *You Can't Take a Duck to Eagle School* (2007) by Mac Anderson. In this book Mac Anderson deals with a very interesting concept—that you can't teach someone to smile, you can't teach someone to want to serve, and you can't teach personality but what you can do, however, is hire people who have these qualities and then teach them all about your products, your culture, and values system and then, more importantly, how to serve your clients.

The trick is to hire attitude, and then mould and train your people to fulfil the role requirements.

*Source: excerpt based on: M. Anderson, You Can't Take a Duck to Eagle School (Illinois; Simple Truths, 2007).

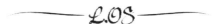

1.7.3. Are you in the right mood to serve or sell?

For unless my mood is right my day will be a failure. Trees and plants depend on the weather to flourish but I make my own weather. Yea, I transport it with me.

If I bring rain and gloom and darkness and pessimism to my customers, then they will react with rain and gloom and darkness and pessimism and purchase naught.

If I bring joy and enthusiasm and brightness and laughter they will react with joy and enthusiasm and brightness and laughter and my weather will produce a harvest of sales and a granary of gold for me.*

The above excerpt Mandino's book *The Greatest Salesman in the World* (1968) sums up the importance of our moods and how they affect the people around us. We are all susceptible to mood swings, and they have a big impact on our attitudes and how we approach each day. Just as sure as we are that the sun will rise and set each day, so, too, will our day be a day of highs and lows, good news and bad news, successes and failures. We need to take comfort in this fact, and do the best we can not to let our mood swings affect our love, relationship, and those around us—our family, friends, and clients.

Let's take it a step further. Are you in the right mood to serve or even sell to your clients? Are you positive, confident, and eager to do the business or are you stressed, intimidated, pessimistic, and/or overwhelmed? These emotions will have a definite influence with your meeting or contact with the client and the successful conclusion of your proposed business transaction with them.

No matter what job you do, which industry you are working in, or what your title is, you can change yourself, your life, your attitude, and, more importantly, your mood. Each morning you wake up the slate is clean. Now it's up to you how you are going to perform during the day.

If you master your moods, you master your destiny. And if you master your destiny you can only be successful in life. *Master your mood or emotions just for one day,* then do it again tomorrow for just one day. **

*Source: O. Mandino, The Greatest Salesman in the World (Hollywood: Frederick Fell, 1968).

**Source: L. O'Sullivan, Client Service Excellence-: The 10 Commandments (Johannesburg: Knowledge Resources, 2010). Page 205

1.7.4. Does attitude override knowledge in a job interview?

"Some people are more talented than others. Some people are more educationally privileged than others. But we all have the capacity to be great."
—philosopher Peter Koestenbaum

If you give me someone with the fire in the belly that needs guidance and polish, I can help. The more success you can help the person achieve, the more the fire tends

to grow. However, give me someone without fire in their belly, and I can't light it.

The above words were a response made by a chief executive officer (CEO) to a question posed to him as to why he chose one particular candidate over another. I can't recall the source, but I do know it made a huge impact on my outlook and approach when interviewing people for a job.

In essence, the article that included those words alluded to the recruitment process adopted by various companies and their senior executives, and a particular CEO of an organization was deciding between two candidates for an important position. The first candidate was described by his reference as polished, focused, and highly competent. However, no one had anything particular to say about his drive, energy, and need to achieve. The second candidate was also described as competent but as a "little rough around the edges" and as someone who "would need some coaching and direction". However, all three of the latter candidate's references described her as energetic, passionate, focused, and as willing to do whatever it takes to succeed. The CEO chose the second candidate.

This just goes to indicate that businesses will more than likely hire a candidate with a positive attitude and a strong drive over someone who just has strong business skills or knowledge. You can't teach attitude, passion, or service, but you can teach a person the skills to perform a job function.

2   Teamwork

2.1. Trust in teamwork

2.1.1. The circus analogy

"Great leaders are made by trusting followers."

—Brian Joffe

There is one event from my childhood that remains indelible in my memory banks: my first visit to the circus. This was an outing that took place more than forty-five years ago but, even today, I recall with awe that evening: the clowns, the jugglers, the trapeze artists, the lion and his tamer, and those high-flying, highly skilled, somersaulting acrobats.

Everything required precision in timing and communication, but, above all, everything required the synergy of the participants' trust and faith in one another.

This synergy of trust and faith is not restricted to the circus. It affects every area of our lives: our relationships, our work, and our characters. One of the core principles of teamwork is *trust*—trust for the leader and trust for one another.

Look around you, and determine how many examples you can find of people who require this very important ingredient of trust in their practise of teamwork: members of the police force, doctors, nurses, gymnasts, ice skaters, sports people, businesses, countries, and even partners in marriages. The list is endless.

What words or actions describe teamwork in your home, marriage, friendship, or organization? Would you include the word "trust" or a synonym of the word like "certainty", "belief", "accountability", faith", "confidence", or "reliance" in your description?

To have trust you have to earn trust.

2.1.2. Get in the wheelbarrow

"Together we stand, together we fall, together we win and winners take all."
—Temple College Volleyball Team

Upon completing a highly dangerous tightrope walk over Niagara Falls in appalling wind and rain, "The Great Zumbrati" was met by an enthusiastic supporter, who urged him to make a return trip, this time pushing a wheelbarrow, which the spectator had thoughtfully brought along.

The Great Zumbrati was reluctant, given the terrible conditions, but the supporter pressed him. "You can do it—I know you can," he urged.

"You really believe I can do it?" asked Zumbrati.

"Yes—definitely—you can do it," the supporter gushed.

"Okay," said Zumbrati, "Get in the wheelbarrow . . ."*

While humorous, the above tale also epitomizes the importance of trust and belief in our team or teammates. So often we sit on the sidelines and offer words of encouragement and support. We profess to be part of the team but don't really help or get involved. If something goes wrong, we are quick to point out that we were dead against the plan in the first place.

Teamwork requires 100 per cent commitment, support, loyalty, courage of conviction, belief, and trust—not a lukewarm association. What type of team player are you? Are you prepared to get into the wheelbarrow with your team or teammates?

*Source: Ric Willmot, Would the team you lead get in the wheelbarrow? Ric Willmot Blog <http://www.ricwillmot.com/index.php/2011/leadership-team-wheelbarrow/> posted 28 July 2011, accessed 2014

2.1.3. Don't have a team of "yes" men or women

"Co-operation isn't the absence of conflict but a means of managing conflict."
—Deborah Tannen

There is an old adage in the corporate world that when someone assumes a very senior position within a company, usually chairperson or CEO, they are reminded of these six words: "Watch how funny the jokes become!"

Sadly, anyone who has ever sat in the boardroom or in a team-build exercise with the leader of their organization will testify to this fact—where the room erupts with laughter when the boss tells a so-so joke.

It seems a fact that the higher up a person goes in an organization, the less honest is the element of direct, open feedback a person receives. People play the "protection" game—aiming to protect their jobs at any cost.

Feedback is usually sugar-coated, massaged, and varnished. One seldom hears of incidents where junior staff members knock on the door of their CEO to tell him or her that they messed up. Those messages are mainly conveyed when a person has nothing to lose or when they have already secured a new job. By then it's too late.

Leaders and managers must try to create a culture of fearless, open feedback or find that trusted adviser who will give you straight feedback despite their rank or position in the company (and who will tell you that your joke isn't so funny). In our personal lives we tend to heed the advice of our friends, mothers, or partners, so why not do the same of finding someone you trust in the business environment?

That's exactly the association that I enjoy with one of my work colleagues, Razanne Kamaar. Two teammates within the same organization, there are vast differences between us in terms of age, gender, race, cultural beliefs, position, and work status, yet her feedback is open, direct, mature, critical, and sometimes brutally honest . . . but very often right and appreciated. This is possible because her feedback is based on mutual respect, and the ground rules allow for this frankness without prejudice or any other agenda.

Don't just have a team of "yes" men or women, as then you have become just an autocratic leader. Encourage open, fearless feedback, and find that trusted adviser.

2.2. The secret of pulling together

2.2.1. Old Warrick

"Alone we can do so little; together we can do so much."

—Helen Keller

A man was driving on a lonely stretch of farm road when all of a sudden he lost concentration, and his car landed up in a ditch. Unable to reverse the vehicle from its plight, the man did the next best thing and headed for help at a nearby farmhouse.

The man was greeted by the farmer, an old man, well into his eighties. Having explained the situation to the farmer, the farmer nodded and said, "Don't worry, Old Warrick will get you out." The farmer then led the man to the stables at the back, where stood a donkey that looked as old and weathered as the farmer.

There was no other choice; there was just this octogenarian and his equally old mule. To cut a long story short, the farmer—with the donkey, a rope, and the man—made his way slowly to the stranded vehicle. The farmer then tied one end of the rope to the car and the other to the donkey and began to shout, "Pull John! Pull Steve! Pull Mike! Pull Warrick!"

As soon as the farmer said, "Pull Warrick!" the mule heaved and pulled the car out of the ditch, much to the delight of the man. Having patted the donkey and thanked the old farmer, the man was just going to move off to get into his car, when he stopped, turned to the old man, and enquired, "Tell me, sir, why did you have to call on all those names before giving **Old Warrick** his instruction to pull the car out of the ditch?"

The old man smiled and replied, "You see, **Old Warrick** is very old—his eyesight is almost gone, his hearing isn't that good, and he struggles to eat and walk—but as long as he believes he is part of a team then he doesn't mind pulling."*

Isn't this a lovely example of teamwork? It doesn't matter what is the age, race, gender, or rank of the person—as long as they feel part of a team, they won't mind pulling. John Murphy, in his book, *Pulling Together: 10 Rules for High Performance Teams* (2010), writes, "The greatest accomplishments in life are not achieved by individuals alone, but by proactive people pulling together for a common good."

By adding your hands to those of others you will be surprised what can be achieved. The trick now is to ensure that your teammates, partners, or colleagues feel part of a team.

*Source: Adapted from: M. Anderson and T. Feltenstein, Change for the Good—You Go First; 21 Ways to Inspire Change (Illinois; Simple Truths, 2007).

2.2.2. Heaven and hell

"Teamwork involves ordinary people working together to achieve extraordinary results."

—Sam Walton

In one room a pot of delicious stew sits in the middle of a big round table. The people at the table are holding unusually long handled spoons, which makes the act of taking the food to their mouths impossible.

The people in this room are starving, despite this lovely meal in the pot, and they are in a bad way—thin, sick, and weak.

The room represents hell.

The next room also has a delicious pot of stew resting on a large table. The people around this table also have those unusually long handled spoons to eat with.

These people are plump, happy, well fed, and remarkably healthy. Why?*

The people in the second room had learnt to feed one another. They used the concept of teamwork and the spirit of serving one another. By helping others they in turn helped themselves. They worked as a team and didn't care who received the credit. As a result the entire team benefited.

This is the essence of teamwork—and it can be the difference between the success or failure of a business or a particular task. One can't do everything oneself. The best way to ensure teamwork is to get the buy-in of everyone (including the support personnel), and the way to achieve this is to develop, train, and give responsibility to them. If you look for the best in your team or employees they will flourish.

Sam Walton was right; ordinary people working together can achieve extraordinary results. With the right teamwork one can get heavenly results.

*Source: Adapted from the fable "Heaven and Hell" (author unknown).

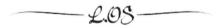

2.2.3. Learn to get on with one another

"Talent wins games, but teamwork and intelligence wins championships."
—Michael Jordan

There is an expression often used to describe a married couple who, seemingly, are a perfect match for each other, their mutual love, respect, and connectivity being an example for all to witness: "Two hearts that beat as one." Sometimes people in a business partnership will similarly enjoy amazing unity of purpose and complement each other's functions perfectly.

While this may be true on the surface you can bet your bottom dollar that everything isn't rosy all the time. There will be those inevitable marital "bust-ups" or partner disagreements, but the one thing these parties have going for themselves is the "level of maturity". They will negotiate, compromise, and agree to differ. They will put aside petty differences and work harmoniously together.

They will look at the "whole", their united team or partnership, rather than letting their egos, selfishness, greed, the desire for power, or even jealously get in the way and mar the good relationships that are necessary for groups, families, teams, and companies to succeed.

They know the secret of teamwork—they learnt how to get on with one another.

2.3. Team support; together each adds more

2.3.1. The porcupine analogy

"We can learn a lot from crayons; some are
sharp, some are pretty, and some are dull.
Some have weird names and all are different colours;
but they all have to live in the same box."

—anonymous

It was the coldest winter ever—many animals died because of the cold. The porcupines, realizing the situation, decided to group together. In this way they covered and protected themselves. However, the quills of each one wounded their closest companions even though they gave off heat to one another.

After a while they decided to distance themselves from one another, and they began to die, alone and frozen. So they had to make a choice: either accept the quills of their companions or disappear from Earth.

Wisely, they decided to go back to being together. In this way they learned to live with the little wounds that were

35

caused by the close relationship with their companion, but the most important part of it was the heat that came from the others. In this way they were able to survive.*

The dilemma facing the porcupines is not unique to that species. The selfsame problems are prevalent in communities, countries, and businesses throughout the world today, each having to deal with their own set of prejudices.

Interestingly, the moral drawn from the porcupine story above coincides exactly with the message in the quote that opened this section: that all the crayons, although different, belong to the same box. Ironically, these two simple concepts provide the world with the solution needed to answer the issues on diversity and ensure that the team functions as harmoniously as possible.

The best relationship is not the one that brings together perfect people, but the best is when each individual learns to live with the imperfections or differences of others and above all, can admire the other person's good qualities.

*Source: Porcupines and the Coldest Winter Ever—Spiritual Short Stories (awaken your spirit) <http://www.spiritual-short-stories.com/spiritual-short-story-738-Porcupines+And+The+Coldest+Winter+Ever.html> accessed 23 May 2014

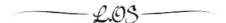

2.3.2. The wingman

"Surround yourself with people who are going to lift you higher."

—Oprah Winfrey

Sometimes it takes a wingman to help us see our own greatness—to reveal that we are more than our fears . . . that we are powerful beings who are capable of doing more than we think is possible.

Asking for help (and being vulnerable) isn't easy. But a "wingman"—someone you trust and who truly wants the best for you—can make it easier. They can be your secret

weapon and give you the courage to take off on the tough missions of life.*

The above excerpt was adapted from the book *Never Fly Solo: Lead with Courage, Build Trusting Partnerships, and Reach New Heights in Business* (2009) by Lieutenant Colonel Robert ("Waldo") Waldman, a fighter pilot who flew sixty-five missions for the Operation Allied Force in Yugoslavia and who helped enforce the no-fly zone (NFZ) in Iraq. Even fighter pilots need the support and encouragement of a trusted ally, a person in their corner, a person who would go into battle with them and would die for them.

Interestingly, Waldo had a different kind of wingman: his best friend in life, his brother. Every time he was about to go into battle he would get a terrible feeling of apprehension that would grip his body, and he would then phone his brother who would calm him down and render the words of strength and encouragement needed for the mission ahead.

Who is your **"wingman"**? More importantly, who can you be a wingman for?

*Source: Adapted from: Lieutenant Colonel R. Waldman, Never Fly Solo: Lead with Courage, Build Trusting Partnerships, and Reach New Heights in Business (New York; McGraw-Hill, 2009).

2.3.3. The power of the pride

"Individuals play the game, but teams beat the odds."

—SEAL team saying

In his book *The Power of the Pride: How lessons from a pride of lions can teach you to create powerful business teams (1992)*, Ian Thomas tells an amazing story of how six lionesses managed to slaughter a buffalo. This occurred when a herd of approximately 250 buffalo were in disarray and some of the sentry bulls had split up. An experienced lioness sprang from her hiding place, charged at the main herd, and then became the decoy runner to lure the remaining bulls on watch away from the heard—leaving enough time for the other five lionesses to kill their prey.

We can learn so much from nature, and Ian Thomas gives us a wonderful illustration of the value of teamwork and communication. We need to act, contribute, and work within the confines of the "pride". There is no open debate on matters like skills, rank, gender, or age when this pride of lions go hunting. Each member has a specific function to perform. Each member knows their responsibilities and each member can be trusted to deliver.

Instil the "power of the pride" concept in your team.

2.4. Teamwork in action

2.4.1. Act clever—stick together

"It's amazing what you can accomplish if you don't care who gets the credit."
—Harry S. Truman

> **I was at a lunch the other day when I heard a commotion at the table near me. The next moment I looked up to notice a gentleman get up from that table, drop to the floor, and commence doing ten push-ups, much to the glee and laughter of his colleagues.**

> **I subsequently learned that this group of people at the table actually work together and have adopted a team strategy on "oneness" and a team motto of "Act Clever—Stick Together".**

> **One of their principles is that they always use the plural format of "we" or "our" in their approach to their work, service ethic, and, more importantly, in their day-to-day communication. Forbidden is use of the words "my", "mine", "me", or "I". Use of the latter words immediately invokes a penalty.**

This approach is so refreshing to note and witness. They have recognized that one of the cardinal rules for a successful business is to work as a team. Their thinking, words, and actions are aligned to their motto and vision. They are practising what they preach and making a public example of this for all to see. They are not filled with **"hot air"** but are committed to the joint approach.

They have also recognized that this principle, over time, will become a good habit, a way of life, which will be the springboard for their success.

There is no **"I"** in **"team"**. This group of people have put aside their individual egos, their personal issues, and personality differences for the team values and rules. They have recognized that **"more"** is better than **"one"**, and that more, in concert, can conquer the seemingly unconquerable.

"Act Clever—Stick Together" is a fantastic motto for this team to have. What is your team motto?

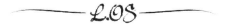

2.4.2. The pig and the horse

"Finding good players is easy. Getting them to play as a team is another story."
—Charles Dillon ("Casey") Stengel

A colleague sent me the following story. I'm not sure of its source, but I'm sure the author wouldn't mind me sharing it with you. The lessons are quite profound.

> **There was a farmer who collected horses. On a particular day one of his horses became ill, and he called the veterinarian, who diagnosed that the horse had a virus. The vet prescribed a three-day course of medication, and said that, failing which, they would have to put the horse down in order to stop the virus from spreading.**
>
> **Nearby, the pig listened closely to their conversation. The next day, after they gave the horse the medicine, the pig approached the horse and said, "Be strong, my friend. Get up, or else they're going to put you to sleep!"**
>
> **On the second day, the medicine was administered to the horse who continued to lie motionless and gravely ill. Again the pig tried to coax the horse to get up and**

reminded him of the dire consequences that lay ahead if he did not show signs of recovery.

On the third day, there seemed to be little improvement. The vet, however, gave the horse the medicine and agreed to call later to see if there had been any improvement or, alternatively, to put the horse down.

After the farmer and the vet had left, the pig approached the horse and said, "Listen, pal, it's now or never! Get up, come on! Have courage! Come on! Get up! That's it, slowly! Great! Come on, one, two, three . . . Good, good. Now faster, come on . . . Fantastic! Run! Run more!"

All of a sudden, the farmer and the vet came back, saw the horse running in the field, and began shouting, "It's a miracle! My horse is cured. This deserves a party. Let's kill the pig!"*

The pig in this story portrays the part of the underrated, unrecognized, and unappreciated employee or member of the team. Sadly, this is a fact of life and is prevalent throughout business and the world in general. Does every employer truly know which employee actually contributes to the success of the organization or which team player is lending the necessary support to other members of the team?

If you are one of those underrated, unrecognized, unappreciated employees, please don't give up—the world needs people like you. Take heart in the following immortal words of Thomas Edison: "Don't look to become a person of success. Look instead to become a person of value."

*Source: The Pig and the Horse: What's the Moral of the Story?—Yahoo Answers <https://answers.yahoo.com/question/index?qid . . . > accessed 19 May 2014

2.4.3. The wolf factor

"It's not the size of the dog in the fight; it's the size of the fight in the dog."
—Mark Twain

A couple lived in an extremely remote area with their two sons in a log cabin they had made by hand. This family also included two wolves they had raised from earliest puppyhood, rescuing them from their den after their mother had been indiscriminately shot and the pups left to die. This was the only family the wolves had ever known, having only lived with humans as their pack mates.

One day the parents were cutting wood about a mile from home when one of the boys accidentally turned over a kerosene lamp (there was no electricity), and a raging fire began to consume the wooden structure. The two wolves immediately dashed towards the flaming cabin where the two boys were trapped inside, immobilized by smoke and fear. The parents were far behind, so the wolves gnawed and fought their way into the cabin and pulled the boys outside to safety. Although both wolves were badly burned, their loyalty to their "pack" meant the difference between life and death for these two members of their human "pack".*

No other mammal shows more spirited devotion to its family, organization, or social group than the wolf. Not only do the members of the wolf pack hunt together to ensure survival of the group, but they also play with one another, sleep as a pack, scuffle with one another, and protect one another. And although generally only the Alpha male and Alpha female produce pups, every member of the pack participates in the nurturing and education of the young. Each pack member assumes responsibility for the food, shelter, training, protection, and play where the pups are concerned, for the pack realizes that the young are their future.

That's truly an expression of the value and spirit of teamwork, highlighting the essence of trust and loyalty. It takes to another level the growth and development of our family, employees, and members of the broader community. Let's learn from the wisdom and unselfish nature of the wolves.

*Source: T. L. Towery, Wisdom of Wolves: Nature's Way to Organizational Success (Michigan; Walnut Grove, 2010).

2.4.4. I love it when a plan comes together!

"Determined people working together can do anything."

—James E. Casey

There is a television series called The A-Team (original run: 1983-7) where four different characters, led by Hannibal Smith, team up in an action-packed endeavour to help the underdog. To achieve this goal, the A-Team had to invariably embark on an obscene, elaborate, and\ or ingenious plan.

As usual, as expected, each episode would end in success, and the final, parting line, would be uttered by Hannibal, "I love it when a plan comes together."*

Yes, Hannibal, the team leader was the brain child behind the plan, but the plan was useless . . . unless implemented. The plan was useless . . . unless accepted, adopted, and had the buy-in of the team. Hannibal couldn't achieve the success by himself; he needed the support of his men, and those he knew and trusted and who were loyal to him.

In a similar vein, people who have produced or organized big, complicated events (for example, matches of the FIFA World Cup, a U2 concert tour, or Kim Kardashian's wedding) face the real test, where their co-ordination, leadership, and communication skills are used to infuse the trust, accountability, and support of others. It requires a lot of different people, all having to work for a cause or vision. Only when the mission is achieved and when things go smoothly can the team leader sit back and say, "I love it when a plan comes together."

*Source: based on the action-adventure television series The A-Team (produced by Universal Television and Stephen J. Cannell Productions).

2.5. It takes all types to make up a team

2.5.1. The boat and propeller

"Coming together is the beginning, staying together is progress and working together is success."

—Henry Ford

A speed boat cruising along the ocean suddenly started "taking in water". The person on board noticed a small leak and began bailing out the water while he signalled for help. But the faster he baled, the faster the water seemed to be filling the boat.

He then realized he had to lighten the boat and began to jettison a few accessories into the sea. Still, the water continued to fill the boat at an alarming speed. The man did the next best thing—he took the propeller and dumped it into the ocean and saw it sink immediately. The weight in the boat was now sufficient for the man to manage the bailing of water process and to keep him afloat while he waited for rescue.

The moment the man threw the propeller into the sea, it sank. Yet, when the propeller was part of the boat, the boat did not sink. All the parts of the boat, including the propeller, were knitted together into one unit—one team.

That is the fundamental of teamwork. All of the team players' strengths and weaknesses, positives and negatives, small and big contributions are banded together into a unit that enables the team to float and perform its mission. This is a more consistent, reliable, and successful approach—unlike the case of individuals that may either sink or swim.

It takes all types to make up a team.

2.5.2. The toaster concept

"In the end all business operations can be reduced to three words: people, product and profits. Unless you've got a good team, you can't do much with the other two."

—Lee Lacocca

Even the most primitive model called for copper, to make the pins of the electric plug, the cord and internal wires. Iron to make the steel grilling apparatus, and the spring to pop up the toast. Nickel to make the heating element. Mica (a mineral a bit like slate) around which the heating element is wound, and of course plastic for the plug and cord insulation.*

Thomas Thwaites, a postgraduate design student at the Royal College of Art in London, discovered just what an astonishing achievement the toaster is when he embarked on what he called the "toaster project". Quite simply, he wanted to build a toaster from scratch, so he started taking apart a cheap toaster, only to discover that it had more than 400 components and sub-components.

In order for this simple product to function and work optimally, each and every component and sub-component has to knit together, truly the essence of teamwork.

*Source: T. Harford, Adapt: Why Success Always Starts with Failure (New York; Farrar, Straus and Giroux, 2011).

2.5.3. Clap and cheer

"There are three types of people in this world: those who make things happen, those who watch things happen, and those who wonder what happened."
—Mary Kay Ash (American businesswoman)

A small boy was auditioning with his classmates for a school play. His mother knew that he'd set his heart on being in the play—just like all the other children hoped,

too—and she feared how he would react if he was not chosen.

On the day that the parts were awarded, the little boy's mother went to the school gates to collect her son. The little lad rushed up to her, eyes shining with pride and excitement. "Guess what, Mum?" he shouted, and then he said the words that provide a lesson to us all, "I've been chosen to clap and cheer."*

Behind every organization or successful person there is some level of support, someone making up a team. Even a sole proprietorship business will have support, by way of a secretary, bookkeeper, driver, marketer, and/or financier. Sometimes the contributions need not be great, time-consuming, or even known, but they are there none the less.

There is a flip side to this analogy, in that people want to feel that they belong to something, to feel that they are part of a team, business, society, or country. They want to make a difference or play a part—no matter how small—that will give them a feeling of achievement and satisfaction and a sense of purpose.

Everyone has a part to play in their team—even if it's to clap and cheer!

*Source: Adapted from: John Slimp, Clap and Cheer!| John Slimp Training and Development <http://ww.createawinningteam.com/clap-and-cheer> date posted 6 May 2010, accessed 19 May 2014

3   Comfort zone

3.1. Aim for the next level

3.1.1. Frank Lloyd Wright story

"We cannot become what we want to be by remaining what we are."

—Max De Pree

The famous architect Frank Lloyd Wright designed many beautiful buildings and other magnificent structures. Towards the end of his career, a reporter asked him, "Of the many beautiful designs, which one is your favourite?"

Without missing a beat, Frank Lloyd Wright answered, "My next one."*

Frank Lloyd Wright understood the "principle of success"—the need to constantly improve, grow, and stretch himself, finding new ways and ideas, relentlessly pressing forward. He was in third and fourth gear, not in neutral or reverse.

He did not sit back and wallow in the successes of the past, but rather he had the ambition and drive to do better—to push himself higher and to achieve more. He was aiming for the next level.

Frank Lloyd Wright's words and thought processes also identify with the wise counsel of Jim Rohn, who said, "Let others leave their future in someone else's hand, but not you."

*Source: Adapted from: J. Osteen, Become a Better You—7 Keys to Improving Your Life Every Day (London; Simon & Schuster, 2007).

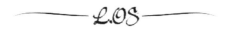

3.1.2. The elephant at the circus

"Patience has its limits. Take it too far, and its cowardice."

—George Jackson

A father took his son to the circus. This was to be the child's first experience of such an event and consequent of the excitement levels the pair arrived at the "big top" more than an hour before the scheduled start.

In order to kill time the dad took his son to see the animals that were secured in their respective cages—all except for the elephant that was tied with a rope, one end to a tree and the other to the foot of the elephant.

The little boy turned to his father and said, "Dad, this elephant is so big and strong, surely he can kick the rope, break free, and run away. Why doesn't he?" The father didn't have an intelligent answer to give his son, so he said, "Good question, my boy. I don't know. Let's go ask the elephant trainer why the beast doesn't try to escape."

They eventually encountered the elephant trainer who confirmed that the creature is strong enough to escape but won't. "You see," said the elephant trainer, "when this elephant was a tiny baby we tied the same rope to his foot and the tree. The elephant didn't like it, so he kicked for days on end to try to break free, but he couldn't; he was too small and weak. *And so, over time, he became conditioned and accepted the rope as a way of life.*"

Isn't it sad that we, too, fall into the trap of old habits and complacency? Are we like that train travelling the same single track, day in and day out, or are we going to change tracks and seek out a new adventure for ourselves?

Break out of the old routine and "snap that rope" that's keeping you tied to a tree like the elephant in the above story. Be free, and explore what life has to offer you.

3.1.3. The pot plant

"If you are not willing to risk the unusual, you will have to settle for the ordinary."
—Jim Rohn

A few years ago my wife and I went to our local nursery and purchased some potted shrubs and trees, the idea being to place them at strategic areas around our pool with them thus creating a boundary fence to offer us the sense of privacy we desired. After a couple of years we noticed that while we continued to water and look after these shrubs and trees they had not fulfilled the screening job we had intended them for.

We then decided to remove them from their pots and move them to the open spaces of our garden; within months there was a noticeable and welcome difference.

You see, in the pots, the growth of the plants and trees was stifled. They could only grow in line with what the pot would allow. Once their roots filled the pot it could grow no further. The pot only allowed water and nutrients sufficient to maintain the plants and trees—nothing else.

By transplanting from the pot to an open bed, the shrubs and trees were set free to reach their full potential. They were no longer stuck in their comfortable "old pot" but had a new beginning, a new lease of life, and grew into something significant and special.

There comes a time when we all must decide to move from the pot to an open bed or garden—when we need to explore our new selves and reach heights we never even envisioned. Now is the time. Your future is waiting.

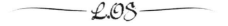

3.2. Sail the unchartered waters

3.2.1. Embrace freedom

"Make up your mind to act decidedly and take the consequences. No good is ever done in this world by hesitation."
—Thomas Huxley

History will list the names of prisoners who, once released, end up back in jail. Similarly, so often birds fly off when their cage is opened, only to return a bit later. Why?

Simply, it's because they are daunted by freedom and then retreat back to what they know or what they know best—their old ways and routine. They shrink back into their comfort zones.

Do we act in the same manner? Remember, we were not created to wallow in captive circumstances. So let's not be the victim of captivity, but rather let's take those opportunities, risks, and/or steps into the unknown, as scary as it may seem.

Embrace freedom. Embrace life. Embrace change. Embrace the adventures and challenges on which you are about to embark. Find the treasures you so dearly seek or want in life.

3.2.2. The horizon effect

"The most dangerous place to hide is in your comfort zone."

—Anonymous

In the old days, sailors believed that Earth was flat. They were too scared to venture too far from land just in case they fell off Earth. Little by little they began to venture further afield and, interestingly, they noticed a new phenomenon, what I will describe as the "horizon effect".

Simply explained, the "horizon effect" is when you reach that point on the skyline, you will inevitably find another horizon, and another . . . and another.

Is this nature's way of teaching us the principles of foresight and vision, the ability to face new challenges, and an appreciation of the fact that there is a big world out there full of opportunity and hope? But how easy is it to take a step into the unknown? It takes courage, faith, and a great deal of excitement or commitment.

It's so much easier if you have a picture in mind of what it is that you want to achieve—a dream or goal. For then, you can take a step towards what you can see. There's an amazing thing that happens when you take a step towards what you can see: More steps are revealed to you. More horizons are opened up to you. The world is open to you.

But you can't achieve this by standing on the shore. Take the action required to reach your goals and dreams. Be your own Christopher Columbus, and look towards your horizon . . .

3.2.3. My life is manageable

"What you are will show in what you do."

—Thomas Edison

My life. My life is familiar. My life is . . . is manageable, every day. I have a thing I do every day. It's all I've ever known and its routine and . . . as long as I have that, I'm OK. If I don't have it, I'm lost.*

The above quote is from the movie *Pay It Forward* and certainly has a message for some of us. Yes, some people love routine and order in their lives. They are creatures of habit, awaking at the same time every day and then like clockwork setting about their daily chores. All they want is their manageable day.

Having some form of law and order, responsibility, or pattern in one's life is OK, and this article is not written with the intention of judging, praising, or condemning any person or their attitudes or lifestyles but merely to provoke consideration.

Are you living a fulfilled and happy life? Are you flexible, creative, and open to change? Do you have a sense of adventure and want to peek into the unknown? And then probably the most important question to consider, "How much control do you exert over your own life?"

Why don't you "pay forward" your life, and see what exciting things await you?

*Source: extract from: Pay It Forward, dir. Mimi Leder (20 October 2000), starring Haley Joel Osment, Kevin Spacey, and Helen Hunt.

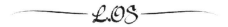

3.3. Change the routine

3.3.1. Burger, fries, and coke

"You can never get to a place of comfort in [(this)] business—as soon as you hit that cushy spot, somebody is going to kick you out."

—Charlize Theron

Sebastian was seconded to work in the United States for a short period of time. He was nervous at this prospect, as his culture and language was very different: He couldn't speak English very well and was unsure as to how he would get around and eke out a living. He was even more concerned that he would feel completely out of place and that people would laugh at him. (Doesn't this sound familiar?)

His friend gave him all the tips he would require for his trip to the West and concluded by informing him that should he want food, he merely had to ask for "burger, fries, and coke", and he couldn't go wrong.

Sebastian duly arrived and found accommodation within walking distance of his temporary job. When he became hungry he ventured into the street and, according to plan, he went up to the first person he met and uttered, "Burger, fries, and coke." He was pleasantly surprised when this passer-by pointed out the nearest McDonald's fast-food facility.

For the next two weeks Sebastian ate hamburgers and fries and drank coke twice a day from the selfsame McDonald's chain.

Eventually, he felt that he couldn't continue in this vane, so he contacted his friend and said to him, "I can't carry on

like this! I need to change! I can't keep on doing the same thing and eating the same meal, day in and day out! What can I do?"

His friend advised a simple change in routine and meal order. Instead of burger, fries, and coke, he suggested a meal of eggs, toast, and juice.

The next day Sebastian took to the street, and, approaching a passer-by, he uttered, "Eggs, toast, and juice." Again he was pleasantly surprised when shown the bistro just across the street from where he was staying.

Once seated, he asked the waitress for eggs. He was taken aback when she said, "Certainly, sir, would you like them fried, hard, boiled, or scrambled?"

Sebastian quickly changed his order and instead asked for toast. Again he became very agitated when the waitress enquired whether he wanted white, brown, or seeded bread and whether and, if so, how, he wanted it toasted. He asked her to cancel his food order and rather bring him juice.

When the waitress started with her selection of juices on offer, Sebastian jumped up in distress and shouted, "Bring me a burger, fries, and coke."*

Isn't it sad that as soon as we become a little adventurous, and things don't work out for us, we become like the tortoise that quickly puts its head back in its shell. We duck out of the pressure, stress, or challenges and run back to our safe environment.

Sadly, if you keep doing this then you will never achieve your goals and dreams or realize self-growth and development. It's like playing a game of *Snakes and Ladders*, and you keep ending on square two. How on Earth will you ever get to square 100?

Perhaps we can take inspiration from these courageous words of Nick Vujicic:

You don't need courage to win. You need courage to fail. If I fail, I try again and again and again. If you fail are you going to try again? The human spirit can handle much worse than we realise. It matters HOW you are going to Finish. Are you going to finish strong?

Make up your mind to act decidedly and take the consequences. No good is ever done in this world by hesitation. You will never get out of your comfort zone unless you try new things and take action. You will never get out your comfort zone unless you accept that you will fail and make mistakes along the way . . . but that doesn't matter. What does matter depends how you finish—finish strong!

*Source: Adapted from a story I once heard on radio many years ago.

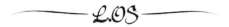

3.3.2. My comfort zone

I used to have a comfort zone where I knew I wouldn't fail.
The same four walls and busywork were really more like jail.

—anonymous

I once worked with a colleague who excelled at his daily tasks. You couldn't find fault with his work, and he rarely made mistakes. This person understood what was in his job description, and he stuck to it religiously. Anything that fell outside of the scope of his work function would not be accepted by him and would be referred to another colleague.

This person didn't have a driver's licence (no reasonable excuse) and was encouraged to obtain one as part of his career development and promotion plan, which he refused. This person would not attend work functions, work overtime, or help colleagues who needed assistance. His work was always 100 per cent up to date and 99 per cent correct. He was out the office at 4.00 p.m. every afternoon.

Sadly, consequent of a restructure within the group, his particular work functions were reallocated and split up

into different areas within the company. There was no place for this employee, and he was given a retrenchment package.

This is a true story and a very good example that one should be cautious of sitting in their comfort zone, especially in the corporate environment. Nothing stands still, and circumstances are always changing. Take every opportunity to better yourself, and stand in contention for that promotion or career-developing movement. Don't let your life or career go by just watching others win.

I came across a poem entitled "My Comfort Zone" that certainly will motivate you into action if indeed there is a degree of complacency in your life or career outlook. Here is an excerpt that could possibly be seen as a "kicker" to take the appropriate action:

> *If you're in a comfort zone, afraid to venture out,*
> *Remember that all winners were at one time filled with doubt.*
> *A step or two and words of praise can make your dreams come true.*
> *Reach for your future with a smile; success is there for you!*
>
> *(Anonymous)*

Kiss your comfort zone goodbye, and close and lock the door.

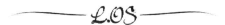

3.3.3. A group of pigs

"Determination is the wake up call to the human will."

—Anthony Robbins

There's an interesting analogy told by Chris Voss on his blog that pertains to a group of pigs who sit all day in their mud puddle complaining about how bad the mud puddle is, yet they stay in it because, deep down, it's comfortable, and they love it.*

The mud gives them comfort. They are as happy as the proverbial pig in the . . .

I'm sure you can recognize these selfsame symptoms in the life of others—those who moan about the state of their property of residence and yet who take no action to fix it or those complainers at work who are unhappy in their jobs, yet not interested in up-skilling themselves or changing their daily routine and outlook?

You have to find ways to stop stagnating and to get out of the rut: those boring, manageable habits of routine and a negative spiral of unhappiness and despair. It doesn't need a mammoth adjustment or need to cost a great deal of money: Just change the order and the way you do things. Drive to work using a different route, leave work at a different time, and try a new restaurant or holiday destination. Continue to change your patterns, and soon you will be re-energized and have a real zest for life.

Get out of the mud puddle! Get rid of that "air of complacency" and spruce up your lifestyle.

*Source: Chris Voss: (CHRIS VOSS)//twitter

—————— *L.OS* ——————

3.4. Don't rest on your laurels

3.4.1. The eagle and the rabbit

"One of these days is none of these days."

—H.G. Bohn

An eagle was sitting on a tree resting, doing nothing. A small rabbit saw the eagle and asked him, "Can I also sit like you and do nothing?" The eagle answered, "Sure, why not."

So the rabbit sat on the ground below the eagle and rested. All of a sudden a fox appeared, jumped on the rabbit, and ate it.*

It just goes to show you that if you sit and do nothing, you must be sitting very high up . . .

There is no room for complacency in business or in life. One of the days could be none of these days. The world is changing faster than ever before.

Business is changing at a speed of knots, and it is likely that your life is a lot less manageable and peaceful than it used to be. It was Pogo who said, "We have met the enemy; he is us . . ."

Don't take things for granted. Don't rest on your laurels.

*Source: Minute Management Course—RIP—Factor—Jokes and . . . . <http://www.rip-factor.com/joke0124.html> accessed 20 May 2014

3.4.2. The bumblebee pin

"When Barbie is in a little girl's hands, she is a vehicle for dreaming, for imagining what girls can be."

—Jill Barad

Jill Barad was given a bumblebee pin by her mother when she first started out in her working career. She joined Mattel Inc, a giant in the toy industry, in 1981 and worked on a brand that changed many lives—Barbie. Jill had risen to be CEO of this institution by 1997. She always wore a "bumblebee pin" to keep her focus and fear aside, to keep her eyes on the first prize, and to beat the odds in order to achieve success. Her motto is "Anything is possible."*

The bumblebee is quite symbolic and represents an oddity, a freak of nature, as, aerodynamically, the creature shouldn't fly, yet it does. Every time she saw the pin Jill was reminded to keep pushing for the impossible . . .

Perhaps you have some other "item" more appropriate to you, or perhaps you feel you don't need an item of reminder. In any event, please ensure that you aren't one of those people plodding along in your comfort zone or accepting mediocrity.

Put your fears aside, and try something new. Broaden your horizons, and push that envelope. If you don't—who will?

*Source: Adapted from: A. Bryant, The Corner Office: How Top CEOs Made It and How You Can Too (London; Harper Press, 2011).

3.4.3. Even lions get ousted

"Comfort zones are most often expanded through discomfort."
—Peter McWilliams

The male lion is king in Africa, but the bush is wild, unpredictable, and dangerous. If he is not aware, alert, and protective of his territory, he may well lose it all to a stronger contender.

The dominant male lion becomes very lazy once his pride is under his command. He sleeps for most of the day, and other lions do the hunting for him. Initially, he can face the challenge from the younger males, but the day will come when his lazy, only-hanging-in-their lifestyle will catch up with him.

A younger, stronger male will take over as the leader, and the king of the jungle will be kicked out to live in isolation.*

Yes, even the king of the beasts will starve to death if he refuses to act or guard himself against the "enemy": competition, time, contentment, and self-satisfaction. So, don't get too comfortable in your job or life; if this can happen to the king of the jungle, it can surely happen to you, too?

*Source: Adapted from: Dr L. Hattingh and H. Claasen, African Wisdom (publisher and date unknown).

4   Opportunities

4.1. Opportunities are like sunrises

4.1.1. Second chances

"Failure is an event, not a person. Yesterday ended last night."

—Zig Ziglar

A man visited an art gallery and was amazed to see a painting of a scene depicting a weather-beaten, rustic-looking rowing boat with its set of oars akimbo, lying stranded on an isolated stretch of beach. That was all— the sea, the beach, and this dejected, lonely, sad-looking boat.

What was more amazing about this painting was the fact that besides the artist's signature it contained a caption that read, "When the tide comes in, I will again be sailing the waters!"

"When the tide comes in, I will again be sailing the waters!" No matter how badly you messed up or how many times you missed golden opportunities, the above painting and its caption tells us you may get a second chance. It's better to be prepared for an opportunity and in the event not actually have one than to have an opportunity but find you are not prepared for it.

There is hope; the tide will come in again—so be ready when it does. You don't want to miss it second time around. You don't have to be stranded on the beach forever; make a better use of your second chance.

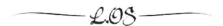

4.1.2. There is seldom a perfect time

"The challenge is not to manage time, but to manage ourselves."
—Steven Covey

I know of a man who was employed to fulfil a strategic role in a company that had just been listed on the South African stock exchange? As part of the man's remuneration package and to incentivize his employment, he was given certain company shares and options at the listed price of R1 per share.

It wasn't long before the share price doubled, and so the man deemed it prudent to purchase additional shares with the hope of a nice profit. Over a few months the share price continued to soar—to R4 per share and then R5 and then more than R6 per share. The man contemplated selling and using his profit to take the family on an overseas holiday. But when was the right time to sell? The share price kept climbing.

Suddenly, the bubble burst; the debt crisis followed by some adverse publicity saw the price of the company's share tumble at an alarming speed. The man was tempted to sell. "Surely," he thought, "the price can't go any lower; it will bottom out."

Sadly, for this man it did go much lower, and so all his plans for a family holiday soon dissipated into thin air.

If you are waiting for the *perfect time* to sell assets, propose to a woman of your dreams, study for that degree, go on that special vacation, or buy that perfect house, you are going to be waiting a long time . . . perhaps even a lifetime. Unless you have that magic crystal ball, don't get caught in the trap of waiting for the "perfect moment": Act, listen to your intuition, go with the flow, and make things happen.

Greet each day with excitement for the opportunities that will come your way; they are plentiful. To paraphrase Richard Branson, *"Business opportunities are like buses; there's always another one coming."* Even problems have opportunities hidden therein, waiting for you to unearth them. But don't wait too long; capitalize on the opportunity before some else "steals" them.

There is seldom a perfect time for opportunities; grab them when you can.

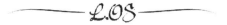

4.1.3. Opportunity only knocks once

"Opportunities are like sunrises. If you wait too long you miss them."
—William Arthur Ward

> **Dan was a single guy living at home with his father and working in the family business. When he found out he was going to inherit a fortune when his sickly father died, he decided he needed a wife with which to share his fortune.**
>
> **One evening at an investment meeting he spotted the most beautiful woman he had ever seen. Her natural beauty took his breath away. "I may look like just an ordinary man," he said to her, "but in just a few years my father will die, and I'll inherit twenty million dollars."**
>
> **Impressed, the woman obtained his business card, and, three days later, she became his stepmother.***

Sometimes, the door of opportunity opens for you. When these rare events occur, one needs to try seize the chance immediately, for, once the door of opportunity closes, one doesn't know if it will open again, if ever.

A specific opportunity usually knocks once, be at home, be alert. It may just be jackpot time!

*Source: Gershon S Lehrer, Dan was a Single Guy |Gershon-Lehrer.be-Family Tree <http://www.gershon-lehrer.be/blog/2012/06/dan-was-a-single-guy> date posted 8 June 2014, accessed 20 May 2014

4.2. Note the signs

4.2.1. The charging elephant

"When you walk on the field of opportunity, you will discover that it is always ploughing time."

—anonymous

The elephant's ears start to flap, and the trunk gets lifted into attack mode. Its whole demeanour starts to change; it mocks and taunts and becomes increasingly agitated. The signs become visible for all to see. Yet . . . it is only when the beast actually charges that one does run for cover.

In business there are many telltale signs that will indicate that the business is in trouble. Besides the obvious financial aspects, factors like employee churn rate, price wars, inroads by competitors, changes in legislation, union matters, fuel shortages, and power cuts are clear and visible indicators that trouble may be brewing, some ominously.

But with these signs comes a wealth of opportunities. Each problem will present a need for corrective actions or alternate strategies to be formed, some very quickly. Some measures may be small or minimal, others large and daunting and calling for change management, creative ideas, or a new vision and focus altogether.

Remember, each challenge presents an opportunity. But with each challenge one must exercise wisdom and a sense of discernment. Read the signs carefully. It is no use expending energy, money, and/or time on useless matters and dead-end opportunities.

4.2.2. The touchstones

"Often we look so long at the closed door that we don't see that it has been opened."

—Helen Keller

The touchstone was a small pebble that could turn any common metal into pure gold. The stone was very rare and would be found lying among thousands and thousands of other pebbles that looked exactly like it. But the secret was this: The real stone would feel warm while ordinary pebbles are cold. A man discovered this truth, sold his few belongings, bought some simple supplies, camped on the seashore, and began testing pebbles.

He knew that if he picked up ordinary pebbles and threw them down again because they were cold, he may pick up the same pebble hundreds of times. So, when he felt one that was cold, he threw it into the sea. He spent a whole day doing this, but none of them was the touchstone. Yet he went on and on this way. Pick up a pebble. Cold—throw it into the sea. Pick up another. Throw it into the sea.

The days stretched into weeks and the weeks into months. One day, however, about mid-afternoon, he picked up a pebble, and it was warm. He threw it into the sea before he realized what he had done. He had formed such a strong habit of throwing each pebble into the sea that when the one he wanted came along, he still threw it away.*

So it is with opportunity. Unless you are vigilant, it's easy to fail to recognize an opportunity when it is in your hand, and it's just as easy to throw it away. Sometimes you may wait a lifetime for an opportunity and then let it slip through your grasp.

At other times you may be looking so long at the closed door that you fail to realize it's been opened. Opportunities are seldom labelled.

*Source: Adapted from: A. Lenehan, The Best of Bits and Pieces (Fairfield, USA; The Economic Press, 1994).

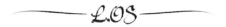

4.2.3. Opportunities do fall into your lap

"Small opportunities are often the beginning of great enterprises."
—Demosthenes

> **Marie and her son Don lived in a trailer park in Huntington Beach in Orange County. Marie baked and sold pies to augment the family's income, with Don delivering pies to customers on his bicycle.**
>
> **Marie soon became infamous for her pies, and this eventually led to her becoming involved in the restaurant business. Even after a number of deals the name of Marie Callender was retained for the food line. It eventually merged with the Perkins Family Restaurants. It's now known as Perkins and Marie Callender LLC and boasts more than 250 locations.***

Marie Callender is one person that defied the odds and put fear out of her vocabulary, albeit consequent of her plight and need to survive. Sometimes adversity in life or pressure in one's business is the catalyst that forces one to find any opportunity they can. In this instance, struggling in a trailer park with a child to keep Marie found an avenue to eke out a living: baking pies. This turned out to be an opportunity that really fell into her lap. Her pies became an overnight success, and her trademark.

The sad thing in life is that people don't always take their opportunities or follow their passions or goals. They get locked into that world of fear and/or conservatism, sometimes through circumstances, at other times through family pressures.

So, prepare yourself for when that moment of opportunity knocks, and be ready to open that proverbial door. Create opportunities by boldly making the move to seize the moment when it appears. Your attitude and mindset will always be the judge on how you view or grasp an opportunity.

But opportunities do sometimes have a strange occurrence of falling into your lap; don't drop them or let them go—grab them. Great opportunities come to those who make the most of small ones.

*Source: Adapted from: Marie Callender's—Wikipedia. The Free Encyclopedia
<http://en.wikipedia.org/wiki/Marie_Callender's> accessed 18 May 2014

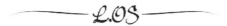

4.2.4. Hoppers and locusts

"We are continually faced with great opportunities which are brilliantly disguised as unsolvable problems."

—Margaret Mead

These young bugs can't quite fly but can jump up to 200 times their height. The hoppers learn to fly by riding the wind. They catch the wind and ride the breeze. Timing is critical.

Adult insects also wait for perfect wind conditions, so they can migrate miles and miles. They don't have aerodynamic bodies but are thick-bodied insects with small straight wings that need to time jumps just right.

Like hoppers and locusts you need to know when it's your time to ride the wind. Your timing needs to be critical, but you must also be very conscious of the fact that there is never a perfect time.

The sad thing about opportunities is that you seldom know upfront if it will work out in a way that you will be happy with. You may have the best of feelings, done the best research, and put all your plans in place, but, ultimately, there are too many variables that can stifle the opportunity. The paradox is that you will never know until you do it.

If hindsight is an exact science, what is vision or foresight? Perhaps it concerns staying tuned to opportunities and timing your jumps just right.

4.3. Fate or destiny

4.3.1. Serendipity

"'Serendipity'—it's one of my favourite words. It's just such a nice sound for what it means: a fortunate accident. Except I don't believe in accidents: I think fate is behind everything."

—*(extract from: Serendipity)*

The above quote is from the opening scene in the romantic movie Serendipity in which a couple (played by John Cusack and Kate Beckinsale) meet, fall in love, and then separate, convinced that they will meet again someday, if it's meant for them—if it's their fate or destiny.*

There are many people I know who believe that if it is meant for them then it will happen. Others believe that things happen for a reason. I must confess that I am one of the latter people.

But is this the right outlook and attitude to have in life? How many opportunities are passed up by this philosophy? Should one not be more persistent instead of waiting for things to drop into one's lap?

So what about you? Do you believe in fate or destiny and waiting for the universe to throw out signs or affirmations, or do you act spontaneously and seize the moment?

*Source: Adapted from Serendipity, dir. Peter Chelsom (2001), starring John Cusack and Kate Beckinsale.

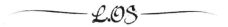

4.3.2. What if?

"If you get too caught up in the 'What if?' part—you will never experience the 'What I can do' part."

—anonymous

"What" and "If" are as non-threatening as any two words can be, but put them together, and it has a totally

different meaning—what if! Side by side, they have the power to haunt you for the rest of your life.*

Do you often play the "What if . . . ?" game with yourself? "What if I did this? Or what if I didn't do that?" When you really analyze it, "What if . . . ?" can only apply to you in your past or something that you need to consider for the future. It's not the present, as you are already in present action mode.

Now you can't do much concerning an event that has occurred; you can only contemplate what could have happened or how your destiny could have been altered. You can only learn from that experience; you can't put back the clock.

Then you have the "contingent" aspect—something that may or may not happen in the future. Yes, it's good to have discernment, wisdom, and a vision or direction for your life with all associated consequences, but don't over-analyze, make excuses, or procrastinate.

Sooner or later you need to step up to the plate. It's your turn for action, and you need to act now. You can't stop time. You can't stop life. Don't wallow in the "What if . . . ?" game like so many.

*Source: Adapted from Letters to Juliet, dir. Gary Winich (2010), starring Amanda Seyfried, Gael Bernal, and Vanessa Redgrave.

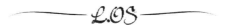

4.3.3. Cast down your bucket

"Effective people are not problem-minded; they're opportunity-minded. They feed opportunities and starve problems."
—Stephen Covey

A ship lost at sea for many days suddenly sighted a friendly vessel. From the mast of the unfortunate vessel was seen a signal: "Water, water, we die of thirst!" The answer from the friendly vessel at once came back: "Cast down your bucket where you are." Not believing the answer received, the crew of the stricken vessel asked a second and then a third time, getting the same response.

At last, the captain of the distressed vessel heeded the injunction; he cast down his bucket and it came up filled of fresh sparkling water from the mouth of the Amazon River.*

Although Booker T. Washington used this metaphor in another context in his famous speech to a white audience on the occasion of the 1895 Atlanta Cotton States and International Exposition, these words are still valid in our world today.

How many times do opportunities lie before you, and all you need to do is cast down your bucket and fill it with the prized possession? There may be times when you think you are down and out, defeated and lost, yet hope lies at your feet—all you need to do is use your bucket, and exchange these sentiments with a new zest for life.

There may be occasions when your goals and aspirations become blurred or lost; all you need to do is fill your bucket, and haul it back with a freshness of ideas and a clear vision. There may be times when you ignored the advice of others or only acted on such words of wisdom at a much later stage when they would have saved you much stress, cost, time, energy, and aggravation. And there are times when you may possibly sit back in utter despair and uncertainty, yet the answer has been right inside your heart or mind from the very beginning.

All you need to do is cast down your bucket into the sea of self-worth, confidence, and knowledge. Take action, and be accountable to yourself—your destiny lies before you.

*Source: Adapted from the "Atlanta Compromise Address 1895" speech by Booker T. Washington. Bounty Books; (2011) 501 Must Know Speeches; London 2011 Bounty Books a division of Octopus Publishing Company (reprinted 2011) page 205.

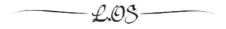

4.4. Take the plunge

4.4.1. Set your sails

"The same wind blows on all of us; it's how you set sail that counts."
—Brian Tracy

> **Have you seen the movie Social Network, a 2010 film directed by David Fincher? It's based on the true-life experiences of Mark Zuckerberg and the original parties to the origins of Facebook. Ironically, it was through Zuckerberg, who, in a more perverse way was intent on executing revenge on an ex—girlfriend, that they stumbled across a phenomenon that has gripped the world and changed people's communication styles and even their lives.***

The world is strewn with examples of pioneers, explorers, inventors, dreamers, and entrepreneurs—from the early days of Leonard da Vinci, Thomas Edison, and Henry Ford to modern-day, household names like Mark Shuttleworth, Steve Jobs, Bill Gates, Richard Branson, and Warren Buffett.

Some of these parties dropped out of school, yet have aspired to reach their dreams, lead a life of fulfilment, and have changed the course of history.

There is still time for you to set your sails, the sails for success, in order to reach those dreams. So play the hand that life has dealt you instead of being hung up on all the petty issues of this world—resentment, revenge, anger, and guilt.

Set your sails; sail on those unchartered waters. Leave your comfort zone, and follow your stars. Find your true North. Place your own star in the sky. Don't be a dis-a-star. Don't be a "night-star" that only lives half a life or a shooting star that fizzles out and dies . . .

Be your own S T A R = Success through Action and Responsibility

*Source: Social Network, dir. David Fincher (2010), starring Jesse Eisenberg as Mark Zuckerberg; adapted from the book Accidental Billionaires by Ben Mezrich.

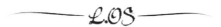

4.4.2. You could have done that

"Each problem has hidden in it an opportunity so powerful that it literally dwarfs the problem. The Greatest success stories were created by people who recognised a problem and turned it into an Opportunity."

—Joseph Sugarman

A thirteen year-old came across a snake up on a rafter of the machine shed on the family farmstead. Panic stricken, she ran for help, and the only person she found was her grandmother.

The grandmother, armed with a shovel, accompanied the teenager to the machine shed and promptly knocked the snake off the rafter with the shovel and chopped its head off. The grandmother then turned to the frightened little girl and said, "You could have done that."*

What an amazing outlook the grandmother has on life—just get it done. Pick yourself up, and move on.

Imagine how great your organization could be if employees spent less time in meetings—just talking about ideas or things—and more time actually doing them. To all those master delegators, procrastinators, dreamers, "time wasters", organizers of meetings, and so on—look inwardly, and consider these wise words: "You could have done that."

To all those trying to break bad habits, change their lifestyles, or who are about to give up on their goals and desires—say to yourself, "I can do it." Don't have people pointing fingers at you or muttering under their breadth, "You could have done that."

*Source: Adapted from: A. Bryant, The Corner Office: How Top CEOs Made It and How You Can Too (London; Harper Press, 2011).

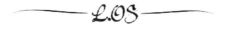

4.4.3 Hadrian's Wall

"If we all did the things we are capable of doing, we would literally astound ourselves."

—Thomas Edison

Hadrian was the emperor of Rome from AD 117 to 138. He is most well-known for building the wall that bears his name. The wall was built in AD 122, measuring 117 km in length, about 5.5 metres in height, and about 2.5 metres in width to protect the Romans inside from the outside barbarians. Not only was the wall a barrier; he built ditches in front and behind the wall, making things difficult for the invading forces.*

You may be wondering: Why the history lesson? Well, the wall was as much a psychological barrier as a physical one and has several lessons for us. By keeping the enemy out, the Romans were trapped inside, driven by fear. I'm sure there are many of us who are in the same situation today: trapped in our own rut, our own comfort zones. We put up invisible walls to keep out opportunities because we may be scared to take a risk, or we think we are not good enough.

Don't let your dreams and hopes lie shattered in the ditch consequent of you being scared to take a chance or worried about what others will say or think. Don't be afraid to try.

What are the states of your relationships, personal or between leader and employee? If some are failing, consider whether you have erected your own Hadrian's Wall instead of embracing open communication and trust. Perhaps you have been deeply hurt or let down by a person, and you now build walls around you in order to keep your emotions in check?

Now is the time to take stock, and see how many walls you have put around yourself and how many ditches you need to climb to achieve your goals or success. Re-ignite that passion, overcome your fears, and breakdown those elaborate fortifications that are holding you back from happiness or your mission.

If you think your problems are "out there" then you will continue to look "out there" for a solution. Look inside. Keep in mind that if you blame someone else for your problems then they have to change in order for you to have what you want and be happy. It doesn't work in reality. If you take the victim road you will end up in the ditch. Don't feed the victim.

Be accountable to yourself. Take action now. Take the plunge.

*Source: Hadrian's Wall—Wikipedia. The Free Encyclopedia <http://www. en.wikipedia.org/wiki/Hadrian's_Wall last> accessed 15 May 2014

5   Passion

5.1. What is your purpose in life?

5.1.1. The protégé and the mentor

"There is no passion to be found playing small, in settling for a life that is less than the one you are capable of living."

—Nelson Mandela

I love the narration told by Barrie Davenport [www. barriedavenport.com] in one of her blog articles of a protégé telling his mentor that he doesn't have a purpose in life. His mentor calmly responds that he most certainly does, as everyone has a purpose in life. The protégé then re-emphasizes the point that he has no purpose, passion, or dreams and has no idea of where to find his goals in life.

The wise old mentor then responds, "Your purpose in life is to find your purpose in life. Once you find your purpose you will find your passion, dream . . ."

Barrie Davenport is spot on with her observation. Once you know yourself it's easier to find your passion in life—that "something" that stimulates and excites your spirit, makes the heart pound faster, and will harness your skills and talents. Sometimes you may not even realize your passions, as you may take your skills and talents for granted.

What is your passion in life? How many of you really know or have truly found that burning desire? Not that easy, hey! Barrie Davenport summed it up so well. She said it's like going into a sweet shop as a child and being told you can have anything you want: You become overwhelmed and can't make a decision.

Passion is not something that falls from the sky. You have to discover yourself first. It's a journey of self-exploration, so give yourself time—it may take decades—but you are never too old to find your passion. It's taken me fifty years . . . So don't be discouraged.

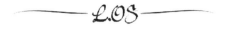

5.1.2. Ice princess

"Wanting something is not enough. You must hunger for it."

—Les Brown

In the movie Ice Princess young Casey Carlyle encounters many setbacks to realize her dream to be a champion ice skater. She is torn between two worlds—to pursue her passion in ice skating or attend Harvard University, the latter being something that her mother has instilled in her from any early age.

At the interview for acceptance into Harvard the Dean asks Casey an all-important question, "Why are you passionate about Harvard?"*

At this interview, Casey comes to the startling realization that she must follow her heart, live her dream and her passion, which is figure skating . . . and not her mother's dream.

You must live your own passions and dreams. Trust yourself. Create the kind of self that you will be happy to live with all your life.

*Source: Ice Princess, dir. Tim Flywell (2005), starring Michelle Trachtenberg, Joan Cusack, and Kim Cattrall.

5.1.3. Willy Loman

"Energy is the essence of life. Every day you decide how you going to use it by knowing what you want and what it takes to reach that goal, and maintaining the focus."

—Oprah Winfrey

Willy Loman is the central figure in Arthur Miller's Death of a Salesman, a poignant but sad story about failure and broken dreams. Willy spent his life chasing his dream of being the best salesperson in the world, so he lived in denial and vacillated between hope and despair,

depression and the illusion of success—it would all happen with the very next sale.

He tortured himself with the belief that if he were persistent or confident enough then he would hit the jackpot and be a success. Sadly he never met his promise to himself and ended up taking his own life.*

Willy did not stop to think about his job or analyze why he was failing. He didn't take the time to consider where his strengths or passions actually lay . . . or perhaps he was chasing the wrong dream altogether.

How many of you are doing just that—studying something because your parents insisted on it or working in the dead-end job as you are too scared to give up your security or just plain bored with life.

Make sure you are following the right dream: your dream, your passion.

*Source: A. Miller, Death of a Salesman: Play in Two Acts, USA, Dramatists Play Service, 1952

5.2. Put passion into action

5.2.1. Handful of keys

"I would rather hire a man with enthusiasm than a man who knows everything."
—J.D. Rockefeller

A few years ago my wife and I were invited by clients to a dinner and show. The show was called A Handful of Keys. On entering the theatre, I must admit we were both taken aback at the stage setting. There was no orchestra and no fancy decor or props; there was just two pianos, alone except for each other on the stage, separated from each other only be a few metres.

Two hours later we were up on our feet, giving a standing ovation to the two musicians who had thoroughly entertained and delighted us. It was one of the most memorable shows we have attended. It was one of

those occasions that we wanted the world to see and experience.

Have you ever come back from live play or show thoroughly enthralled and "blown away" by the acts and cast you have just witnessed? If so, you will identify with me, and I'm sure you will be equally quick to recount the highlights of the event to your family, friends, or colleagues and will add a recommendation that they, themselves, do attend the show.

What is more amazing is that this was well over the 100th performance of this show, yet, to us, it was like opening night; the passion, energy, and brilliance displayed by the cast were exceptional.

When it comes to your business or work environment, the same principle must apply. People will recommend you or your business to their sphere of influence. You have to display that attitude of positivity, professionalism, and fresh interest. You have to stand out from the rest of the "cast". That's exactly what it should be like when serving or selling to a client. Serve with a sense of freshness, energy, passion, and professionalism—like an opening night performance.

Put passion into action.

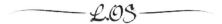

5.2.2. Hein Wagner—a passion for life

"Being driven is not the same as being passionate. Passion is a love for a journey. Drive is the need to reach the destination."

—Simon Sinek

Hein Wagner (aged thirty-eight) is married, a business owner, and a motivational speaker. He also holds the Guinness World Record for land driving at 322.5km/h in a Mercedes-Benz SL65. He has tackled the Cape to Rio yacht race, soared mountain peaks, parachute jumped, ran the Hong Kong and New York marathons, completed the 39 km Construction du Cap cycle race in Cape Town and 180 km on a tandem cycle in Korea.

Not bad for someone born blind.*

Isn't this a truly inspirational story of someone who has a passion for life? Hein Wagner has overcome severe adversity and handicap to achieve more than most of us able-bodied, full-sighted, and conservative folk. How many of us tend to complain at the slightest headache, too much rain, or Monday mornings, yet we have so much to be grateful for?

If you are in that guilty bunch, then it's time to stop and express gratitude for blessings you have in your life instead of being part of the "herd", complaining and blaming and bemoaning their circumstances or problems. It takes courage and a strong mindset, but it can be done.

We can learn so much from Hein Wagner—that life isn't about having, complaining, or moaning. It's about *being*: being part of life, enjoying life, and living life. Leo Buscaglia once said, "*Life is a paradise for those who love many things with a passion.*" Hein adopted this approach, and he does things that make him come alive, and in so doing he shows the world what it's like to be alive and live with that zest and passion. Hein chooses to win each day—to defy the odds, to embrace his challenges, and not let adversity steal his dreams.

Perhaps it's also time to be a "Hein Wagner", and put that passion and fire back into your lives, hobbies, or work chores. Re-ignite that flame of emotion, and get back to what once was the true love for what you do. Show the world that you, too, are alive.

*Source: Adapted from: "See I Can Do Anything", You (a South African publication—Media 24 Weekly Magazines), 8 April 2010.

5.2.3. Ed Roberts

"What colour is in a picture, enthusiasm is in life."

—Vincent van Gogh

Despite polio and several near death experiences Ed Roberts fought for fifteen years to make the world a better place for the physically challenged, which included wheelchair access ramps, special parking places, and grab bars.

He also became the first quadriplegic to graduate from the University of California, Berkeley, and held the position of director of California State Department of Rehabilitation—again pioneering this position for the disabled.*

The above is a very brief outline of the wonders performed by the late Ed Roberts that aptly illustrate the power of a positive attitude, and his passion to make a better life for so many disabled people in this world.

There is a valuable lesson for all of us. Ed did not sit with a victim mentality—he had the victor belief and mentality. He used every fibre of energy in his disabled body to champion rights for others. He has left an indelible mark on this world. His actions and continued lobbying during his lifetime has made life so much easier for handicapped people for the years to come.

Allow Ed to be an example to you—that you also will find a way to overcome any hurdles or dead ends in your life and will ignite your passion and desire to help and serve others in some way or other.

*Source: Ed Roberts (Activist)—Wikipedia. The Free Encyclopedia <http://www.en.wikipedia.org/wiki/Ed_Roberts-(activist)> accessed 19 May 2014

5.2.4. The tone is in your fingers

"You can't start a fire without a spark."

—Bruce Springsteen

In the book Rework by Jason Fried and David Hansson there is a wonderful chapter entitled "Tone is in Your Fingers". They concur that you can buy the same type of guitar, related equipment, and amplifier that Eddie Van Halen uses, but when you play it's still going to sound like you.

Likewise, Eddie could plug into a "crappy" setup at a pawn shop, and you would still be able to recognize Eddie playing.*

Fancy gear can help, but the bottom line is that your tone comes from you. People tend to obsess over "tools" and fancy equipment—instead, use the tools you have, but use them properly—as an aid, not a crutch. Concentrate on your abilities, gifts, and talents, and make your own music.

Everyone is gifted—but some people never open their package. Talent is only the starting point in business, sport, music, or your life's passion. To be a success you also need to keep working that special talent or inherent gift you have discovered. It takes thousands of hours of self-discipline, practice, hard work, or studying. It's not solely reliant on the accessories or type of equipment around you.

The tone is in your fingers.

*Source: J. Fried and D. Hansson, Rework (London; Vermillion, 2010).

5.3. Do you love what you are doing?

5.3.1. The diamond merchant

"Passion is the secret sauce that makes the impossible probable."
—Robin Sharma

A wealthy merchant was seeking to buy a diamond of a certain kind to add to his collection. A famous dealer found such a stone and called him to come and see it.

The merchant flew immediately to the dealer where the seller had assigned his best diamond expert to close the transaction. After hearing the assistant describe in perfect technical detail the diamond's worth and beauty, the merchant decided not to buy it.

Before he left, however, the owner of the store stepped forward and asked, "Do you mind if I show you that stone once more?" The customer agreed.

The store owner didn't repeat one thing that the salesman had said. He simply took the stone in his hand, stared at it, and described the incredible beauty of the stone in a

way that revealed why this stone stood out from all the others he had seen in his life. He passionately described the stone's radiance and how he felt about the stone.

The customer bought it immediately. Tucking his new purchase into his breast pocket, the customer commented to the owner, "Sir, I wonder why you were able to sell me this stone when your salesman could not?"

The owner replied, "That salesman is the best in the business. He knows more about diamonds than anyone, including myself, and I pay him a large salary for his knowledge and expertise. But I would gladly pay him twice as much if I could put into him something I have that he lacks. You see, he knows diamonds, but I love them."*

The above story is a reminder to us of the importance of that sense of passion, energy, and pride in our work. It's got to be 110 per cent at all times. It must show in your eyes, your face, your tone of voice and your whole being—your inner core.

The way you act, serve, and work—your passion forms part of your personal branding. Being good or knowledgeable in your particular field is not good enough. You have to offer more. You need to present the whole package. It's what's inside, in your heart, which makes you as a person and that will manifest in your other roles—as a salesperson, parent, coach, or sportsperson. It's your DNA.

What makes up your DNA?

*Source: unknown

——— *L.OS* ———

5.3.2. The taxi driver

"Don't ask yourself what the world needs; ask yourself what makes you come alive. And then go and do that. Because the world needs people who have come alive."

—Howard Thurman, author and philosopher

Some may say that I'm "just a taxi driver". But, to me, I help visitors create memories that enrich their lives. I have the chance to show people some decency in a world where so many among us long for more human connections. I get to put smiles on the faces of my customers—and leave them better than I found them.

In my mind, work is a vehicle for discovering more of our gifts, displaying more of our potential and being of use to other human beings.*

The quotes above put everything in perspective. What makes you come alive? What excites you? What gets your juices going? Have you ever noticed when you ask someone about their interest or passion what their reaction is like? Their eyes light up, they start talking faster, their hand movements are more pronounced, and you can't shut them up. They go on and on and on.

Someone once said that if you love what you do you have never worked a day in your life. Find that thing or job that makes you come alive, and then go and do it. Steve Jobs understood the need to be happy at work. He stated on many occasions that he loved what he did, and he worked with real passion. Take note of the wise words that he left for us:

> *You've got to find what you love. And that is as true for your work as for your lovers. Your work is going to fill a large part of your life, and the only way to be truly satisfied is to do what you believe is great work. The only way to do great work is to love what you do. If you haven't found it yet, keep looking. Don't settle. As with all matters of the heart, you will know when you find it.*

*Source: Adapted from: R. Sharma, The Secret Letters of the Monk Who Sold his Ferrari (London; Harper Element, 2011).

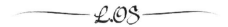

5.3.3. The Vince Lombardi story

"There's only one way to succeed in anything, and that is to give it everything. I do, and I demand that my players do."

—Vince Lombardi

The above quote was the cornerstone of the philosophy that shaped the life of the great Vince Lombardi, not only from a coaching or football aspect but from the general principles of sport, business, and life.

It's been more than forty years since the passing of Vince Lombardi, yet his famous speech, "What It Takes to Be Number One", continues to inspire and motivate a countless number of people and athletes.

In the book *What It Takes to Be # 1* Vince Lombardi's son shares nine key principles that shaped his father's philosophy of coaching and of life. Here is an excerpt on passion:

> **Zeal and passion are emotions that move you. My father was once described by the late Wellington Mara, one-time co-owner of the New York Giants, as having "the zeal of a missionary". And although the Packers** [THE *Green Bay Packers, an American football team based in Green Bay Wisconsin*] **held a special place in his heart, my father's passion and enthusiasm extended into all corners of his life. He could get excited about dinner at a good restaurant, a sunset, Christmas with family, and, especially, a game of golf.**
>
> **His passion overflowed. It was an enthusiasm that could be neither corralled nor fended off. "If you said 'good morning' to him the right way," said a friend, "you could bring tears to his eyes." His emotional ups and downs as an assistant coach with the Giants earned him the nickname "Mr Hi-Lo".**
>
> **Lombardi said in response, "If you can't get emotional about what you believe in your heart, you're in the wrong business."**
>
> **Passion and enthusiasm are the seeds of achievement. Enthusiasm is like an ocean tide; there's a certain inevitability about it. Zeal sweeps obstacles away. To motivate people, there must be a spark, some juice, desire, zeal, inspiration. It's rough to be a leader if you can't energize yourself, and then your people. They need**

to be able to tap into your emotional energy—and you need to be able to tap into theirs.

It's called passion today. In my father's day, it was called "emotion". No matter what you choose to call it, I doubt you could find someone who was as passionate—and this is important—as effective, as my father. Having a plan is important, but along with a plan there must be a hunger and a zeal to achieve the vision.*

*Source: Adapted from V. Lombard and V Lombardi Jnr, What It Takes to Be # I (Edinburgh; Thomas Nelson, gift edition, 2012).

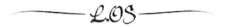

5.3.4. Colonel Saunders

"Nothing in this world is impossible to a willing heart."

—Abraham Lincoln

He was nothing but a retiree with a fried chicken recipe. That's all. No organization. No nothing. He owned a little restaurant that was going broke because the main highway had been routed elsewhere. When he got his first social cheque, he decided to see if he could make some money selling his chicken recipe. His first idea was to sell the recipe to restaurant owners and have them give him a percentage of the proceeds.

He drove around the country, sleeping in his car, trying to find someone who would back him. He kept changing his idea and knocking on doors. He was rejected 1009 times and then something miraculous happened. Someone said yes. The Colonel was in business.*

Colonel Saunders built the Kentucky Fried Chicken (KFC) Empire that made him a millionaire and changed the eating habits of a nation.

He had the belief and faith in both his product and himself. He was driven by his passion. He had the ability to hear the word "no" more than a thousand times but still possessed the determination and strength of his conviction to carry on until his goal was achieved. His dream became his passion, and his dream came true.

How many of you have a recipe for success—that passion, faith, and belief in yourself? How many of you give up on your goals or hopes at the first hurdle? There is a valuable lesson to be learned from Colonel Saunders. Nothing is impossible to the willing heart.

*Source: A. Robbins, Unlimited Power (London; Simon & Schuster Ltd 1988).

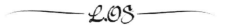

6   Values

6.1. Ethics

6.1.1. Fishing and ethics

"I think we all have a little voice inside us that will guide us . . . If we shut out all the noise and clutter from our lives and listen to that voice, it will tell you the right thing to do."

—Christopher Reeve

The above words by the late Christopher Reeve are quite apt when it comes to values that one should listen to that little voice inside them, that echo in their conscious and unconscious state that tells them what is the right thing to do.

There is a story (that I believe to be a true one) that was sent to my inbox some years ago. I don't know its origins, but its message about values is very powerful, and I would like to share it with you. The moral of this story re-enforces the comments made by Christopher Reeve in the quote above.

> **On the day before the bass season opened, a young boy and his father were fishing early in the evening, catching some fish with worms. When his pole doubled over, the boy knew that something huge was on the other end. His father watched with admiration as the boy skilfully worked the fish alongside the dock.**

> **Finally, he very gingerly lifted the exhausted fish from the water. It was the largest one he had ever seen, but it was a bass. The boy and his father looked at the handsome fish, shining in the moonlight. The father lit a match and looked at his watch. It was 10.00 p.m., two hours before the season opened. He looked at the fish and then at the boy. "You'll have to put it back, son," he said.**

> **"Dad!" cried the boy.**

> **"There will be another fish," said his father.**

"Not as big as this one," cried the boy.

He looked around the lake. No other fishermen or boats were around in the moonlight. He looked again at his father. Even though no one had seen them, nor could anyone ever know at what time he had caught the fish, the boy could tell by the clarity of his father's voice that the decision was not negotiable. He slowly worked the hook out of the lip of the huge bass and lowered it into the black water.

I'm not sure if that boy ever again caught such a magnificent fish as the one he landed that night long ago. But I do know that that boy—now a man—does see that same fish—again and again—every time he comes up against a question of ethics or when his value system is questioned. And, in doubt, I'm sure he will still hear his dad's voice quietly whispering into his ear, "You'll have to put it back, son."

Ethics and our values are simple matters of right and wrong. It is only the practice of ethics that is difficult. Do we only do right when someone is looking?

So, when tempted, remember to listen to that little voice inside you, and, if necessary, to put the fish back into the water. Always do the right thing, and be an example to others.

6.1.2. The sweep stake

"My basic principle is that you don't make decisions because they are easy; you don't make them because they are cheap; you don't make them because they're popular; you make them because they're right."

—Theodore Hesburgh

Young Simon responded to the farmer's advert to sell a donkey for $100. He met the farmer, paid the money, and arranged to collect his donkey the next day.

The following day the farmer informed him that, regrettably, his donkey had died during the night. Even

worse, the farmer had spent the money at the pub that evening and was unable to refund young Simon.

Simon asked the farmer to keep the corpse in the shade for a few days and eventually phoned the farmer, saying that it could now be buried, as he had sold the donkey for a profit of $898. The farmer was blown away and asked how Simon had achieved this.

"Simple," said Simon. "I raffled it. Sold 500 tickets at $2.00 each."

Didn't anyone complain when they found out the donkey was dead asked the farmer. "Only the winner," replied Simon, "and I refunded him."*

How shrewd of Simon. In this instance he managed to get away with the deal and still make a handsome profit. In life not every deal will work out favourably or go according to plan. What will happen when others learn of Simon's shortcut or unethical dealings? And then there is the reputational risk to both Simon's own name and his organization to consider.

The poet Dale Wimbrow, in his poem "The Guy in the Glass", offers advice in the ethics of doing business. He warns us not to cheat or fool ourselves or others but to be a person of strength, good values, and manners and to live with our conscience. This fits in so cleverly with the wise words of Theodore Hesburgh in the quote mentioned above: Don't make decisions because they are cheap, easy, or popular—make them because they are right.

*Source: Adapted from a joke that appeared in You. (a South African publication—Media 24 Weekly Magazines), date unknown

6.1.3. Codes of conduct—the Birkenhead drill

"Be sure you put your feet in the right place, then stand firm."

—Abraham Lincoln

> **On 26 February 1852 the Birkenhead, mainly carrying British soldiers to fight in the English Frontier War, struck an unchartered rock 3 km off Danger Point. The ship was torn in half, and there was barely time to get the handful of women and children into the few lifeboats along with some of the crew.**
>
> **Afraid that the soldiers, who had streamed on deck, would panic and swim to the boats and swamp them, Colonel Alexander Setan, their commander lieutenant, ordered the soldiers to "stand first" as the sea rose.***

That act of courage became known as the Birkenhead Drill and marked the start of a tradition of saving woman and children first from a sinking ship. It became entrenched as the unwritten rule in navigation—the code of conduct, the code of ethics, the rule of the sea. Despite this, there have been recent instances, the *Oceanos* and *Costa Concordia*, where the respective captains had disregard for this code and were the first to abandon ship—to much ridicule and public outcry.

In the same manner, businesses have traditions, codes of conducts, and even unwritten laws that set the tone and culture for its operation. Believe it or not, they are also the barometer that measures the relationship, spirit of engagement, integrity of the business, and degree of trust between employees and employers on the one hand and between the employees and clients on the other.

Businesses have the responsibility to ensure these codes of conduct or unwritten rules are true to their morals and can withstand scrutiny from the press and public.

*Source: Adapted from: an article by Paul Ash in The Sunday Times, 11 March 2012.

6.1.4. Trust is like a mirror

"Trust is like a mirror. Once broken it can be fixed, but you can still see the cracks."

—anonymous

Just before my mother went into a retirement home my sister and I tried to find a suitable "helper", that is, a person with nursing experience who could also be a companion and assistant to her daily needs. I recall interviewing a number of perspectives and found the ideal candidate—a person who could drive, was strong to help bathe her, had nursing experience, could cook, and so forth The only problem was that this person was still employed and had to give one month's notice.

The candidate was so eager for the room and job that she said she would just give her current employer 24 hours' notice and that she simply wasn't going to wait the month.

This comment immediately led to the candidate's downfall and not getting the job, based on the question of ethics, trust, and even loyalty, coupled with the premise that *if she could do this to her current employer, she could certainly do it again—to us.*

It's the small things in life, as in this example, that make a person and determine their sense of ethics, trust, loyalty, and character—so guard your reputation.

Trust is like a mirror; once it has been broken, it may be patched up, but it will never be the same again.

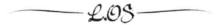

6.2. Personal strength of character

6.2.1. The R20.00 Seminar

"What lies behind us and what lies before us are small matters when compared to what lies within us."

—Ralph Waldo Emerson

A well-known speaker started off his seminar by holding up a R20.00 note. In the room of 200, he asked, "Who would like this R20.00 note?" Hands started going up.

He said, "I am going to give this R20.00 to one of you but first, let me do this." He proceeded to crumple up the R20.00 note. He then asked, "Who still wants it?" Still the hands were up in the air.

Well, he replied, "What if I do this?" And he dropped it on the ground and started to grind it into the floor with his shoe. He picked it up, now crumpled and dirty. Still the hands went into the air.*

The above anecdote portrays a very valuable life lesson. No matter what the speaker did with the money, it did not decrease in value. It was still worth R20.00.

Many times in your lives, you may be crumpled, stood on, or ground into the dirt by the decisions you made and/or by the circumstances that come your way. You may be feeling as though you are worthless. Stop for a minute and realize that no matter what has happened or what will happen to you, *you* will never lose your value—you are a priceless commodity.

The worth of your life comes not in what you do or who you know but in *who you are*. You are special and unique and have your own personal brand—don't ever forget it.

*Source: The R20.00 Note—Johan Campbell <http://www.motivate.co.za/BnP/Bnp-118.shtml> accessed 18 May 2014

6.2.2. Be your own true, authentic self

"There is a fountain inside you. Don't walk around with an empty bucket."

—Rumi

We must break free of the seductions of society and live a life on our own terms, under our own values and aligned with our original dreams. We must tap our hidden selves;

explore the deep-seated, unseen hopes, desires, strengths and weaknesses that make us who we are . . . .

Every decision we make, every step we take, must be informed by our commitment to living a life that is true and honest and authentic to ourselves and ourselves alone.*

It is through Robin Sharma in his work *The Secret Letters of the Monk Who Sold His Ferrari* that we are reminded that the most important gift we can give ourselves is the commitment to living our own true, authentic life.

To understand yourself it's important to understand your value system. Self-awareness is key to your ability to understand yourself, and, in so doing, you will appreciate the various sides of your existence—your physical, spiritual, emotional, and mental sides. You will soon realize your strengths and weaknesses, needs and desires, loves, passions, attitudes, and why you are at peace—or not.

You are also responsible for your own success or failures, actions or lack of action. So look in the mirror and see yourself—your own friendly authentic, kind, gentle, and loving unique self.

*Source: R. Sharma, The Secret Letters of the Monk Who Sold his Ferrari (London; Harper Element 2011). Page 44

6.2.3. The picture of "you"

"Nearly all men can stand adversity, but if you want to test a man's character, give him power."

—Abraham Lincoln

There is a lovely story that I once read whereby a father was trying to watch his favourite motor-racing idol one Sunday afternoon but was continually being interrupted by his five year-old son who was bored and demanded his father's attention. Trying to occupy his son with a game, the father found a picture of the world in the newspaper. He knew that this would keep his son occupied until after

the Grand Prix, so he cut it up into about fifty pieces, scattered the pieces all over the living-room floor, and said, "Son, see if you can put this puzzle back together."

The father was astounded when his son came back some fifteen minutes later with the puzzle completed. "You're kidding," said the father (who knew his son didn't know the positions of all the countries in the world). "How did you do it?"

"It was easy," replied the son. "There is a picture of a person on the back of the map, so when I got the person put together, the world looked just fine." *

In the same manner, people are piecing together the various attributes that decide you as a person. Your values, emotions, mannerisms, ideologies, feelings, ambitions, hurts, beliefs, and character are strewn all over the living-room floor, and each and every person you come into contact with is piecing this giant jigsaw puzzle of "you" together.

What picture or image are you allowing people to piece together about you?

*Source: unknown

6.2.4. Values are not always determined by background

"Courage doesn't always roar. Sometimes courage is that little voice at the end of the day that says I'll try again tomorrow."
—Mary Anne Radmacher

Have you heard about an African-American girl born into poverty in rural Mississippi, USA? She was born to unwed parents, and, shortly after conception, her father took off, never to be seen again. She initially lived with her grandmother and wore dresses made of potato sacks. At age six she moved back to her mom who worked as a maid with very little income. At nine, she was abused by her cousin, uncle, and a family friend.

She ran away at age thirteen, miscarried a year later.

Today she is probably the most influential woman in the world—Oprah Winfrey.*

Oprah did not let her past nightmares get the better of her, and she didn't let her standards and values become influenced by the family or community she grew up with or be tainted by her childhood experiences and upbringing.

She has risen like the phoenix and has developed a new set of beliefs and strength of character that has empowered her and taken her to the top of the ladder. She is now a wonderful role model to so many. If Oprah can do it—so can you!

*Source: Adapted from: Oprah Winfrey—Wikipedia, The Free Encyclopedia. <http://en.wikipedia.org/wiki/Oprah-Winfrey> accessed 13 May 2014

6.2.5. It's what's inside that counts

"Good timber does not grow with ease. The stronger the wind the stronger the trees."

—J. Willard Marriott

There's an old joke of a woman who battled to find a man to marry her. She regarded herself as fat, ugly, and unwanted—surely no man would marry her in this state? So she makes a pact with God that if she saved sufficient funds to beautify herself, he would send her a man of her dreams.

After a couple of years this lady had sufficient funds saved to start reconstructive surgery to her face and body. She consulted the world's leading plastic surgeon who did a most wonderful job; this lady could now enter the Miss World contest and have a good chance of winning.

Being discharged from hospital this lady was crossing the road to buy new clothes from a fashionable boutique

when she was hit by a truck and was killed instantly. On her arrival at the Pearly Gates she quizzed St Peter as to why God had called her now before she had found the man of her dreams. St Peter calmly replied, "You changed so much that not even God recognized you."

St Peter's answer was a real jolt to bring us back to our senses. People sometimes spend large amounts of money trying to make themselves look younger or more beautiful. Others take courses to develop their characters and social skills. Alas, to be well groomed or beautiful looking doesn't compensate for the inner values, emotions, and character of the person.

Looks can be deceiving, beauty is only skin deep, and first impressions are merely that—it can be just cosmetic, sometimes all an illusion. What counts is a person's deep-down authentic self—their self-assurance, self-belief, and self-love. You are not a clone, and you are not unimportant, so get in touch with your inner self.

Guard your reputation. First, be true to yourself: *It's what is inside that counts.*

6.3. Values in general

6.3.1. Cast in stone

"Values, in matters of style, swim with the current; in matters of principle, stand like a rock."

—Thomas Jefferson

In 1927 the Danish-American artist and sculptor, Gutzon Borglum, started the process in carving the renowned "four figures" in the steep rises of Mount Rushmore, South Dakota. He was responsible for the surveying, planning, modelling, and sculpting of these four faces—a task that consumed the last fourteen years of his life. He was supported by his son, and the work was completed just before he died.

Tens of thousands of tons of debris were carefully chiselled from the mountain to expose the four faces of Washington, Jefferson, Lincoln, and Theodore Roosevelt.*

In essence, the carving revealed that the presidents were always in that mountain, looking down at the valley, buried in the solid rock face of nature. All that Borglum did was to clear some of the rubble, so their faces became visible.

There is a profound moral for everyone in this story. If a person could expend the time and energy to remove the "rubble"—the fears, negativity, or vulnerability that hinders their true feelings, values, and strength of character—can you imagine the effect that this would have on their personal life, their career, their family, or community as a whole?

Make sure that your values are righteous, consistent, and steadfast—cast in stone for all to see and witness. Perhaps then everyone would see your beautiful face embodied in the stone of the earth, looking down the valley—at them—as a living example, a source of inspiration, or a role model for all to follow.

*Source: Adapted from: Gutzon Borglum—Wikipedia, The Free Encyclopedia <http://www. en.wikipeadia.org/wiki/Gutzon-Borglum> accessed 19 May 2014

6.3.2. Your character role

"You tell on yourself by the friends you seek, by the manner in which you speak. By the way you employ your leisure time, by the use you make of dollar and dime."

—anonymous

I recently read an article on the life and acting career of Julianne Moore. What struck me the most are the various roles she plays and the different characters she assumes, both on and off the screen, from being an actress in movies like Saving Grace or Chloe to being a mum and wife or a daughter and human being such as dealing with the emotions of her mother's death.

In the same manner, are we not actors assuming various roles in our family, work, and life situations? Likewise, we wear different hats every day and during the day, each with its own set of rules and responsibilities. The big question to ask when we play these roles is, "Are we living up to our value system and expectations?"

There is a short poem entitled "You Tell of Yourself" (author unknown) that deals with the attributes that one would look at to appreciate a person's character. The words are profound and the underlying concept is a wonderful way for us to measure ourselves and our values for we show ourselves to the world by the friends we keep, the way we work, eat, speak, walk, and the manner in which we bear defeat; all the things we do and don't do. These daily actions and behaviours reflect our true character and principles.

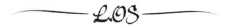

6.3.3. What goes around comes around

"There is one word which may serve as a rule of practice for all one's life—reciprocity."

—Confucius

I once read a story about a man and his son hiking along a mountain top when the lad slipped and slid a few metres, only to be caught up by the shrubbery. In his panic, the boy called out, "Help! Somebody help!"

No sooner had he uttered these words, a voice called back, "Help! Somebody help!"

The boy, surprised by the voice, shouted back. "Who are you?"

The voice shouted in return, "Who are you?"

By then the boy's father had reached the lad, and he pulled him to safety. The boy looked up at his father and said, "Dad, who was that answering me back?" The boy's father smiled and explained to the boy it was an echo.

It's an echo but also a factor of life. What you send out to the universe comes back to you. If you send out honesty and good values you will reap the benefits of some form of reciprocation. If you send out signals of fear and negativity then these will also return back to you in some form or another.

So be careful to send out the right signals, and bear in mind the law of attraction and all its benefits. Keep your internal dialogue and thoughts as positive as possible.

Perhaps the best advice that one can give is to treat others as you yourself would want to be treated. What goes around comes around.

6.4. Guard your thoughts and your words

6.4.1. Choose your words carefully

"Let's all be ambassadors of our mouths so we won't be slaves of our words."
—anonymous

> **Once upon a time, an old man spread rumours that his neighbour was a thief. As a result, the neighbour was arrested and later released, as he was proven innocent. After being released he sued the old man for wrongly accusing him.**
>
> **In court the old man told the judge, "They were just comments; I didn't mean harm to anyone."**
>
> **The judge, before passing sentence on the case, told the old man, "Write all the things you said about your neighbour on a piece of paper. Cut it up, and, on the way home, throw the pieces of paper out. Tomorrow, come back to hear the sentence."**
>
> **The next day, the judge told the man, "Before receiving your sentence, you must now go out and gather all the pieces of paper you threw out yesterday, and bring them back to me."**

The old man protested, "I can't do that! The wind would have scattered them, and I won't know where to find them."

The judge replied, "In the same way that the wind would have scattered the pieces of paper, simple comments may destroy the honour of a man to such an extent that one is not able to fix it."*

If you can't speak well of someone, don't say anything about them. Once you utter a word or comment then it's out there in the universe; you can't retract it. In the words of Frank Outlaw, watch your thoughts, for they become words, and, in turn, your words will become your actions, your habits, your character, and, ultimately, your destiny.

Labels can be hazardous. In today's world we are very quick to judge or be judged. We are also very quick to diagnose or label a person—whether it relates to issues concerning a person's disease, character, social behaviour, or career ambitions. Labels can be hazardous and can stick to a person for the rest of their lives. So remember there is a person under that label. Choose your words carefully.

Protect your reputation that you too don't be wrongly labelled.

*Source: Adapted from: RUMOURS—'Let's all be masters of our mouths . . .' CiteHR.com Motivation and Improvement <http://www.citehr.com/177663-rumours-lets-all-masters-our-mouths-so.html> date posted 11 July 2009, accessed 12 May 2014

6.4.2. The fence

"Values are like fingerprints. Nobody's are the same, but you leave them all over everything you do."

—Elvis Presley

There once was a little boy who had a bad temper. His father gave him a bag of nails and told him that every time he lost his temper, he must hammer a nail into the fence. The first day the boy had driven thirty-seven nails into the

fence. Over the next few weeks, as he learned to control his anger, the number of nails hammered daily gradually dwindled down. He discovered it was easier to hold his temper than to drive those nails into the fence.

Finally, the day came when the boy didn't lose his temper at all. He told his father about it, and the father suggested that the boy now pull out one nail for each day that he was able to hold his temper. The days passed, and the young boy was finally able to tell his father that all the nails were gone.

The father took his son by the hand and led him to the fence. He said, "You have done well, my son, but look at the holes in the fence."*

The fence will never be the same. When you say things in anger, they leave a scar just like the holes in the fence. Similarly, you can put a knife in a man and draw it out, but it won't matter how many times you then say, "I'm sorry," the wound will still be there.

Someone once said it's not the snake bite that kills you; it's the spread of the poison. Dr Laurence J. Peter wisely commented that if you speak when you are angry you will make the best speech you'll ever regret. So, make sure you control your temper or the words or tone of your message the next time you are tempted to say something you will regret later.

*Source: Adapted from: Nails In The Fence—Inspiration Peak <http://www. inspirationpeak.com/cgi-bin/stories.cgi?record=50> accessed 20 May 2014

6.4.3. Your own value system

"To be yourself in a world that is constantly trying to make you something else is the greatest accomplishment."

—Ralph Waldo Emerson

Lynda Kau, a recognized coach and psychologist, wrote an interesting article, "Connect with the different parts of yourself". She mentions that each of us is not a solo

instrument, but we are more like a choir or orchestra with several voices.

So what is your mind, heart, body, or gut saying? Let these different voices or parts of you co-exist and speak to one another. In this way you will find an answer that comes from your whole self.

Let each voice and part of you be compatible to your own value system. Get to know the real *you*. In so doing you will uncover your belief system.

The following poem is a set of affirmations that could easily be incorporated into your value system:

> *If you plant honesty, you will reap trust*
> *If you plant goodness, you will reap friends*
> *If you plant humility, you will reap greatness*
> *If you plant perseverance, you will reap contentment*
> *If you plant consideration, you will reap perspective*
> *If you plant hard work, you will reap success*
> *If you plant forgiveness, you will reap reconciliation*
> *So, be careful what you plant now; it will determine what you will reap later.*
>
> *(source unknown)*

7   Challenges and problem solving

7.1. Find the source of the problem

7.1.1. The monkey story; that's how things are done around here!

"There are no limits on what you can achieve with your life, except the limits you accept in your mind."

—Brian Tracy

A group of scientists placed five monkeys in a cage, and, in the middle of that cage, a ladder with bananas on the top. Every time a monkey went up the ladder, the scientists soaked the rest of the monkeys with cold water. As a result, it soon became evident that every time a monkey went up the ladder, the other monkeys would turn on the monkey ascending the ladder and beat him up. After some time, no monkey dare go up the ladder regardless of the temptation.

Scientists then decided to substitute one of the monkeys. The first thing this new monkey did was to go up the ladder. Straight away the other monkeys started to beat him up. (There were still bananas and still the intention to soak the monkeys). After several beatings this new monkey learned not to climb the ladder, even though he didn't know the reason as to why the other monkeys turned on him.

The scientists carried on with this experiment, and the second substituted monkey got beaten up when climbing the ladder. Even more surprising, the first substituted monkey also took part in beating up the second substituted monkey.

Over time, the scientists rotated and exchanged the original set of monkeys with a new set of substituted monkeys—with the same result as above. The newest

monkey started to climb up the ladder, only to get beaten up by the others. In the end there were five substituted monkeys, and although they didn't get the cold shower, they beat up the monkey who attempted to climb the ladder.*

There is some debate as to whether this particular experiment actually occurred. There is, however, data to substantiate the fact that experiments involving monkeys and bananas took place; please see one particular reference in a self-help book *Competing for the Future* by Gary Hamel and C. K. Prahalad (1996). Nevertheless the storyline and experiment offers an interesting insight into the psychology of group behaviour, and the need not to upset the status quo.

If it was possible to ask the monkeys why they would beat up all those who attempted to go up the ladder then I bet the answer would be: "I don't know—that's how things are done around here!"

Does it sound familiar? And what about you or your team or organization?

Do you/your team challenge the status quo?

Do you/your team members just accept everything you are told or taught?

Are you/your team open to change or new, innovative ways of doing things?

Do you/your colleagues teach others or impart knowledge in a clear, distinct, and value-added format?

*Source: Adapted from: _Michael Basilico, *Monkeys by Michael Basilico—Robot: Mafia* **<http://robotmafia.com/five-monkeys-by-michael-basilico/ I Dec 2011>** **accessed 20 May 2014**

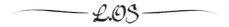

7.1.2. The rock

"Every problem contains the seeds of its own solution."

—Stanley Arnold

An old farmer had ploughed around a large rock in one of his fields for years. He had broken several plough shares

and a cultivator on it and had grown rather morbid about the rock.

After breaking another plough share one day, and remembering all the trouble the rock had caused him through the years, he finally decided to do something about it.

When he put the crowbar under the rock, he was surprised to discover that it was only about six inches thick and that he could break it up easily with a sledgehammer. As he was carting the pieces away he had to smile, remembering all the trouble that the rock had caused him over the years and how easy it would have been to get rid of it sooner.*

John Foster Dulles once said, *"The measure of success is not whether you have a tough problem to deal with, but whether it's the same problem you had last year."* That is exactly what the farmer did; he went on for years avoiding the rock, and, yet, in the end, the solution was so simple. So much aggravation and stress could have been eliminated.

If you stand too close to an elephant all you see is grey matter. In like manner, if you stand too close to your problems you can't see the "wood for the trees" or, in the case above, how to remove the "rock" from the path. Even small things become big issues and over-bearing. Try taking a step back and looking at things with fresh eyes.

There are always solutions; the secret is to break big problems into smaller, much more manageable "bites". Remember, one can't solve problems by complaining about it; do something about it. The world loves a problem solver, so . . . be a good one.

*Source: B. Cavanaugh, The Sower's Seeds—120 inspiring stories for preaching, teaching and public speaking (Mahwah; Paulist Press, 2004).

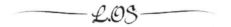

7.1.3. The lost keys

"There are two equally dangerous extremes—to shut reason out, and to let nothing else in."

—Blaise Pascal

Did you hear the story about a person who lost his car keys one night on the way home from a function? He spent more than 15 minutes searching, in a well-lit area under a street light, without any success.

A passer-by approached and asked the man what he was looking for. He then proceeded to help the man and joined the search for the missing car keys. After a while the passer-by posed a question to the man, "Are you sure you lost the keys in this spot?"

"Oh, no," replied the man. "I lost the keys around the corner . . . I'm just looking here because the light is better."

When it comes to problem solving we must ensure we get to the source of the problem, the root cause, not to go looking where "the light is better": By taking short cuts and finding the quick and easy way out.

Einstein said, "Problems cannot be solved at the same level of thinking at which they were created." We can't solve the problem by just "scratching the surface" or assuming the problem has been identified. We need to drill down to the "root" of the issue, and only then will we be able to present an acceptable solution.

We need to reframe the problem, and look at it from a different perspective while simultaneously checking for the opportunities that may abound. Put the problem "to bed" once and for all, so it doesn't come back and "bite" you. And if, for some reason, we discover that the issues can't be solved, or if they are completely out of our control, then we must change our attitude to the problem, and accept the circumstances.

7.2. How do you handle problems and challenges in your life?

7.2.1. Peter Van Kets

"I'll defeat you yet . . . be aware you're as big as you're going to get—but I'm still growing."

—Sir Edmund Hillary (explorer)

Peter van Kets, a South African adventurer and motivational speaker, single-handedly sailed across the Atlantic, a distance of approximately 5,500 km in a 7-metre boat. He encountered many setbacks, including storms and an aching body along the way, but that didn't deter him. He remained resolute and focused on the end goal.

He rowed harder instead of relaxing. So instead of 12 hours a day, he did 18 hours a day. It took him 76 days to complete the odyssey.*

On completion of the event, and in response to a question on how he achieved this remarkable feat, he said, "If you want to get to know yourself, spend at least 24 hours with yourself." One will be surprised what inner strengths and attributes are contained in the inner sanctum of our bodies, heart, and mind, and when the "chips" are down we know we can come up trumps. We can prevail.

There is always an adventure on the horizon, and invariably there will also always be another storm to spoil those well-laid plans. How do you handle the storms in your life? Do you batten down the hatches, wait for them to blow over, or row harder?

No storm lasts forever, and a downpour is normally accompanied by a rainbow—a glimmer of light, hope, and possibility.

Don't be too quick to surrender. Dig deep within your being, and draw on that remarkable strength and courage.

***Source: Adapted from: Peter Van Kets, adventurer and motivational speaker . . . —Speaker Inc <http://www.speakersinc.co.za/en/motivational-speaker/petervankets.html> accessed 20 May 2014**

7.2.2. Fly your kite

"You can learn to forgive yourself. You can't change your shortcomings until you accept yourself despite them."

—Dr Bernie Siegel

There is an unusual custom that occurs in Japan. At the end of the year, people take to the streets to fly a kite. What's unusual about this event, however, is that they write on the kite a certain "quality" or "failing" about themselves that they are not happy with, for example, laziness.

Then once the kite is up in the air they cut the string, sending their kite and their affliction into oblivion.

I'm sure there are other alternatives that you can use, but this physical act of letting go of one's problems, bad habits, faults, resentments, worries, or jealousies helps clean the slate so that you can start afresh.

Don't be too hard on yourself. Author and poet B. J. Gallagher, in her poem, *Staying the Course*, reminds us that *our journey of life is about progress, not perfection; it's not about doing one thing 100 per cent better—it's a matter of doing 100 things, 1 per cent better each day*. Progress is evolutionary not revolutionary, and most days we measure our progress in inches, not miles.

You can't change your shortcomings until you accept yourself despite them. Perhaps it's not a bad idea for you to go find your kite, and . . . fly your kite, and learn to forgive yourself.

7.2.3. Robin Sharma's words of wisdom

"Problems exist only in the human mind."

—Anthony de Mello

Once and for all, come to the realization that pain is a teacher and failure is the highway to success. You cannot learn how to play the guitar without hitting a few wrong

notes and you will never learn how to sail if you're not willing to tip the boat over a few times.

Begin to see your troubles as blessings, resolve to transform your stumbling blocks into stepping stones, and vow to turn your wounds into wisdom.*

The above words by Robin Sharma have certainly made a significant impression on me, and I would incorporate these words of wisdom into my personal top ten quotes of all time. It's a very profound message of hope and inspiration that succinctly tells us not to be discouraged if we mess up. We are not infallible, and, yes, we will err, and make mistakes from time to time.

Robin Sharma also tells us that our problems are challenges that can be overcome, and we can grow and develop from these hurdles. But we must turn the stumbling blocks into stepping stones, and we can learn from our errors and experiences . . . turning "our wounds into wisdom". We must learn our lesson well the first time, for we will have no sympathy for repeating the same mistakes.

Turning stumbling blocks into stepping stones, moving forward inch by inch, and developing and growing from storms in our life—that's how we will handle the challenges that confront us daily.

*Source: Sharma R, (2002) Who Will Cry When You Die? Life Lessons from the Monk Who Sold His Ferrari, (California USA, Hay House, 2002).

7.3. Dealing with problems and complaints

7.3.1. One problem, two solutions

"Don't find fault, find a remedy."

—Henry Ford

Mark Brownley, in his book, The Things Big Business Do, shares a very interesting concept when it comes to advocating solutions.

His motto is: "One problem—two solutions." *

In essence, his advice is that one should come up with two possible solutions to any problem. This affords one a wider choice and ensures an intelligent and well thought out decision to the problem at hand.

Today, in the service or sales fields, customers are not interested in excuses or even the reason as to why things happen or don't happen. They are not interested if you have power cuts or staff shortages; they only want solutions or answers. You must become solutions-oriented. That is what will differentiate you or your organization from your competitors. The "*buck stops with you*".

Clients see you as "*the face*" of your organization. Your ability to resolve issues or complaints promptly and professionally is what sets you apart from the rest of the pack. *There is always a solution, even to the most complex problem.*

Keep a positive attitude when it comes to problem solving. Don't shortcut the solution—it will come back to bite you and possibly give you extra stress and cause more embarrassment for you with your client. Be flexible in your approach to solving problems or finding solutions without compromising yourself or your business.

Remember the world needs a problem solver; be that person.

Source; Brownley M; The Things Big Businesses do: What you can learn from top organizations. Cape Town, (2006) Zebra Press (Struik Publishers) Page 66

7.3.2. Instead of going to your boss with problems . . . Go with solutions

"Accept responsibility for your life. Know that it's you who will get you where you want to go, no one else will."

—Les Brown

The Japanese use a wonderful concept called "Quality Circles" where a group or team of employees bind together to first identify the problem and second offer suggestions or answers to the problem.

While they may not be fully privy to company policy, budgetary, compliance, or other issues, at least they haven't just complained, thrown their hands in the air, and become dejected and full of apathy. At least they are "buying in" to the business vision or goals, embracing change, being creative, looking at the bigger picture, and being proactive in their thinking.

Why must you always rely on your boss, a committee, or colleague for the solution? Take a leaf out of the book offered by the Quality Circle (or other problem-solving techniques), and the next time an opportunity presents itself, grab it and attempt a solution or even part-remedy.

This is a sure way to score "Noddy" points. It demonstrates your creativity and commitment and interest to resolve the matter for the benefit of the company or client. Know that actions like this will not only catapult your career; it will also make you a "king" or "queen" in the eyes of your client and superior.

Accept responsibility. Instead of going to your boss with problems, go with solutions.

7.3.3. The Victoria Falls trip

"One of the surest signs of a bad declining relationship is the absence of complaints from the customer."

—Theo Levitt

My family and I recently returned from a wonderful trip to Victoria Falls and Chobe National Park. The area was frequented with tourists, and we heard many lodging complaints. We had a few ourselves that we eventually, happily resolved.

I recall a time when my son turned around and said to me, "Gee, Dad, all I have heard from that person . . . is her bitching and complaining. I wonder if she is really enjoying herself?"

This got me thinking. I always believed that complaints are good for business, as they act as a measurement, a barometer, on how the business is performing; they provide information on how the business's service model is working and how its product or service offerings are selling and/ or being accepted. The old adage applies: If it can't be measured, then how can it be managed or fixed?

Then, what about the reputational aspect? Unhappy clients may be telling others about their dissatisfaction.

Some unhappy customers will probably "sidle off" to the competition rather than being candid and complaining in an effort to avoid confrontation.

But there is a flip side to this. Too many complaints can have negative and reverse consequences. Instead of attending to the problems and putting them to bed, once and for all, the business can "switch off" and no longer pay attention to the complaints. Their rationale, as in the example of my trip mentioned above, could be—"Bloody tourists again . . . All they do is complain, and find fault, even if it is not justified. We may as well just leave things exactly as they are."

How do you or your business deal with complaints?

7.3.4. Lipstick kisses on the mirror

"It all depends on how we look at things, and not on how they are themselves."
—Carl Jung

A school head was alerted by the caretaker to a persistent problem in the girls' cloakroom: Some of the girl students were leaving lipstick kisses on the mirrors. The caretaker had left notices on the toilet walls asking for the practice to cease, but it had been to no avail; every evening the caretaker would wipe away the kisses, and the next day lots more kisses would be planted on the mirror. It had become a bit of a game.

The next day, the school head asked a few girl representatives from each class to meet with her in the cloakroom.

"Thank you for coming," said the head. "You will see there are several lipstick kisses in the mirrors in this washroom . . . As you will understand, modern lipstick is cleverly designed to stay on the lips, and so the lipstick is not easy at all to clean from the mirrors. We have therefore had to develop a special cleaning regime, and my hope is that when you see the effort involved you will help spread the word that we'd all be better off if those responsible for the kisses use tissue paper instead of the mirrors in future."

At this point the caretaker stepped forward with a sponge squeegee, which he took into one of the toilet cubicles, dipped it into the toilet bowl, and then he used it to clean one of the lipstick-covered mirrors.*

The head teacher took a creative approach to problem solving. Yes, you can bet that the word spread like wildfire, and the kisses on mirrors ceased immediately. This school head didn't use the autocratic, disciplinary approach to solve the problem, something that would lead to a great deal of stress, rebellion, and energy-expenditure. Rather, she put into place a system or practice that had the culprits voluntarily cease their modus operandi. She still left the girls with a choice, but the emotional and psychological factors in play were sufficient to ensure that the problem dissipated without too much fuss and bother.

*Source: Adapted from Leadership LaunchPad|Lipstick on the Mirror, <http://www.leadershiplaunchpad.co.za/articles/36> accessed 20 May 2014

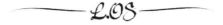

7.4. Sometimes problems are over-exaggerated

7.4.1. The camel

"Justifying a fault doubles it."

—French proverb

In 2005 George Steinmetz took a photograph that was considered as National Geographic's "Photo of the year for 2005". At first glance, there appeared nothing striking about this photo; it depicted a large group of camels walking through the desert, their black outlines clearly visible against the reddish-brown sands of the desert.

On closer inspection, however, one noticed that underneath each camel was a very small white line just visible with the naked eye. It transpired that these white lines in the photograph were, in fact, the camels.

The black outlines were just the camels' shadows!

Sometimes our "problems" seem to be as big as those big black shadows, but in reality we have exaggerated them out of proportion. Sometimes we hear of problems being encountered by others that make ours pale in significance.

In fact, we wouldn't swap our problems for all the gold in South Africa.

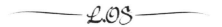

7.4.2. Things could be worse

"The principles are the same whether you add zeroes to the problem or not."
—Brian Joffe

Husband: *Why do you always carry my photo in your handbag to the office?*

Wife: *When there's a problem—no matter how impossible—I look at your picture, and the problem disappears.*

Husband: *You see how miraculous and powerful I am for you?*

Wife: Yes, dear. I see your picture, and I think, "Things could be worse."

Isn't this true in your life? I know it happens in my household. Recently my car was overheating, and it seemed to me (an untrained mechanic) that the radiator had developed a leak. I took my vehicle to a nearby radiator specialist, half-expecting the radiator to be replaced, and there to be a massive bill to settle. You can imagine my relief when they replaced the washer of the plug, for gratis, and I was on my way without having paid a cent. It could have been worse.

Don't exaggerate the problem. Don't add zeroes to the problem. Rather, let your imagination run wild for some novel, creative, and innovative idea.

7.4.3. Stick to the facts

"Solving problems is like sanding furniture. Once you remove the outer layer you will get to the core."

—anonymous

> **I heard about a man who gave up his career to pursue a passion of pottery. He signed up for a six months' course at a pottery school out in the countryside with accommodation provided. But when he got there he was bitterly disappointed.**
>
> **The pottery wheel was lopsided, the accommodation was rustic with holes in the wooden walls that let in a cold breeze and bugs, and there was no hot water.**
>
> **Having complained to his friend, he was wisely advised that if he stuck to the facts, things wouldn't seem as bad as he was making out. All that had to be done was to get the pottery wheel levelled, the holes in the wall plugged, and someone to fix the hot water.**

If he did the things advocated by his friend then he would still be able to pursue his passion and goal. You see, so often we tend to exaggerate the problem; we tell ourselves that things are much worse than they actually are because we allow the facts to get extorted by our emotions.

The same thing happens when we procrastinate in the face of a big task. If we just broke down the task into small bites, it would be noticeable that there are smaller facts to consider in each stage, making it a lot easier to manage each individual task and ultimately the total project.

7.4.4. The dark clouds of life are only temporary

"We are continually faced with great opportunities brilliantly disguised as insoluble problems."

—Lee Lacocca

He dropped out of high school because he couldn't wait any longer to become a musician. By the age of twenty-two he feared that he had made a mistake, and no one would love his music. He played in piano bars and was flat broke. He battled depression, and, in 1970, personal problems and a downturn in his music career caused him to attempt suicide by drinking furniture polish.

Fortunately, his drummer assistant, Jon Small, was on hand and rushed him to hospital. He later spent time in a mental institution. Today, Billy Joel is the sixth best-selling recording artist in the United States.*

The above is a brief summary of the earlier life of the great Billy Joel. Billy managed to lift himself from "rock bottom" to being a singing great in this world. His secret to "pulling" himself out of that state of depression concerned adapting a new belief, a new mindset. He overcame his personal life-threatening problems and challenges.

We can learn from the Billy Joel story. No matter what problem, challenge, or setback we are currently experiencing, it too can be overcome. So often we tend to feel sorry for ourselves, perhaps exaggerating the problem or looking for excuses. I'm not saying that it will be easy, and, as in the case of Billy, you may need to seek help (professional, medical, and other) to do so. But in my experience, dark clouds are only temporary.

When faced with your challenges or dilemma consider these three matters:

What is the real problem, the bottom line?

What does this mean to you—the impact?

What can you do to resolve it—in spite of the challenges that may appear to limit you?

Perhaps if you give adequate consideration to the above issues then you may realize that the issues are not as bad as originally anticipated and that the dark clouds are only temporary.

*Source: Adapted from: Billy Joel-Wikipedia, The Free Encyclopedia <http://en.wikipedia.org/wiki/Billy_Joel> accessed 19 May 2014

7.5. You have the power to overcome

7.5.1. Nancy McKinstry story

"Attitude is the one thing that anyone can control, even if it seems like everything else is outside of their control."

—Adam Bryant

Nancy McKinstry grew up without a lot of money. Her parents were divorced when she was fairly young, and life wasn't a bed of roses, as her mum supported the family on a basic teacher's salary.

What Nancy learned from her mum and her early childhood was the value of education and that hard work can make a difference. Because the family didn't have much she worked all the time. In college she had two or three different jobs to fund her way through her education. That ability to keep a lot of balls in the air and keep adapting to situations to try to make things happen every day was something that helped her make her career a success.*

Here was someone that didn't become the victim of her circumstances or poor background. But it wasn't an easy ride. It took strength of character, a steely determination, considerable hard work, and a desire to master the adverse conditions that she had found herself in. Today, Nancy McKinstry is the CEO of Wolters Kluwer N.V., the global information services and publishing company.

Interestingly, when hiring or promoting people within her organization she looks for this selfsame quality in others, that is, she is looking for evidence that they have persevered and can handle difficult challenges. When interviewing candidates she asks them the following three important questions:

Give me an example of some adverse situation you faced?

What did you do about it?

What did you learn from it?

How would you answer these questions? How resilient are you? How will you react when "the going gets tough"? It doesn't matter what hand you have been dealt in life; you can rise from the ashes and fly again. And, if you fall, you can get up, dust yourself off, and carry on. Stay optimistic in the face of adversity.

*Source: Adapted from the interview with Nancy McKinstry. A. Bryant, The Corner Office: How Top CEOs Made It and How You Can Too (London; Harper Press, 2011) Page 26 & 27.

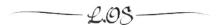

7.5.2. Locus of control

"I have learned that success is to be measured not so much by the position that one has reached in life as by the obstacles he has overcome to achieve while trying to succeed."

—Booker T. Washington

If you place a carrot, an egg and a coffee bean into a pot of boiling water, each reacts in a completely different manner to their conditions.

The carrot goes into the boiling water hard and comes out soft; the egg goes in fragile and comes out hardened; while the coffee bean turns the hot water into coffee by releasing its flavour and aroma!*

What is it that makes people, faced with similar adversity, become weakened or hardened or stronger? In life, as in business, people will be confronted with challenges, but it's how they embrace these events and overcome these obstacles that will provide the answer to the above question.

During the early years of World War II, more than 300 British military and merchant ships were sunk on the waters of the North Atlantic Ocean with an appalling number of casualties. While interviewing the survivors, an interesting pattern emerged. The survival rate for the younger, presumably more physically fit, sailors was a great deal lower than that for their older, more mature shipmates. The study concluded that the older, mature shipmates had overcome adversity before and, therefore, they had developed greater confidence in being rescued than their younger peers.

In psychology, there is a concept known as "Locus of Control", which in general, refers to a person's outlook and belief about what leads to success or failure in their life. For example, some may apportion blame to factors they can't control while others have the conviction to shape events and circumstances by making the best of what they can control.

Don't let circumstances or personal setbacks get the better of you. Stare them down, and make things happen.

*Source: John Boe, Adversity Gives You Strength, By John Boe <http://www. johnboe.com/articles/adversity_gives_strength.html> accessed 24 May 2014

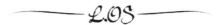

7.5.3. Get up . . . and up again

"There is a difference between interest and commitment. When you are interested in something, you do it only when circumstances permit. When you are committed to something, you accept no excuses, only results."

—Art Turock

In his book, A View from the Zoo, Gary Richmond describes how a newborn giraffe learns its first lesson in life. At birth the baby giraffe falls 10 feet from its mother's womb and usually lands on its back. The mother giraffe lowers her head long enough to take a quick look that everything is alright, and then a few minutes later she

starts the most incredible process to ensure that her little offspring adapts to the challenges of life.

She positions herself directly over her calf, and then she swings her long, pendulous leg outward and kicks her baby, so that it is sent sprawling, head over heels. When it doesn't get up, the violent process is repeated over and over again. The struggle to rise is momentous. As the baby calf grows tired, the mother kicks it again to stimulate its efforts. Finally, the calf stands for the first time on its wobbly legs.

Then the mother giraffe does the most remarkable thing. She kicks it off its feet again. Why?*

Because the mother giraffe wants its offspring to remember how it got up. In the wild, baby giraffes must be able to get up as quickly as possible in order to stay with the herd, where there is safety. Lions, hyenas, leopards, and wild hunting dogs all enjoy young giraffes.

The late Irving Stone understood this concept perfectly well. He spent a lifetime studying greatness, writing novelized biographies of such men as Michelangelo, Vincent van Gogh, Sigmund Freud, and Charles Darwin.

Stone was once asked if he had found a thread that runs through the lives of all of these exceptional people. He said, "I write about people who sometime in their life have a vision or dream of something that should be accomplished and they go to work. They are beaten over the head, knocked down, vilified, and for years they get nowhere. But every time they're knocked down they stand up. You cannot destroy these people. And at the end of their lives they've accomplished some modest part of what they set out to do."**

As someone once said, life always gives us lemons. A fool remains bitter and grows more lemons. A wise man borrows sugar and makes lemon meringue pie.

*Source: Adapted from: G. Richmond, A View from the Zoo (Edinburgh; W Pub Group, 1987).

**Source: C. B. Larson, Illustrations for Preaching & Teaching; from Leadership Journal (Michigan; Baker Pub Group, 1984).

7.5.4. Find your second wind

"The way I see it, if you want the rainbow, you gotta put up with the rain."

—Dolly Parton

Michelangelo *is probably* considered *one of* the greatest living artists *of all time*. A number of his works in painting, sculpture, and architecture rank among the most famous in existence, including the Sistine Chapel, which took more than four years to complete and covered more than 300 figures over an area of approximately 500 square metres.

I read an account by the late Lewis Smedes, author, ethicist, and theologian, *who indicated that* even the great Michelangelo was weary and sore as he descended from the scaffolding, where he had been lying on his back since dawn painting the chapel ceiling. At times it's stated that Michelangelo became doubtful about his painting ability.

But when the sun shone again, Michelangelo got up from his bed, climbed up his scaffold, and laboured another day on his magnificent vision of the Creator.

Even the great Michelangelo became tired (physically and mentally), sore and discouraged at times . . . but then he found his "second wind" . . . and so can you. We are all human, and we all get tired, bad tempered, and stressed and start questioning issues about our jobs and life in general.

It's amazing what we can do after we have rested or taken a break and how clearer our tasks or surroundings appear. Sometimes we need that space in order to regain perspective so that we see things in a different light.

If you have had a bad day, put it behind you. Tomorrow the slate is clean. Tomorrow will always bring with it a degree of freshness, the opportunity to start anew, and thus hope.

Find your second wind.

7.5.5. The storm

"When a man has to put a limit on what he will do, he has put a limit on what he can do."

—Charles R. Schwarb

One day a young lady was driving along with her father. They came upon a storm, and the young lady asked her father, "What should I do?" He said, "Keep driving."

The storm got worse, and cars began to pull over to the side. Up ahead, she noticed that even eighteen-wheelers were pulling over. She told her dad, "I must pull over, I can barely see ahead. It is terrible, and everyone is pulling over!"

Her father told her, "Don't give up, just keep driving!" Now the storm was terrible, but she never stopped driving, and soon she could see a little more clearly. After a couple of miles she was again on dry land, and the sun came out. Her father said, "Now you can pull over, get out, and look back at all the people that gave up and are still in the storm. Because you never gave up your storm is now over."*

Just because everyone else, even the strongest, gives up, it doesn't mean you need to surrender. If you keep going, soon your storm will be over, and the sun will shine upon your face again.

It's not easy to keep on driving when things look bleak and hopeless. It's not easy to continue driving when everyone around you is giving up. But that's exactly the time to be doing so. Storms, setbacks, and problems will not persist day after day, 24/7. There will always be a breakthrough, and when it does happen you will find yourself in pole position. Keep driving!

*Source: Adapted from: motivational/educational message, Never Give Up . . . CiteHr—CiteHr Human Resource Management <http://www.citehr.com/290111-never-give-up.html> accessed22 May 2014

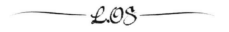

8   Success and being the best

8.1. Talent is never enough

8.1.1. Talent is only the starting point

"The toughest thing about success is that you've got to keep on being a success. Talent is only the starting point in business. You've got to keep working that talent."

—Irving Berlin

When we mention talented people our minds spring to Tiger Woods, Celine Dion, Jacques Kallis, Houdini, Michael Jordan, William Shakespeare, Michelangelo, Beethoven, or the late Dr Christiaan Barnard, the South African surgeon who performed the world's first heart transplant in humans. Yet that list is not correct. You see, everyone has been blessed with certain gifts and talents.

Unfortunately, when you take a closer look around, you will notice that there are so many people in the sports, academic, musical, and other fields who have extraordinary talent and yet end up with mediocre careers or achievements. In every field certain people have failed to capitalize on their talents. Why? Is it laziness, lack of belief or passion, lack of support or funds, lack of time or lack of determination and focus?

When you think of it, most of the above drawbacks can be overcome if one really took full responsibility and applied their mind to achieving their goal or the task in hand. If you are really "hungry" for something (particularly success) you will find the time, motivation, and perseverance required to reach your dream. You don't have to wallow on excuses, bad circumstances, and change in legislation to dash your successful ambitions. Make a way.

The trick is to recognize, develop, and then enhance your "gifts" to reach your desire. But talent is only the starting point on your journey. To achieve success you've got to make the rest of it work for you. Talent is meaningless without effort, confidence, practice, and the development of your gifts. Use your strengths, and concentrate on these rather than stressing about your weaknesses.

Don't just allow your talents to remain dormant and your dreams to die. Don't let excuses rule your life. Start today to maximize your special gifts to reach your full potential and promise.

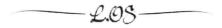

8.1.2. Henri Matisse

"Above all, be true to yourself, and if you cannot put your heart into, take yourself out of it."

—Hardy D. Jackson

I read somewhere about the maestro painter, Henri Matisse, who in his later years succumbed to a crippling arthritis that really affected the joy and skill of his work. Just wrapping his fingers around a brush was painful, and painting was extremely difficult.

When someone asked him why he continued painting under such distress his answer showed his true passion, attitude, and strength of character. He said, "The pain goes away; the beauty endures."

There are more than 100 quotes from this great man, many to do with painting and his success. His view on talent and success is quite interesting: "An artist is an explorer. He has to begin by self-discovery and by observation of his own procedure. After that he must not feel under any constraint."*

To enjoy success we have to go through the pain barrier. Success comes with lots of sacrifices and hard work. Talent is only the starting point for there is a long road of self-discovery—gaining experience, knowledge, and skills.

Some people may argue that luck plays a part; others will quote examples of someone who became an overnight sensation. Yes, it's true these events and examples do exist, but if one "drills down" much deeper one will recognize the effort, sacrifices, and pain already endured in their accomplishment.

Some wise person once said, "There is no elevator to success; you have to take the stairs."

*Source: Adapted from: Henri Matisse quotes—Art Quotes <http://quotes. com/auth_search.php?name=Henri+Matisse> accessed 16 May 2014

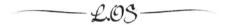

8.1.3. H.L. Hunt

"Successful people ask—what can I learn from this situation?"
—Mark Victor Hansen

The great oil man, H.L. Hunt, a self-made billionaire, was once asked by a journalist for his "secret of success". He replied, "There are only three requirements for success:

1. **Decide exactly what it is you want in life.**
2. **Determine the price you are going to have to pay to achieve it.**
3. **Resolve to pay the price."***

Many people carefully avoid discovering the secret of success because deep down they suspect the secret may be hard work. The great John D. Rockefeller's secret to success was to do the common things uncommonly well.

What is your answer to success? The answer I'm afraid is very subjective and personal. What one person does won't apply to the next. Timing, luck, resources, opportunity, hard work, and perseverance are all factors that may have resulted in someone's success. It's like the old economist joke—ask a room of seven economists one question and you will get eight different answers.

Look around you. Look at successful people—positive role players or inspirational leaders. How do they do it? Study their "winning" traits, and determine what they do differently to you. How do they think? How do they act? It may not guarantee you the exact same results, but they will certainly point you in the right direction. Even if you improve a mere I per cent by following their ideals you are I per cent better off.

Success breeds success, just like money produces money. So does vision. Visualize the things you want. See it. Feel it. Believe in it. Make your blueprint, and begin. The secret for success lies in your hands, heart. and mind.

Your destiny awaits.

*Source: paraphrased from: H L Hunt Quotes—Brainy Quote <http://www. brainyquote.com/quotes/authors/h/h_l_hunt.html.> accessed 20 May 2014

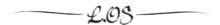

8.1.4. The little fish

"Everyone is gifted—but some people never open their package."

—anonymous

> **A little fish swims up to an older and wiser fish and says, "You go on about water, but where is it? I have been looking everywhere for it and can't find it. I have read about it but still can't find it."**
>
> **The wiser old fish answered, "Yes, dear, as I always tell you, not only are you swimming in it right now, but you are also composed of it."**
>
> **The little fish shakes his head, and, swimming off, murmurs, "Someday I will find it."**

Sometimes we are like that little fish. We search everywhere outside of ourselves. We look for acceptance, appreciation, knowledge, happiness, and even love . . . and yet the answer is there all the time—within us.

We tend to compare ourselves to others and resent their achievements and success. Well I have news for you—the only person who can make you a success (or instil happiness, peace, or love in your life) is you.

The answers lie within each and every one of us, staring us in the face . . . but sometimes we don't like it. We can't accept the truth. At other times, we know deep down in our conscience what needs to be done, but will we have the courage and strength of character to do the right thing—for us?

8.2. Key to success

8.2.1. Self-discipline

"Even though it's all perfect, there is still room for improvement."

—Zen master

> **Pablo Casals continued to practise the cello five hours a day even though he was recognized as the world's greatest cellist. Despite his advanced age and the fact that the exercise tired him out, he believed that practice was a way to get better or stay on top of his game. He believed it was the key to his success. It became part and parcel of his daily routine.**
>
> **He defended his action with this quote: "Don't be vain because you happen to have talent. You are not responsible for that; it was not of your doing. What you do with your talent is what matters."***

Pablo Casals understood the importance of self-discipline, and he continued to practise and hence improve himself. He practised for hours on end. He also recognized that one cannot take their talent and gifts as the be all and end all of everything; it's only the starting point to success.

According to Brian Tracy, America's leading author on the development of human potential, the number one key to success in anything you do is *self-discipline*—your ability and willingness to discipline yourself, and take personal responsibility.

You cannot foist this responsibility onto others. You are completely responsible for your own life, actions, happiness, health, achievements, or success. You are in charge; take charge.

Without self-discipline, success is impossible.

*Source: Adapted from: Pablo Casals Quotes (Author of Joys and Sorrows),— Good reads <htpp;//www.goodreads.com/author/quotes/198277.Pablo_Casals> accessed 17 May 2014.

8.2.2. Become indispensable

"We are held prisoners only by ourselves. Our own thoughts and actions are the jailers of our fate."

—James Allen

Sally Bedell Smith, in her book on William Paley and CBS talks about an incredibly ambitious individual, Frank Stanton, who attained his goals and success in his career.

Frank was twenty-seven years old with a PhD from The Ohio State University when he joined the research division of a company consisting of two people. Seven years later, he was vice-president of CBS in charge of the research department that had grown to more than 100 people. But it didn't end there; he was also in charge of advertising, sales promotion, public relations, building construction, operations, and maintenance as well as overseeing the group's owned radio stations.*

What did Frank do? How did he achieve this incredible rise to fame?

One of Frank's strategies was to become "indispensable". He worked as hard as he could, gathering as much information as possible on any and every topic of possible interest to senior CBS management. For example, he researched who listened to various radio stations and why. He studied demographic information and data on various media markets and was able to give valuable input on matters concerning his industry, especially to his senior management. He became the "go-to person".

The above is a wonderful example that one shouldn't just rely on one's status in the workplace. A job title won't keep you employed. You need to believe in yourself, and add value to clients, your colleagues, and, ultimately, the business. You also need to be a positive influence, knowledgeable, and be trusted by all around you.

Most people, according to Geoffrey Colvin's 2009 book *Talent is Over Rated, What really Separates World Class Performers from everybody else,* learn their jobs in the first year of their employment, and then they never get better. Don't let this happen to you. When you leave a concern or retire you want to hold your head up high and be saluted for the person you are. You want to leave a legacy and don't want people expressing their glee that you have left the business.

Become a leader without title. Make a name for yourself. Stay employable—become indispensable.

*Source: Adapted from: S. B. Smith, In all his glory. The life of William S. Paley the legendary tycoon and his brilliant circle (New York; Random House Inc 2003).

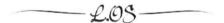

8.2.3. Let go of your crutch

"When I let go of what I am, I become what I might be."

—Lao Tzu

> **Trappers use a crafty technique to catch monkeys. They begin by hollowing out a coconut, making a small hole in the one end, just enough for the monkey to squeeze its flat unclenched hand inside. They then tie a treat to the inside of the coconut, and hang it from a tree.**
>
> **The monkey comes along, notices the treat and squeezes its hand inside and grabs the "loot". The monkey's hand holding the treat becomes a clenched fist, and it cannot remove its hand in this position through that tiny hole. As long as that monkey holds on to the treat, it remains trapped.**

If the monkey was to simply let go then it would instantly be free. How many of us are like that monkey that has to hold on to things so tightly that we don't want to let go? It could pertain to our relationships, familiar processes, techniques, or technology, our employees, thoughts, ambitions, dreams, or habits. Perhaps it's more sinister and includes those false support mechanisms like drugs or alcohol to boost one's confidence levels and help one "get through" the day or circumstances.

In life we all have some form of "crutch" that we hold on to, believing it's the warden to set us free and out of jail. Sadly, many times it's the bars of the jail house that keep us trapped—trapped like that monkey who won't let go of its treat. While we are trapped we tend not to think of other options, ideas, or opportunities; we will never get the chance to explore our true worth and value or if we can achieve success.

Who pulls the strings in your life? Are you a puppet or a puppet master? Let go of your crutch, and become the person you have the potential to be.

8.2.4. Keep your focus

"Of all the liars in the world, sometimes the worst are your own fears."
—Rudyard Kipling

> **A tightrope walker was once interviewed by a TV and radio reporter and was asked the question, "What is the key to walking the tightrope?"**

> **In response, the tightrope walker said, "The key is to keep your eyes fixed on where you are going. You don't look down for there will be a good chance you will fall. Where the head goes the body goes."**

Where the head goes the body goes; you always need to look to where you want to go. This same principle can be applied to one's life or business model. It's no use looking back on all one's hurts, mistakes, lost dreams, and opportunities, but there is much to be gained by focusing on what is coming ahead like the tightrope walker.

Have your dream or vision firmly in your mind, and look through the windscreen of hope, excitement, and accomplishment and not the rear-view mirror of regrets, self-pity, and negativity. It was Sam Walton who said, *"Capital isn't scarce; vision is."*

Vision is not enough. It must be combined with venture. Vision without action is a daydream, and action without vision is useless.

To be a success, keep your vision, and keep your focus!

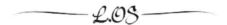

8.2.5. Learn to tell better stories about yourself

"Trust yourself. Create the kind of self that you will be happy to live with all your life. Make the most of yourself by fanning the tiny, inner sparks of possibility into flames of achievement."

—Golda Meir

Most of us are guilty of using pretty lousy language when we speak to ourselves, causing serious damage to our self-belief and confidence. In fact, if we spoke to other people the way we speak to ourselves, we'd struggle to make friends. Sometimes we place high value on people who are kind and supportive of us on the one hand and then curse and belittle ourselves with something dumb, on the other.*

The above except caught my eye. It appeared in an article by Colin Browne entitled "Learn to Tell Better Stories about Yourself" published in a recent edition of the *Sales Guru Magazine*. It made a big impact on me.

The stories or lies we tell ourselves can affect our success or goals. So often, we make those self-limiting, stereotypical comments about ourselves. Changing the way you talk about yourself may be the biggest, most positive, most life changing thing you can do.

Cease telling bad stories about yourself with immediate effect. Make a "revolutionary" positive change in your behaviour; you are more powerful than you realize. So the next time you hear yourself say, "I can't" or, "I'm no good at that" ask—Why not? Give yourself a fair chance.

Colin Browne advocates that perhaps the best way to start is to keep a notebook. Every time you say anything negative about yourself out loud or in your head, make a note. Come the end of day, you may be stunned by seeing how much you self-sabotage.

If you want success—real success—then you ought to find some better stories to tell about yourself, your abilities, and your personality—everything.

*Source: Adapted from: Colin Browne, "Learn to Tell Better Stories about Yourself", Sales Guru Magazine, 2013.

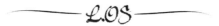

8.3. Self-leadership

8.3.1. The best of whatever you are

"If you can't be a pine on the top of the hill, be a scrub in the valley—but be the best little scrub by the side of the rill."
—excerpt from "The Best of Whatever You Are" poem by Douglas Malloch

> **So to those who think, "I can't achieve my ambitions," I say think again. A good education, a stable family; yes, of course these help to provide the bedrock of a successful life. But if you are not blessed with these things, never become a prisoner of your background. The past is just that—the past. Don't let it limit your future . . .**

> **Success depends on what lies deep within us. If you spend your life never daring to go where your hopes and dreams might take you, you will end your days in a dark valley of frustrated hopes, looking up at what might have been. You are ultimately responsible for your own actions. Only you can decide the path you take. Misfortune and mistakes will knock you back, but keep on moving, look up, and turn the page.***

The above is an extract from the book *Management in 10 Words* by Terry Leahy and a stirring example of the attitude we should have for success. One shouldn't be a prisoner of their background or level of education for that part is history. What counts is the now and future—that burning drive and fire inside you to achieve.

How many times do we experience that haunting self-doubt, that sense of inadequacy, that fear of not coping or not meeting both our or the expectations of others? Isn't it strange that we are much harder on ourselves than others are on us? The deeper our self-awareness and self-confidence, the greater is our capacity to befriend these concerns.

Let's maintain our perspective and not measure our delivery against unattainable, perfection-driven standards. If we do our best, what else is there? Don't undervalue your worth. Until you make peace with who you are . . . you will never be content with what you are.

Be the best of whatever you are.

*Source: T. Leahy, Management in 10 Words (Random House Business, 2012).

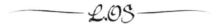

8.3.2. Stand out in a crowd

"Our greatest victory is not in falling down, but getting up every time we do."
—credo of Natalie du Toit
(Olympic Gold medallist)

Most of us can run 100 metres. If I had to try it today I would probably do it in 59.60 seconds—about 50 seconds longer than Usain Bolt's record of 9.60 seconds. The end result will be the same—we both will have completed the 100-metre race. The big difference, however, is that no one will remember who Larry is! To take it a step further, no one will care who I am or what I represent.*

You have to be ahead of the pack to be remembered.

How much time, practice, and dedication does Usain Bolt put into his training schedules to reach peak performance and success? The answer is the same for every top athlete, sportsperson, musician, or artiste who has ever achieved success. Conditioning and training, experience, a positive attitude, and the drive to be a success are paramount.

Above all, they need a game plan, a good coach or manager, and, of course, a strong support structure. Their only goal is being number one—being ahead of the pack.

You don't have to wait to be successful—to "stand out in a crowd" or to be ahead of the pack, because, by then, you are already there: You have already achieved, are different, and no longer need to worry about the competition.

So the time to make that decision is today as you journey to the top. Differentiate yourself from your peers and competitor. Be the best you can be! Establish your own brand—your own unique, personal brand!

Source: Adapted from: L. O'Sullivan, Client Service Excellence: The 10 Commandments (Johannesburg; Knowledge Resources, 2010).

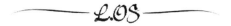

8.3.3. The prerequisite to success

"What separates the winners from the losers is how a person reacts to each new twist of fate."

—Donald Trump

As a boy, Charles Dickens knew he wanted to be a writer, but since his family was poor, he did not get much schooling. By the age of twelve, he was earning money for his family by "gluing labels on bottles". He did not, however, give up on his dream to write. A little later he worked as a law clerk and stenographer, becoming a court stenographer at the age of eighteen.

Then he worked at newspapers, where he practised hard and became a capable reporter. He subsequently moved on to creative writing and developing "sketches" of people under the pen name "Boz". This led to his first book of sketches by Boz. One thing led to another, and he became the world's most popular writer.*

How did he do it? Through hard work, developing himself, believing in himself, practising, and honing those special writing skills and then by finding the right breaks and opportunities. He built up confidence and became better and better. He took responsibility for his own actions and career.

He didn't sit back and say to himself that he was talented, and everything would come to him. He made it happen. He got into a position where people could see his writing and then respect and acknowledge his talent.

The prerequisite to success is the ability to be special, unique, and different. You need to develop your own personal brand, and take responsibility for your own career or life. Don't give others your power, be your own driver, your own leader. Become your own career capitalist, and take care of your "marketability".

*Source: Adapted from: **Charles Dickens-Wikipedia, The Free Encyclopedia** <http://en.wikipedia.org/wiki/Charles_Dickens> accessed 20 May 2014, and

Sketches by Boz—Wikipedia, The Free Encyclopedia <http://en.wikipedia.org/wiki/Sketches_by_Boz> accessed 20 May 2014

8.4. Don't accept mediocrity

8.4.1. The 100 per cent theory

"I've got a theory that if you give 100% all the time, somehow things will work out in the end."

—Larry Bird

A boy and a girl were playing together. The boy had a collection of marbles. The girl had some sweets with her. The boy told the girl that he will give her all his marbles in exchange for her sweets. The girl agreed.

The boy kept the biggest and the most beautiful marble aside and gave the rest to the girl. The girl gave him all her sweets as she had promised.

That night, the girl slept peacefully. But the boy couldn't sleep as he kept wondering if the girl had hidden some sweets from him the way he had hidden his best marble.*

There is a simple moral of the story: If you don't give your 100 per cent in a relationship, you'll always keep doubting if the other person has given his/her 100 per cent. This is true for any relationship, including family, friends, and that of employer-employee or between client-employer/employee.

But the above scenario doesn't only apply to relationships: It also affects our values, passion, attitude, service ethos, communication and listening skills, and so forth. Every day we are challenged to give it 100 per cent or fall short, so aim high. It's better to aim for "gold" than "bronze, for if you miss what you considered to be gold then you will still have a chance of consolation medals. And, if you miss the mark, don't despair, for the slate gets cleaned at night, giving you another day and thus another chance . . . tomorrow.

By giving your 100 per cent to everything you will not only live or sleep peacefully, you will also be successful.

*Source: Humari Chahat: A Boy and a Girl Playing Together <http://humarichahatein.blogspot.com/2013/04/a-boy-and-girl-were-playing-together.html> accessed 20 May 2014

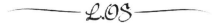

8.4.2. And then some . . .

"When we have done our best, we can await the results in peace."

—anonymous

> **The top people always do what is expected . . .**
> **and then some.**
> **They are thoughtful of others; they are considerate and kind . . .**
> **and then some.**
> **They meet their responsibilities fairly and squarely . . .**
> **and then some.***

The above excerpt is from the book *Charging the Human Battery* by Mac Anderson.

Take note of the three words *"and then some"*; they are the secret to success and an example of the attitude that needs to be practised, daily.

They are the difference between average people and top people in most companies. It means you don't just do the job, you do something more—something special, to the best of your ability. This philosophy is the core difference between average people and top performers in all aspects of life and business.

To my mind there is no better satisfaction one can experience than that feeling of peace when a person knows in their heart that they have done their best. Because, win or lose, they know that they are more prepared for the next battle, be it in life, the job, or other.

Doing your best is essentially committing to excellence, and committing to excellence is not merely the act, it's an attitude and a promise to oneself. All excellence begins with the decision that we must be and will be excellent. Great things are not done on impulse; they are a case of a series of small things brought together, moving from good to great to excellence.

So, let's adopt a daily habit of *"and then some"*. Do that little bit extra. Go that extra mile. Be a success!

*Source: M. Anderson, Charging the Human Battery (Illinois; Simple Truths, 2008).

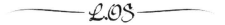

8.4.3. Keep pushing the envelope

"Change 'I don't know' to . . . 'I don't know yet.'"

—anonymous

None of our men are "experts." We have most unfortunately found it necessary to get rid of a man as soon as he thinks himself an expert because no one ever considers himself an expert if he really knows his job.

A man who knows a job sees so much more to be done than he has done, that he's always pressing forward and never gives up an instant of thought to how good and how efficient he is.

Thinking always ahead, thinking of always trying to do more, brings a state of mind in which nothing is impossible. The moment one gets to "expert" state of mind a greater number of things become impossible.*

The above quote epitomizes the key elements in the composition of successful people: the hunger for knowledge, the drive to better themselves, and the open-mindedness to know that all goals and dreams are achievable.

Someone wisely once said that to achieve success in life we must stay within our strength zone, but move out of our comfort zone. One way to improve on that strength zone is to push the envelope—that continued yearning for knowledge, skills, and experience on the one hand and flexibility and creativity on the other. It also includes finding new, innovative ways or changing old behaviours or processes to ensure success.

Don't let the sameness or monotony of your job cause mediocrity, for as Henry Ford has indicated there is so much to learn or excite you in your job functions. Find ways to stimulate yourself, or the way you undertake your tasks.

Keep pushing the envelope. Change your "I don't know" to "I don't know yet."

*Source: Quote by Henry Ford: "None of our men are 'experts.' We have most . . . <http://www.goodreads.com/ . . . /306037-none-of-our-men-are-experts-we—have-most-unfortunately> accessed 19 May 2014

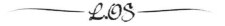

8.4.4. Burglar concept

"Every child is an artist. The problem is how to remain an artist once he grows up."

—Pablo Picasso

There is a story about a world-class burglar . . . if I can call someone that. The thief in question successfully broke into homes for more than twenty years, until he was caught. How did he manage to elude the police for

so long? How did he manage to get away with hundreds of jobs over such a long time span? Certainly, he was considered a master at his trade!

When the thief was arrested, the police and press couldn't help but notice that he looked just like an ordinary citizen—like a normal banker or accountant you would pass in the street.

When asked why he resorted to thieving the burglar claimed, "I knew no better."

Now isn't that sad. If this thief used his skills in a positive, more concrete, manner, just think what he could have achieved. If he realized that there was so much more to life or his purpose in life, he would have been a great success.

For more than twenty years he used the core skills of any successful leader, banker, accountant, or any other person, albeit for the wrong trade and reasons. He learnt the essence of:

> planning and goal setting
> research and doing one's homework
> use of his talents and skills (in a negative or perverse sense)
> the essence of trade/marketing (how to get rid of his stolen artefacts)
> negotiation—sell goods at the right price
> pride in his work—did not get caught

What about you? Are you living your purpose, or are you just like the burglar who knew no better and used his skills and talents for the wrong purpose or less than his potential? Don't achieve success and fame for the wrong reasons.

More importantly, don't achieve success and fame by compromising your sense of values, reputation, and ideals.

8.4.5. What is your blind spot?

"Argue for your limitations and, sure enough, they're yours."

—Richard Bach

> **If we can stop, listen and think about what others are seeing in us, we have a great opportunity. We can compare the self that we want to be with the self that we are presenting to the rest of the world. We can then begin to make real changes that are needed to close the gap between our stated values and our actual behaviour.**

I love the above quote by Marshall Goldsmith in *What Got You Here Won't Get you There; How Successful People Become Even More Successful (2007).* Perhaps you need to re-read it to grasp its content and message.

We all have blind spots whether we like to believe it or not. It could be the words we say or our actions or mannerisms that have a negative impact on others. The best solution to dissolving blind spots is to make sure you have people in your life (spouse, partner, or trusted friend) who are willing to speak up and tell you the truth about your behaviour or faults.*

Of course, this can leave you very vulnerable, and it's natural to feel defensive or even angry when you hear feedback different from the way you see yourself. If you do become defensive or angry you push away the other person and effectively shut down communication. In the process you rob yourself of valuable feedback and can damage the relationship.

However, if you take the plunge and welcome such feedback, listen calmly, and thank them for bringing the matter to your attention then you could gain a lot of insight with regards to your behaviour or character.

Remember that when people talk to you about your blind spots it's because they care enough about you and the relationship to risk holding up a mirror, so you can see yourself as they see you.

*Source: Adapted from: Meredith. Bell, "Your Voice of Encouragement", 25 June 2013.

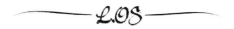

8.5. Self-belief

8.5.1. The realm of possibility

"Ordinary people believe only in the possible. Extraordinary people visualize not what is possible or probable, but rather what is impossible. And by visualizing the impossible, they begin to see it as possible."

—Cherie Carter-Scott

Ornithologists say birds have three methods of flight. First there is the flapping of wings, mainly to counteract gravity. This requires the greatest amount of effort and is probably the most ungraceful motion. Then there is gliding, which doesn't last forever. Finally, there is soaring, where the thermal winds send them effortlessly into the heavens.

In like manner, we also have three modes of movement—crawling, walking, and running. Just as we need to crawl before we can walk or run, let's not stay in this baby state but grow and develop by using all our gifts and talents.

Perhaps there is a fourth mode of movement—soaring. Perhaps if you soar like an eagle then you will push your boundaries. Have you ever noticed that when it rains most birds head for shelter, but the eagle flies above the clouds and rain? It does what others do not; it takes the road less travelled. Winners push their limits until the new limits become the norm. The more we push or extend ourselves, the more our beliefs and limits will expand.

Yes, we can achieve greatness and success; we can overcome obstacles or soar to new heights. The realm of possibility always exists.

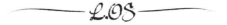

8.5.2. Dream a new dream

"Successful people aren't afraid of the heights they attain."

—James Waldroop and Timothy Butler

She was the youngest of seventeen children, born in South Carolina to slaves. In spite of all the odds she received a

good education and even went to college. From the time she was a little girl, she dreamed of going to Africa to teach the children on that continent. After graduation she applied for a missionary post to Africa, but she was devastated when she wasn't accepted.

Instead of sitting around and sulking, she decided that since she couldn't teach the children in Africa, she would do so in the United States. She decided to open her own school, but she lacked funds. But where there is a will there is a way, and so she gathered cardboard boxes to be used as desks and strained berries to use the juice as ink. She and her students raised money for their books by hauling thousands of pounds of garbage to the local dump.

Her name is Mary McLeod Bethune. Several years went by when a college nearby noticed what was going on and asked Mary to join forces. The two schools became known as the Bethune-Cookman College, which is now known as Bethune-Cookman University in Daytona Beach, Florida.

Mary went on to become the first African American woman to be college president. In 1932 President Franklin Roosevelt appointed her advisor to his cabinet, making her the first African American woman to serve as a presidential advisor.*

So if things don't work out for you, if your dreams feel that they are falling apart or being dashed, don't sit around, and mope with a defeatist attitude.

There is a lovely little poem by Walter D. Wintle entitled "Thinking" that talks about the defeatist attitude. Take note of the opening lines:

> *If you think you are beaten, you are;*
> *If you think you dare not, you don't.*
> *If you like to win, but think you can't,*
> *It's almost certain you won't.*

If you think you'll lose, you're lost
For out in the world we find,
Success begins with a fellow's will
It's all in the state of mind. **

So turn that defeatist attitude around. Have that self-belief like Mary McLeod Bethune. Dream another dream. Change course. Do something. Don't give up hope.

*Source: Adapted from: J. Osteen, Become a Better You—7 Keys to Improving Your Life Every day (London; Simon and Schuster).

**Source: Walter D Wintle, Quote by Walter D Wintle: "If you think you are beaten . . . -Goodreads, <www.goodreads.com/ . . . /327729-if-you-think-you-are-beaten-you-are-if-you >accessed 20 May 2014.

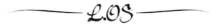

8.5.3. Muhammad Ali

"I am the greatest."

—Muhammad Ali

Do you remember the great boxer Muhammad Ali, also known as Cassias Clay, arguably the most celebrated boxer of all time? In 1974 Ali challenged George Foreman for the heavyweight championship of the world in the famous "Rumble in the Jungle". Ali had been in jail for refusing to fight in Vietnam and was past his peak. Foreman was a giant of a man who had destroyed every other contender leading up to the fight and was the clear favourite to win.

All the fight pundits believed that Ali would lose, virtually everybody, except Ali himself.

If you look at the fight footage of the bout, Ali was battered around the ring, ending up on the ropes and just covering his head for all he was worth while taking punches on his arms from the ferocious Foreman onslaught. All the while Ali taunted and goaded Foreman

who was becoming tired and frustrated. In round six, Ali suddenly landed a serious punch for the first time in the fight, and in the next round Ali knocked out the giant Foreman. Ali was once again champion of the world.

Mohammad Ali is a prime example of a person who had the self-belief to succeed; he believed in himself. Only you need to believe in yourself. Whatever people say about you, whatever setback you are experiencing, keep believing in yourself, and never lose courage. What others say should not concern you that much, unless they hit your blind spot. In fact, whatever they say should serve to make you more determined than ever. They will try to make you doubt your personal power, but you know better.

When you next doubt yourself, think of these people:

- Thomas Edison's teacher told him that he was too stupid to learn anything.

- Walt Disney was fired as a newspaper reporter because he "lacked imagination".

- Winston Churchill had to repeat a school year.

- The Beatles were turned down by more than one recording studio with the words, "We don't like your sound."

- Michael Jordan was cut from his high school basketball team (and went home and cried).

- Albert Einstein could not talk before the age of four.

Everyone gets knocked down. The ones who find a way to get back up—they become somebody. All of these greats were successful for one primary reason—they believed in themselves!

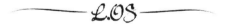

8.5.4. Fear of failure

"It's impossible to win the race unless you venture to run, impossible to win the victory unless you dare to battle."

—Richard M. DeVos

In the movie *Chariots of Fire*, English runner Harold Abrams runs against Scottish champion Eric Liddell and loses for the first time in his life. The pain of failure is so great he decides he cannot race again. Harold struggles to accept the fact he has lost. "I don't run to take beatings—I *run to win. If I can't win, I won't win.*"

His girlfriend, Cybil, then firmly reminds him, *"If you don't run, you can't win."**

To run your best race you need to give it everything that is in you—if you want to win. To run the race, giving your best, and to then lose, well that's certainly painful, but it's not failure. Failure is refusing to run the race at all. That is the mindset that separates the winners from the losers. Winners aren't afraid to run the race. A quitter never wins, and a winner never quits. If they don't dare they will never win.

Sadly there are many of us who have a fear of success or are afraid of making a fool of ourselves. Many of us, similar to the English runner, Harold Abrams, have this fear that we will fail and embarrass ourselves or let down our team or supporters. Well, I have news for you. Show me a single person in this world who hasn't failed at some venture, event, or task they were doing.

Consider these wise words by Marianne Williamson, which form the opening stanza of the poem "Our Deepest Fear":

> *Our deepest fear is not that we are inadequate.*
> *Our deepest fear is that we are powerful beyond measure.*
> *It is our light, not our darkness*
> *that most frightens us.*
> *We ask ourselves*
> *who am I to be brilliant, gorgeous, talented, fabulous?*
> *Actually, who are you not to be?***

When it comes to success and leadership realize it's impossible to win the race unless you run, and it's impossible to have victory unless you do battle. Don't be inhibited by the fear of failure.

*Source: J. Ortberg, If You Want to Walk on Water, You've Got to Get Out of the Boat (Michigan; Zondervan Publishing Company, 2003).

**Source: Marianne Williamson, Our deepest fear is not that we are inadequate. Our . . . -ThinkExist.com, <http://en.thinkexist.com/quotation/our-deepest-fear-is . . . /397505.html> accessed 18 May 2014

9 Mistakes, accountability, and excuses

9.1. Don't be slow to apologize

9.1.1. Say sorry—make the call now!

"An apology is the superglue of life. It can repair just about anything."

—Lynn Johnston

A man and his wife had been arguing all night, and as bedtime approached neither were speaking to the other. It was not unusual for the pair to continue this war of silence for two or three days, but on this occasion the man was concerned; he needed to be awake at 4.30 a.m. the next morning to catch an important flight, and being a very heavy sleeper he normally relied on his wife to wake him.

Cleverly, so he thought, while his wife was in the bathroom, he wrote on a piece of paper: "Please wake me at 4.30 a.m.—I have an important flight to catch." He put the note on his wife's pillow, and then he turned over and went to sleep.

The man awoke the next morning and looked at the clock. It was 8.00 a.m. Enraged that he'd missed his flight, he was about to go in search of his errant wife to give her a piece of his mind when he spotted a hand-written note on his bedside cabinet.

The note said: "It's 4.30 a.m.—get up."

Communication breakdowns play one of the biggest roles in our personal, social, and work relationships and environments. One just has to look at the underlying reasons for today's high divorce rate, wars, bad service, unresolved problems, office conflict, and stress, and one will note communication (or should I say, lack thereof) ranks well up there with trust, respect, and other related emotions and values.

To ensure openness of communication one needs to be aware of issues causing miscommunication or distrust and not to be slow to correct any misconceptions or faults. At the same time, don't be slow to admit you were wrong, or apologize for the folly of your ways. One is not right all the time, and one must never be ashamed to apologize—it takes a "real man/ woman" to do so, and it shows you to have greater courage, commitment, and strength of character than those who do not.

Make that call now.

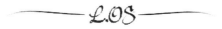

9.1.2. Own up—pay up

"Customers don't expect you to be perfect. They do expect you to fix things when they go wrong."
                            —Donald Porter, vice-president British Airways

A wise person once said, "Admitting a mistake *defines.* **Not admitting a mistake denies. Lying about a mistake** *destroys.* **Repeating a lie will not make it true."**

Like pulling off a plaster (the quicker the better), admit your error as soon as possible, and then move swiftly in resolving the problem. Work to re-instil trust in you or your organization's creditability and reputation.

Mistakes happen. We all make mistakes. They can be painful, embarrassing, or costly. Mostly, it's not the end of the world for us. Put them down to experience and knowledge gained. As long as you learn from these, you will be much more street wise and successful. They can be the stepping stones to greater opportunities. *You can't unscramble eggs, but you can still make an omelette from the situation.*

It's easy to judge the mistakes of others but difficult to recognize our own mistakes. Mistakes are painful when they happen, but years later, a collection of mistakes is called experience, which leads to success.

Admit when you are wrong or have made a mistake. Face up to your mistakes or errors in judgement. It's not a sign of weakness but rather a sign of personal strength, mental maturity, and individual character. It also fosters trust and confidence for people to deal with you.

Own up. Pay up.

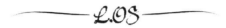

9.1.3. Fix immediately—sleep better

"A man who has committed a mistake and doesn't correct it is committing another mistake."

—Confucius

Did you hear about a woman who noticed that she dropped a stitch while knitting the back of a jersey for her husband? Instead of stopping there and then and going back to mend it, she continued knitting. Once completed, she looked at the completed work.

All looked good, and if she hadn't known that she had dropped that stitch it would have been perfect. In fact, the error was so small and would in 99 per cent of cases go unnoticed. But this error kept gnawing at this woman.

Eventually she couldn't take it any longer, so she undid all her hard work to re-knit that part of the jersey.

Some days we are just like this woman. We make mistakes and try ignoring them or smoothing them over. Sometimes we lie about it; at other times our conscience gets the better of us. Sometimes we make so many mistakes that it becomes second nature to us, and our level of work or standard of output is just plain poor.

It's your choice, your conscience! Just like the knitting . . . you can keep to the pattern, or change the pattern. Take accountability for your actions. The secret in business and life is to never do anything that keeps you up at night.

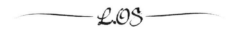

9.2. Experiences/Mistakes will be your education

9.2.1. Trying, learning, and failing . . . and then trying again

"The greatest mistake you can make in life is to continually be afraid you will make one."

—Elbert Hubbard

The book called *Art and Fear* indispensably portrays how failure is tied to learning. A ceramics teacher divided his class into two groups. One group would be graded solely on quantity of work (50 kg of pottery would be "A" symbol; 40 kg of pottery a "B" symbol, etc.). The other group would be graded on quality. Students in that group had to produce only one pot—but it had better be good.

Amazingly, all the highest quality pots were turned out by the quantity group. It seems that while the quantity group kept churning out pots, they were continually learning from their mistakes and growing as artists. No pot was an outright failure but a process of getting that much sought "A" symbol.

While the first group were experimenting and learning, the quality group sat around theorizing about perfection and worrying about it—but they never got any better.*

In this example of pottery it's proven that trying, learning, and failing . . . and then trying again is so much better than waiting for perfection—a concept that no doubt can be used in many areas of our lives, including in our workplace.

The outcome of the above experiment bears testimony to the indelible words by Jim Rohn, *"You can't hire other people to do your push-ups."* You can't go through life delegating or relegating work and responsibility. You also have to try to fail; get your hands dirty, and experience, and then learn from these scenarios.

Sometimes you need to take responsibility, and do things, even if you fall or fail. You can't know everything, and you can't do everything yourself. Put your ego and vulnerabilities aside. You can't go through life being spoon-fed or working like a martyr. Cynthia Copeland Lewis said it best: *"If you wait until you are really sure, you'll never take off the training wheels."*

If you haven't experimented, taken action, or attempted the work, then how else will you be able to make informed decisions, accept responsibility, or teach or guide others? Knowing the theory is one thing—but experiencing the practical is another. Keep trying, learning, and failing . . . and then trying again.

*Source: Adapted from: D. Bayles and T. Orland, Art and Fear: Observations on the Perils (and Rewards) of Artmaking (Oregon; Image Continuum Press).

9.2.2. Regrets

"Never regret yesterday. Life is in you today, and you make your tomorrow."
—L. Ron Hubbard

> **In a television programme the audience were given the opportunity to ask a successful actor, dramatist, and director, the great Peter Ustinov, questions about his work. One such question was, "Looking back over your career, are there pieces of work which you have accepted that you wish you hadn't, or those you refused and when you wished later you had accepted?"**
>
> **His reply was so refreshing and perhaps a lesson to all of us—the right attitude to live life. "What's the point of having regrets? I have made mistakes—we all do. But no, once a decision has been made, there it is . . . It is no good living with regrets."***

If we are brutally honest with ourselves, I'm sure we can all recount a number of decisions we made or statements we said that we regret. It is hoped that they are like the words contained in the theme song from the album *My Way* released by Frank Sinatra in 1969: "Regrets I've had a few but, then again, too few to mention."

Now, we can either dwell on these, or let them eat at our spirit and conscience like a cancer, or we can adopt the same attitude as the successful actor and dramatist, as above. The past can hurt; you can either run from it, or learn from it.

Someone once said, "Yesterday is already a cancelled cheque, tomorrow is a promissory note, but today is cash." Learn from yesterday, live for today, hope for tomorrow. Let's "cash in" from this day forward, and live a life free of excuses and past errors.

*Source: Adapted from: F. Gay, The Friendship Book of Francis Gay (Dundee; UK D.C. Thomson & Co Ltd, 1983).

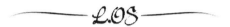

9.2.3. Mistakes—what is the cost?

"If you don't have the time to do it right, when will you have the time to do it over?"

—John Wooden

> **Plumbers put in pipes and then the electrician accidently drills through the odd pipe. You hope the fault is found or admitted before the tiling or plastering takes place; otherwise an even bigger problem will occur, resulting in the need to rip off the tiles or chip away the cement, replace the pipes and then redo all that work over again.***

The above occurrence, according to Toby Shapshak, author of the article from which this is taken, is one of many scenes that unfolds in the construction industry. And, of course, it's never anybody's fault; the blame gets passed, and the buck never stops at anyone's door.

These mistakes are costing time and money; in fact, according to Shapshak, it's estimated that 30 per cent of any project is wastage. Now that's a gigantic proportion. Can you imagine the impact on the bottom line, beside the costs associated with new material, labour, and even penalties for late completion?

How much wastage goes on in your company? Do you, as an employee, know the cost of each error you make, not only in time and money, but in those intangible measurements of trust, reputation, and consistency of service or delivery? That's the crux of the matter, and the point I'm trying to get across—it's not only the cost of material, labour, or time; it's the cost to your brand.

*Source: Tony Shapshak, Sunday Times (South African weekly newspaper), 11 March 2012.

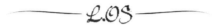

9.2.4. You are not a humpty-dumpty

"Life is 10% what you make of it and 90% how you take it."

—Stephen Covey

> **Humpty Dumpty sat on a wall,**
> **Humpty Dumpty had a great fall.**
> **All the kings' horses and**
> **All the kings' men couldn't put**
> **Humpty Dumpty back together again!**

You are not Humpty Dumpty, so when you fall or fail the only direction to go is . . . up. We all have those good days and then those days you want to forget. Don't let those difficult times shake your confidence and self-worth. Separate your true worth from a lousy event, experience, or mistake.

Everyone gets knocked down in life, but that doesn't mean you must give up. The ones who found a way to get back up became somebody. They became successful, as they believed in themselves.

Get up, and believe in yourself—you are not Humpty Dumpty. Remember: *Winners never quit, and quitters never win.*

9.3. No to excuses

9.3.1. The pointed finger

"Blame is just a lazy person's way of making sense of chaos."

—Doug Coupland

> **On New Year's Day a person I know dived into their**
> **swimming pool to cool off, only to establish that he had**

forgotten to take his cell phone out of his swimming trunks. He got out of the pool fuming. "Who in their right mind puts pockets on swimming costumes?"

It's never our fault! We blame our parents, teachers, bosses, clients, friends, or even the person who sewed a pocket on to a costume . . .

Perhaps it's time we stop the blame game, and take personal responsibility for our lives instead of pointing fingers or revelling in the cult of victimhood. Watch how you react to circumstances. Accept the situation you find yourself in, and work out a solution to get out of the mess.

Have you ever noticed what a pointed finger is really "saying"? If you are not sure, please try this experiment. Extend your right arm directly out in front of you. No matter how you twist your arm, you will notice that while you are apportioning blame to someone else, there are always three fingers pointing back at you. This symbolizes that you too are not entirely blameless. You need to look more closely at yourself, and determine what part you may have played in the error, delay, or failure. Perhaps it was some degree of miscommunication, lack of training, or even incorrect delegation on your part.

There is one thing I know for certain: When it comes to making excuses or apportioning blame, if we say them enough times then they become the truth by which we live. Don't build a library of excuses or scapegoats.

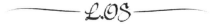

9.3.2. Never explain, never complain

"Some men have thousands of reasons why they cannot do what they want to, when all they need is one reason why they can."
—Willis Whitney

Greg Hickman decided to tape a piece of paper containing the phrase "Never explain, never complain" to the wall of his office, at the same time as he made a personal challenge that as soon as an entire day went by without him voicing a complaint or offering an excuse, he would take the message down.

Five years later this message is still pasted on the wall.*

The message of "Never explain, never complain" is really refreshing and sums up the philosophy of *winners*. A winner doesn't waste his or her valuable time complaining or making excuses or blaming others. They divert their energies and mindset to the task at hand. If their path becomes stymied, they look for alternative solutions.

Unfortunately, there is a Greg Hickman in many of us. At some stage during the day we start blaming people or the circumstances or we start working out an "Oscar" of an excuse—something plausible and yet not used by us before. Worse still, we become hyper-critical and start blaming ourselves and calling ourselves "stupid", an idiot, or a lot worse.

Perhaps it's high time someone beats Greg Hickman at his own game—let it be you!

*Source:—Greg Hickman, Never Complain, Never Explain, self help.com <http://www.selfgrowth.com/articles/Hickman3.html> accessed 22 May 2014

9.3.3. I tried that once, and it didn't work

"If you learn from defeat, you haven't really lost."

—Zig Ziglar

I was at the gym one day when a man was terminating his gym contract. As part of the exit strategy the man was required to complete a questionnaire, airing the reason for him ceasing his membership and to comment on certain aspects so as to enhance the service and facilities offered by the gym.

The person attending the final formalities glanced through the survey form and noticed that the man's comment and reason for closing his gym membership was one sentence, eight words long—"I tried that once, and it didn't work."

The gym instructor then asked the man to elaborate on this statement, to which the man replied, "I came into

your gym once, got onto the treadmill for 20 minutes, did spinning for 20 minutes, and then rowed for 20 minutes. I then got onto the scale and lost not a gram in weight. *I tried it once, and it didn't work.* That's it! I'm not coming back again."

How many of us are like this man in the above example that try a thing once and give up if it doesn't work? Other than a fluke or the odd lucky experience, I'm afraid there is no magic wand that one can wave and all of our hopes, dreams, goals, and desires will be instantaneously fulfilled. Very often in life, success and achievement is a long-term process of self-discipline, determination, passion, and, most importantly, a positive attitude.

There is an age old question that's applicable here: "How does one eat an elephant?" The answer, of course, is: "Slowly, very slowly." So, don't be discouraged, as tangible and measurable results take time. At a minimum, give yourself a true, realistic chance before deciding to throw in the towel.

9.3.4. The Bear Bryant concept

"Let others lead small lives, but not you. Let others argue over small things, but not you. Let others cry over small hurts, but not you. Let others leave their future in someone else's hands, but not you."
—excerpt from *The Challenge* by Jim Rohn

When Bear Bryant, the legendary Alabama football coach, was asked what was important in his coaching success, he replied, "When we win I give them [the players] all the credit, and when we lose I take all the blame."*

I love the excerpt on responsibility presented by Robin Crow in his book entitled *Rock Solid Leadership*. It demonstrates the essence of accepting responsibility and is a wonderful illustration as to why successful people focus on responsibility rather than blame. It's a concept I try to practise when dealing with my subordinates every day.

It's human nature to "pass the buck" and to play the blame game. We blame others—the economy, politicians, this and that—but invariably one can always find the culprit by looking in the mirror. In many instances, it invariably comes back to the choices we made or the things we did or did not do properly.

In my case, if my subordinate fouls up then I need to question myself: "Did I explain the task clearly?" and "Did I give them the correct training to carry out the task, or did I throw them into the 'deep end' too soon?"

There a lot of merit in the Bear Bryant concept—something you can apply in your career and life.

*Source: Adapted from: R. Crow. Rock Solid Leadership: How Great Leaders Exceed Expectations (Illinois; Simple Truths, 2006).

9.4. Don't pass the buck-take responsibility

9.4.1. RARE

"Few things can help an individual more than to place responsibility on him, and to let him know that you trust him."

—Booker T. Washington

> **Herby Rosenberg, the deputy chairman of Afrika Tikkun, a charitable organization, used the following words when addressing a fundraising strategy session.**
>
> **"Everything we as an upliftment organization engage in should be 'RARE'. In other words, all our endeavours should be Responsible, Accountable, Relevant, and Ethical. These are the traits we strive to infuse into all our activities."***

How simple and yet so profound is this message. These four words are the foundation of every business's principles and every life's values. Herby's message is clear: We cannot pass the buck for the buck starts with us. We must all be responsible, accountable, relevant, and ethical in our dealings each day.

Let's take it to heart, and adopt this RARE approach in all facets of our business and personal life.

*Source: Adapted from: Herbert Alex Rosenberg, Afrika Tikkun newsletter.

9.4.2. The lighthouse keeper

"Whenever you become empowered, you will be tested."

—Caroline Myss

There is a well-known story of an old lighthouse keeper. The man had a limited amount of oil to keep his beacon lit so that passing ships could avoid the rocky shore. One night a man who lived close by needed to borrow some of this precious commodity to light his home. And sure enough the lighthouse keeper gave him some.

On several other nights the lighthouse keeper was similarly approached by other members of the community requesting some oil for some particular reason. The lighthouse keeper obliged each one.

Then one night all the oil was used up, and the beacon ran dry. There was no warning to be given to the passing ship, which ran aground.

Many lives were lost.

The lighthouse keeper neglected his key responsibility area. This good-natured soul forgot his primary mission and priority: to ensure the safe passage of passing ships and ultimately to protect the lives of the ship's crew and passengers. He let down those who trusted him, and the crew and passengers of a particular vessel paid the ultimate price for his trust.

But there is another very important lesson we can learn from the above experience. With accountability there comes a time when we have to say *no*. We will be tested, and we need to keep a level, mature, and honest head on our shoulders. With accountability comes responsibility, commitment, and integrity.

There is a price a person pays for accountability, and it's a bit of a paradox. The more power, fame, or superiority a person achieves the greater is their level of accountability and responsibility.

9.4.3. Accepting responsibility is a promise

"Promises are like babies: easy to make, hard to deliver."

—Anonymous

A businessman borrowed $100 million from the bank. A reporter/analyst asked him how he managed to sleep given the worry he should have in repaying the interest and capital of this loan. He answered, "Oh, I sleep well at night, but my bank manager doesn't. There is no point to us both being up at night."

The banker-client joke is not an example or invitation that you should shirk your responsibilities. Rather, the message is to accept them in the manner that they do not consume you—that you do not over-commit yourself and that you have the sense of values, peace of mind, and ability to meet what you have undertaken to do. Accept responsibility with your eyes wide open and your heart in the right place.

Accepting responsibility is a promise: a promise by you to others and a promise by you to yourself that you will deliver.

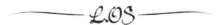

9.4.4. Let others solve their own problems

"Never tell people how to do things. Tell them what to do and they will surprise you with their ingenuity.

—George Patton

I read of a man, well into his forties, who was still living with his parents. However, this man was lazy, wouldn't work, or contribute in any manner, financial or other, to the household. All he did was sit and watch TV and play video games, all day, all year. To compound matters

he wouldn't listen to his parents and denied he had a problem.

After a year his parents sought professional help and were shocked at the psychologist's response. "You are right; your son doesn't have a problem—you do! You have protected him, fed him, and helped him avoid responsibility for his own life. If you want your son to get better—give him back his problems."

If you want people to succeed in life or in the workplace then you cannot shelter and protect them. You have to let them loose to find their own ways, make their own mistakes, and be accountable for their actions. It's not always the best approach to solve a person's problem; you may be doing them a disservice. They need to stand on their own two feet. How else will they grow and develop? How else will they gain experience and confidence?

Sadly there are many who rely on others to solve their problems, and, similarly, there are many who, for addictions, stubbornness, and other reasons, won't change their ways or listen to reason. Unfortunately, there comes a time when if you continue to help somebody who is refusing to help him or herself then you are actually hurting that person more than you are helping them.

10 Decisions/Choices

10.1. Take a chance

10.1.1. You can't cross a chasm without a big jump

"Often you just have to rely on your intuition."

—Bill Gates

> **Question: There were once three frogs on a log, and one of them made a decision to jump into the water. How many were left on the log?**
>
> **Answer: There are still three frogs on a log. He only made a decision, and he took no action.**

The above is a simple illustration of the importance of making a decision. We are all decision makers, but the question to be answered is what type of decision maker are you? Are you consistent, head strong, adamant, certain, and unchanging . . . or more empathetic or flexible?

Some decisions are impulsive, others are premeditated, and others yet again are well thought out. Some decisions are easy to make. Others, however, cause great deliberation, stress, and upheaval in our lives. When we look back on our lives we note where we made some wonderful decisions and equally some bad decisions. We will also recall when we took a chance, and things worked out for us.

We will also, of course, regret those times when we didn't take that chance—we were too scared of the risks or too preoccupied by what others may have said or thought about the matter.

And then there are those decisions that you know you need to make today—those decisions that have been eating at your conscience and causing you sleepless nights. Have the strength and courage to make that decision today, as "no decision" is, in reality, a decision, a tacit acceptance of the current situation. Indecision is the killer; it shows lack of confidence, and you lose out on opportunities.

Remember: You can't get to second base if one foot is on first. Don't be one of those people who looks back on their life and says, "If only." Take a chance, and make that decision today.

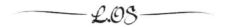

10.1.2. He who does not risk cannot win

"When you have to make a choice and don't make it, that is in itself a choice."
—William James

Have you ever seen those game shows on TV—Who Wants to be a Millionaire? or Deal or No Deal? In each case the contestants are pitied against the choice of risk or reward. As the game unfolds, and the stakes get higher, the decisions become more and more difficult.

Some may call it gambling, others greed, luck, or stupidity; there is no scientific formula to beat the bank. There have been some happy endings and some devastating results, but one common theme has prevailed throughout the game of chance—choice.

The contestants have the choice to stop the game at any stage and take their accrued winnings. Therein lays the crux; he who does not risk, cannot win or see significantly better rewards.

Sadly, you are not equipped with the "magic formula" to make the right decision every time. Mostly, your intuit or common sense will be your guide; you will know what is right for you. At other times, you need to take a risk.

Weigh up the issues carefully before deciding. There is no need to do anything reckless; there is no need to stake your life or your entire wealth on a project, but you do need to sacrifice something to earn the reward. Each decision you make (or do not make) will change the direction of your life, affect who you may become, or move you closer to or further away from your goals and success.

He who does not risk does not win.

10.1.3. Risk—lock

"We gain strength, and courage, and confidence by each experience in which we really stop to look fear in the face . . . we must do that which we think we cannot."

—Eleanor Roosevelt

Larry Laudan, a philosopher of science and guru on risk management has coined a phrase "risk-lock". Similar to traffic coming to a standstill in a "gridlock" situation, "risk-lock" is a condition of where we are so risk-averse that fear paralyzes us to the extent that we don't really live.

We can't hide in our cocoon and be sheltered from life. It is not that we need to go to the other side of the spectrum—consciously putting ourselves in dangerous situations and searching out adrenalin "extremes" like partaking in bungee jumping or abseiling, but we do need to temper risk with the perceived advantages that will emanate from the event. It's a package deal—like the "positive" and "negative" on a battery; you can't have one without the other.

Risk comes with a price . . . but without risk there is no life; so choose life.

10.2. Your destiny is in your hands

10.2.1. Toddler at poolside

"There is only one thing more painful than learning from experience and that is not learning from experience."

—Archibald MacLeish

On my recent vacation to Sun City, I witnessed a little toddler standing by the side of the pool watching his father who was already in the pool. "Jump!" the father said with open arms. "Don't be afraid, I will catch you."

The little boy, in that moment, was a bundle of conflict—his body, and everything inside him, was saying, "Stay put—don't jump. The water looks dangerous and cold. I have never done this before, so don't start now. What if Daddy misses and doesn't catch me? I can't swim. I will drown."

Then the mind "kicks in" and so does love, trust, and security. "That is Daddy in the water. He loves me. He will protect me. He would rather die for me than see me get hurt or drown. He will catch me."

The battle was between one's values and emotions—confidence and trust, fear and love, courage and security. Trust said, "Jump!" Fear said, "No!" What did the little boy do? He couldn't stand at the pool edge forever. It was decision time—action was required. His destiny was in his hands. Would he jump or back away?

Whichever choice this little toddler made would have a profound effect on his future. If he jumped he would become more confident and trusting of his dad, believing in his ability to catch him the next time. There would be a new barrier that would have overcome. There would be a new experience that he could chalk up in the learning curve of his life. On the other hand, if he decided not to jump, he would have lost that opportunity to discover if his father could be trusted. Fear would have won the day and . . . what would it have done for his confidence and growth?

And so, how will you deal with your everyday choices? Like the little boy in the story above, you can't remain on the pool edge indefinitely. While you can't afford to be frozen by fear, procrastination, and indecisiveness you also have to be responsible, proactive, and decisive.

Your destiny will be shaped by the choice/s you make.

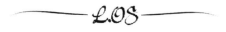

10.2.2. Follow your dreams

"Men have in their minds a picture of how the world will be. How they will be in that world. The world may be many different ways for them but there is one world that will never be and that is the world they dream of."
—Cormac McCarthy (author of *Cities of the Plain*)

But then, at the end of a very long day, Lluis walked out the hotel and saw an old friend from his taxi driving days opening the door of his cab for a hotel guest. He smiled at Lluis and waved, then hopped in the cab and drove off. Lluis watched with a heavy heart as the tail-lights disappeared down the street.

Lluis had got to work that morning before the sun was up. He was just leaving as the sun slipped the horizon. He had barely left the office all day; he hadn't once stepped outside. It felt as if he had spent his work hours in some sort of suspended animation. And all the time, the world was spinning. Clouds were moving across the sky, birds were calling, people were moving back and forth and were alive, while he had been without a pulse.*

The above quote is from the book *The Secret Letters of the Monk Who Sold his Ferrari* by Robin Sharma. I'm sure that many of us can identify with Lluis in the above excerpt, and I'm equally sure that many of us are stuck in a dead-end job or working long tedious hours in a stressful environment to make ends meet. Perhaps many of us are working in a job we hate but are too scared to leave?

And then there are those who will forgo happiness and quality of life for greed or selfish or ambitious reasons—to climb the proverbial ladder of success. I know there are many people, in the corporate world or their own business, who could be classified as workaholics or diagnosed as suffering from stress, depression, or burnout.

I don't have the magic formula for you, as there are so many scenarios and reasons, and each individual will need to do some soul-searching. Perhaps to end let me remind you of the old Arabian riddle that goes, "Who is richer—the man with a million dollars or the one with seven daughters?"

The answer is, "*The man with seven daughters for he has enough, and he knows it.*"

Steve Jobs was a great example of a man who followed his dream. One of his famous sayings was:

> *Being the richest man in the cemetery*
> *doesn't matter to me . . . Going to bed at night*
> *saying we've done something wonderful . . .*
> *that's what matters to me.*

So follow your dreams; your destiny is in your hands.

*Source: R. Sharma, The Secret Letters of the Monk Who Sold his Ferrari (London; Harper Element 2011). Page 132.

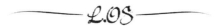

10.2.3. You can choose to be positive in a negative environment

"There are two major types of change that tend to challenge us and disrupt our day-to-day lives. The first happens to us. The second happens within us. We can't control the first, but we can and should control the second."
—Nick Vujicic

Vultures fly over the desert, looking for dead animals. Hummingbirds fly over the same desert, looking for flowers growing from a cactus or near a pond. Vultures and hummingbirds fly over the same desert, but one bird looks for death and the other looks for life.*

So it is in life. Are we choosing death or life, failure or success, the negative or the positive? It's your choice!

The above is an excerpt from "How to Create a Positive Business Outlook" by Joey Faucette. In her article, Joey introduces an interesting approach to choice: the slant and psychology of being positive.

She advocates that when you choose to think about your business, think about its best qualities, not the worst. Similarly, when it comes down to the people element, think of ways to praise your employees instead of moaning and belittling them and think of the exciting way in which the majority of your customers buy your products and use your services, not the ugly few who demand a refund.

Eileen Taz, in her eBook, *The Inspirational Moment* (www. Theinspirationalmoment.com 2013) advocates that if we can't change the situation we are in, we can make the very best of it. If we can't solve our problems we can change the way we see them, or the manner in which we allow them to affect us. Life is all about perspectives. Life is all about choices.

Staying positive in a negative environment can change not just your business, but your entire life. It's your choice.

*Source: J. Faucette, Work Positive in a Negative World: Redefine Your Reality and Achieve Your Business Dreams (California; Entrepreneur Press, 2011).)

10.3. Get comfortable with your decisions

10.3.1. Amateur photographers

"In every single thing you do, you are choosing a direction. Your life is a product of choices."

—Dr Kathleen Hall

My wife and sons are keen birders, and what I call amateur photographers. I accompanied them recently on a "field trip" and am proud to say that I spotted certain species before their trained eyes.

One thing that struck me about the day's excursion was the frequency of the choices they had to make and how each decision would have a huge influence on the outcome of the picture to be taken. Which lens to use? What settings, angle of photo, or light reading would be best to influence the finished product? What shall I allow to appear in the background? They had to see, visualize, encapsulate, and imagine the "big picture".

Their whole focus was on making the photograph "great" or having the satisfaction of that "perfect shot". Yes, there were some duds or blurred pictures, but these were be intermingled with some "winners" or "masters of Art".

Every day, all day, we are faced with a multitude of choices that will affect the various areas of our life, and each decision will affect the final outcome. With practice, experience, and time we will become better and better at it.

The choices made by my family today are as a result their learning experiences, and it's these choices and experiences that are moving the photography status of my family from that of amateur—to professional. That's something you should strive for, and you should apply to your trade or profession in order to become a champion in your own field of expertise. Become a professional, a guru; grow your own personal brand or image. Become a go-to person.

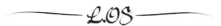

10.3.2. Decide to live life today

"Control your own destiny or someone else will."

—Jack Welch

I recall an incident many years ago when my family attended a children's birthday party. The child in question was the youngest daughter of a very good friend of the family. There was an atmosphere of excitement when we arrived, as already quite a number of the children and their parents who had gathered prior to us were in party mood. The kid in question was excited to greet us and receive well wishes and the gift we had brought along.

To our surprise, however, the child took the gift, and, without opening it, she went and locked it away in her cupboard. She had no clue as to what present we had given her, or, for that matter, what effort we had made to purchase and wrap the gift for this occasion.

Have you ever let your mind wander back in time to some great event that happened in your life? It could be your wedding day, the birth of a child, the first day at a new job, or your first plane trip. Do you sometimes think that had you the opportunity all over again, you would have done something differently on that day or at that event?

You don't know how tomorrow will unfold. You can try to visualize or imagine it, or the event that is forthcoming, but you have no degree of certainty (unless you are psychic) on how tomorrow will unfold. You may not even live to see tomorrow.

The past is history, and the future is, in reality, a promise of things to come. So the best day in your life is today. You can still act, be proactive, or counteract things. You can change your day in a split second by the choice you make at that moment.

Don't be like that man who spent most of his life longing to go to heaven. When he died he was met by an angel who took him on a conducted tour of the greatest and most beautiful mountains, streams, forests, and valleys, and of people laughing and having fun, and of many wonderful and thrilling events. The man was truly impressed and asked the angel if this was heaven. "Oh, no!" exclaimed the angel. *"This is the world in which you lived and never saw."*

So how are you going to spend today? Today is a gift. Be thankful for it, and unwrap the gift from its wrapping, and make use of it. Do not be like the child who takes the gift simply to lock it away with the other toys. You can decide to live and not merely exist—there is a difference. The choice is yours . . . make it count.

Live today to the best of your ability.

10.3.3. The Susan Lyne story

"I don't buy a dog and bark for it."

—John Evans

Susan Lyne was newly promoted to chief editor of the Premiere magazine. She was new to the responsibility, uncertain of herself, and needed input on an issue or two. Previously, as managing editor, there was always a person

she could go to for advice or confirmation, now she was alone. Susan eventually decided to approach her superior, John Evans, who was running Murdoch magazine at that time, for feedback.

A little later John called her and demanded to know what the problem was and why she couldn't handle it. Susan explained that it was her editor's letter and believed he wanted to review it first before publication. John's response was so powerful and thought provoking: "I don't buy a dog, and bark for it. Don't ever send me your editor's letter again."*

The above excerpt is a true story, shared by Susan Lyne of Gilt Group, from the early days working at a magazine. She learned a valuable lesson that day: that—no longer a number two—she would in future live and die by her own decisions. So she got comfortable with her own decisions, her own voice.

That's something we can take from the extract above. Accept responsibility, and take responsibility; get comfortable with your own voice, and your own decision-making abilities. The buck stops, and, in fact, starts, with you. Don't expect people to "bark" for you.

*Source: Adapted from: A. Bryant, The Corner Office: How Top CEOs Made It and How You Can Too (London Harper Press 2011).

10.4. Freedom of choice

10.4.1. You have a choice

"Your reputation is what you're perceived to be; your character is what you really are."

—John Wooden

"Did I make a bet? Yeah, I made a bet. bet that I could take an average everyday girl,

> **"Did I make a bet? Yes, I made a bet . . . a bet that I could take an average everyday girl, who happens to sell fish, and turn her into a model because I thought I could change anyone. I thought I could change her . . . but I can't.**
>
> **"She is Dessi [(her name]) on the inside, and that's why she is on the cover. I thought I could change her. but . . . she changed me."***

The above is a quote from the romantic movie *Tricks of a Woman* where a fashion photographer takes a bet that he can turn a plain girl into a model. He teaches her all the tricks of the trade—about how to be a beautiful woman and how to star in her new role. Despite all the tricks and lessons, Dessi remained Dessi. She wasn't everyone's ideal of what a model should be but . . . she was herself.

You see, no one can effect change in your life or career, but you. People can teach, guide, mentor, encourage, and/or show you what to do, but you have to do it. Circumstances can be forced on to you, but you still have a choice to accept those circumstances or not.

*Source: Tricks of a Woman, dir. Todd Norwood (2008).

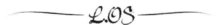

10.4.2. Whichever he chooses

"Choice, not chance determines your destiny."

—Aristotle

> **One evening an old man told his grandson about a battle that goes on inside people.**
>
> **He said, "My son, the battle is between two 'wolves' inside us all. One is the human Ego. It is anger, envy, jealousy, sorrow, regret, greed, arrogance, self-pity, guilt, resentment, inferiority, lies, false pride, and superiority. The other is the Divine Light. It is joy, peace, love, hope, serenity, humility, kindness, benevolence, empathy, generosity, truth, compassion, and faith."**

The grandson thought about it for a minute and then asked his grandfather, "Which wolf wins?"

The old man simply replied, "Whichever he chooses."*

The above famous Native American Cherokee fable sums up our daily thought processes. From the clothes we wear, the work we do, the food we eat, to the time that we go to sleep, we are free to choose. There is no sitting on the proverbial fence—the fence is electrified. You are either this side or the other. It comes down to choice.

Like the story of the wolves, you have the power to choose—good or bad, positive or negative, fear or faith, success or failure.

Choose wisely.

*Source: Adapted from: Native American Cherokee story, wolves within—Roger Knapp <http://www.rogerknapp.com/inspire/Wolveswithin.htm> accessed 20 May 2014

10.4.3. Be your own person

"As human beings, we are endowed with freedom of choice, and we cannot shuffle off our responsibility upon the shoulders of God or nature. We must shoulder it ourselves. It is our responsibility."

—Arnold Toynbee

I know of a man who had become estranged from his family because he didn't go into the family business. The irony of this situation was that the man's father hated his job. His grandfather had forced his own father into the family business, and now his father is just counting the days until he can retire.

This, unfortunately, is a story that resonates with so many of us. While you may not have been forced into the family business you may currently be in a job (or some other situation) that you hate and looking for a way out or counting the days to your retirement.

Now is the time to question your thinking and be led by what the heart really wants. There are only two primary choices open to you—and each choice hinges on the word "change" with its own set of circumstances and consequences.

First, you can take the plunge, and change jobs, and start something new, and chase your dreams, or, second, you can change your attitude and work ethic, and stay exactly where you are. You have freedom of choice, but choice without action is meaningless. There is a wonderful quote by Nick Vujicic that highlights the importance for action in both choice and change:

> *No matter how dire your circumstances may appear, you can rise above them. To wish for change will change nothing. To make the decision to take action right now will change everything!*

Don't be paralyzed by fear or guilt or the wishes of others. Once you have made a decision, own it. You can't expend your energy second guessing and doubting yourself. You are not a slave; you have freedom of choice. However, choice comes with consequences, so you need to be discerning and need to choose wisely.

Have confidence in your decisions. Be your own person.

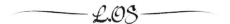

10.4.4. We choose how we live

"Life is comprised of days. Enjoy and focus on the now. You can deal with tomorrow, tomorrow."

—anonymous

A wise man, addressing an audience, cracked a joke— and all of them laughed like crazy. After a moment he repeated the joke, and a few people laughed. He then cracked the same joke again, and no one laughed.

The wise man smiled and said, "When you can't laugh at the same joke again and again, why is it that you cry over the same thing . . . over and over again?"

Choice is a concept introduced to us at a very early age, albeit on a limited scale, and it develops over our formative, teenage, and adult years. It's something that plays a huge part in our lives; there are continual battles in most of our lives regarding what we want and what stands in our way.

But choice also plays a significant role in our outlook in life. It affects our attitude and passion, whether we embrace change or are creative, our goals and our dreams, and whether to be positive or negative—to cry over the same thing over and over again.

The way we live is a choice. Joseph Epstein understood this concept better than many.

> *We do not choose to be born.*
> *We do not choose our parents,*
> *Or our country of birth.*
> *We do not, most of us,*
> *Choose to die; nor do we choose*
> *The time and conditions of our death.*
> *But within this real of choicelessness,*
> *We do choose how we live.**

*Source: Joseph Epstein, 9 February 2010, We do not choose to be born . . . . Quotegasm . . . <http://www.quotegasm.com/joseph-epstein-we-do-not-choose-to-be-born/> accessed 20 May 2014

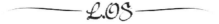

10.5. Theory versus practice

10.5.1. Communication and collaboration in decision making

"Well, it may be all right in practice, but it will never work in theory."
—Warren Buffett

A little field mouse was lost in a dense wood, unable to find his way out. He came upon a wise old owl sitting in a tree. "Please help me, wise old owl. How can I get out of this wood?" asked the field mouse.

"Easy," replied the owl. "Grow wings, and fly out, as I do."

"But how can I grow wings?" asked the mouse.

The owl looked at him haughtily and sniffed disdainfully. He said, "Don't bother me with the details; I only decide the policy."*

Over the past six years I have delivered a countless number of talks to businesses, conferences, and team builds and have been amazed by how many organizations implement policies or processes without consultation with their employees, that is, those in the trenches, those serving the business's clients, and those fielding all the abuse and problems hurled at the company.

Author Sarah Cook estimates that only 4 per cent of all complaints about the organization reach the upper echelons of senior management. What happens to the other 96 per cent of complaints? Who attends to these, and puts out the fires while protecting the brand and reputation of the organization?

What I also find very fascinating is that businesses spend so much time, money, and energy on hiring and employing personnel (some having three or four interviews, and many new recruits receiving sign-on bonuses in order to move jobs), yet when policies are dictated, their input is often overlooked or ignored.

While there may be a need for some top-down decisions, it's important that every business takes note of the concerns, practicalities, and issues raised by its team members. Sometimes the reasons are not black or white (like financial implications) but more abstract and harder to define (like reputational risks). There are, at times, vast differences between the theory and the practice that need to be clearly understood.

Communication and collaboration plays a vital role in understanding these differences and ultimately in reaching the fair and correct decisions.

*Source: Adapted from: Growth |Seefin Coaching|Page 4 <http://www. seefincoaching.com/category/growth/page/4/> accessed 23 May 2014

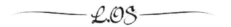

10.5.2. Limit the number of choices; less is better

"A man is too apt to forget that in this world he cannot have everything. A choice is all that is left him."

—Harry Matthews

Nelson Mandela Square is a very prominent and affluent landmark and tourist attraction, nestled in the suburb, north of Johannesburg. While walking through the shopping centre one day I passed a retailer who just sold ice creams—vanilla, bubblegum, and other flavours, in pink, green, and even yellow. In total, there must have been a selection of twenty-five to thirty from which members of the public could choose.

I recall watching a family who took their four children for a treat. The children were wildly excited and running amok, from one end of the store to the other, trying to make up their little minds which ice-cream combination they wanted.

They had a choice, but the choice was far too wide. In fact, ironically, it was so broad a choice that they couldn't make a choice . . .

Would it not have been easier for these little children if the store or their father had limited the selection to three or even five ice creams? Does the same principle not hold in the sales or marketing environment? Would a client faced with say three products or service offerings be able to make a better informed decision than from a greater multiple choice?

From a business point of view, would it not be more cost effective and prudent to limit the range of products and service offerings where the focus of attention can be delivered?

10.5.3. Do some "effortful processing"

"Chains of habit are too light to be felt until they are too heavy to be broken".
—Warren Buffet

> **We are all creatures of habit. Our days are full of habits, and much of what we do is without what psychologists call "effortful processing". We do things routinely, without even realizing it. In fact, a Duke University study found that more than 40 per cent of the actions people performed each day were not actual decisions but habits.***

The above statistic could be quite scary if the habits we do are not attributing to our success, good health, goals, and self-development. The odds are good, however, that our daily decisions or even our habits (which can be automatic or subliminal decision) are a mixture of good and bad, positive and negative. As many of these are in robotic rhythm, the challenge is to identify which action or nuances need to be addressed.

Changing those bad or negative habits requires discipline and vigilant monitoring. That is the theory, but how good is it to put into practice?

*Source: Adapted from: D. Neal, T. Quinn, and W. Wood, Habits: A Repeat Performance (New Jersey; Wiley Blackwell, 2006).

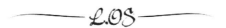

11 Leadership

11.1. What type of leader are you?

11.1.1. The Chinese poem

> A leader is best when people barely know he exists,
> Not so good when people obey and acclaim him,
> Worse when they debase him.
> Fail to honour people and they fail to honour you.
> But a good leader (is one) who talks little
> (And) When his work is done, his aim fulfilled,
> They will say, **WE DID IT OURSELVES.**

The above poem, believed to have been written by the great Chinese philosopher Lao Tzu (also known as Tao Te Ching) way back in period 600 BC, is still relevant in today's thinking of leadership and still offers wonderful advice for any leader. The essence in leading is so subtle—to take back stage, and make the people feel they did it themselves.

Stan Toler, in his book *Minute Motivators for Leaders: Quick Inspiration for the Time of Your Life*, hints that there are three ways to motivate people: guilt, flattery, and inspiration, either by word or by deed. The best leaders are those who can inspire others to reach for something greater than themselves while at the same time making everyone in the team feel valuable, motivated, and focused on achieving the vision and goals of the team or organization.

Leaders need to be self-controlled and great communicators, visionaries, listeners, team builders, and problem solvers. They also need to be courageous, supportive, flexible, and blessed with a degree of emotional intelligence. They need to be able to work with all kinds of people, and, most importantly, they need to earn their respect. An authentic leader will be just as excited with the success of their people as they are with their own success.

The list of leadership attributes goes on and on. Yes, I'm the first to admit that it's impossible for a human to possess all of these wonderful characteristics (can you imagine the type of world we would be experiencing if this was the case?), but it's important that you know what type of leader you are. In so doing you will also recognize the way forward for self-development.

*Source: Reference to Chapter 17, Laozi—Wikiquote <http://en.wikiquote.org/ wiki/Laozi> accessed 24 May 2014

11.1.2. Know your strengths and weaknesses

"Nothing so conclusively proves a man's ability to lead others as what he does from day to day to lead himself."

—Thomas J. Watson

> **"Did you hear the tale of the hippo who tried to paint a stripe on his body, so he would look like the zebra? But he fooled no one. Then he tried to put a spot on his body to be like a leopard, but everyone knew he was a hippo.**
>
> **"So, at a certain point, he looked at himself in the mirror and said, 'Hey, I am a hippopotamus, and there is nothing I can do about it.' And, as soon as he accepted this, he lived a happy, fulfilled life."***

For someone in a leadership role, it's vital that they "know themselves" better than their subordinates or team members. Like the hippopotamus in the above tale, a leader will have to find his or her own style of managing, guiding, and influencing others. They can learn from others, but they can't be a clone of someone else, as leadership is very personal in nature; they need to find their true self.

Leaders need to identify their strengths and weaknesses. They need to establish where they are vulnerable and where possibly they may be exploited. Forewarned is forearmed. They must capitalize on their strengths, and find ways of overcoming weaknesses. A leader's education doesn't end for there are always gaps to fill and heights to reach.

Harvey Mackay offers some sound advice when it comes to dealing with weaknesses; his motto is: *"Don't water your weeds."* How profound. You know, we tend to spend too much time in self-doubt or worrying about our bad habits or weaknesses that they consume us and take over. Instead, turn it all around. Accept your unique strengths, talents, and attributes. Concentrate on these, and once you have established a positive base and self-esteem, only then concern yourself with improving your weaknesses. For if you only concentrate on your weaknesses then you run the risk of diminishing the power or uniqueness of your strengths.

It was Donna Harrison that said, "*Great leaders are never satisfied with current levels of performance. They are driven by possibilities and potential achievements.*"

*Source: paraphrased extract from: Along Came Polly, dir. John Hamburg (2004).

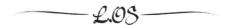

11.1.3. "Management by walkabout"

"I not only use all the brains that I have, but all I can borrow."
—Woodrow Wilson

The then chief technology officer (CTO) of Sun Microsystems, Inc. and now CEO of Google, Eric Schmidt, went for a walk around the lab one day and discovered that a coder at Sun had invented Java.

That little piece of nearly forgotten software is now a key component of many internet experiences and has enabled software industries to exist. If he hadn't done his walk about he may have missed that "pot of gold".

There's a wonderful lesson for us from the above event. Businesses are so focused on their day-to-day matters that they forget what they have in their hands: the talent in their workforce and the ideas being incubated by their employees.

And what about those niggling problems (including complaints and red tape) that are often ignored with the hope that they will go away or are brushed under the carpet? Sometimes it's those small issues that manifest into something big and could be the start of a "cancer" spreading throughout the organization.

I'm a great advocate of the concept of "management by walkabout", a tool that can help managers, leaders, and senior executives to witness what is happening at the coalface of their business. It allows them to hear first-hand and experience how their staff are coping, how they deal with clients and processes, the problems they are faced with on a day-to-day basis, and their ideas or gripes.

The advantages of this concept are immeasurable:

- *Visible for all to see instead of executives/managers sitting behind their desks or hiding in their corner office. It reminds people who they are being led by and why.*
- *Demonstrates great leadership and the human element.*
- *Fosters buy-in and team spirit.*
- *Closes the gap between executives/management and employees.*
- *Achieves an instant feel for how things are going in the trenches and how clients see the business.*
- *Provides instant feedback on what's happening at the coalface, and the attitude of one's staff (how staff are speaking to clients over the telephone, the neatness of the office, stress levels, corridor talk, and so on).*
- *It's an opportunity for one's staff to ask questions in a less intimidating space (in the employee's comfort zone).*

"Management by walkabout" elicits more direct, honest, and open feedback from the trenches. It's an opportunity for the staff to ask questions and be open regarding what's on their mind. Generally staff won't go knocking on the CEO's/senior executive's door to tell them what's wrong.

11.1.4. How do you make people feel?

"I've learned that people will forget what you said, people will forget what you did, but people will never forget how you made them feel."

—Maya Angelou

When Apple computer fell on hard times, Steve Jobs went from California to New York City. His purpose was to convince Pepisco's John Sculley to run his struggling company. Sculley said, "You have to give me a million-dollar salary, a million-dollar bonus, and a million-dollar severance."

Jobs instead issued a challenge to Sculley. "Do you want to spend the rest of your life selling sugared water, or do you want a chance to change the world?"*

In his autobiography, *Oddesy*, Sculley admits that Jobs' challenge knocked the wind out of him and resulted in him accepting the Apple position. Jobs, as a leader, used a great deal of psychology and appealed to the emotions of Sculley. That's what leaders do, especially if they want to extract the best out of a person or achieve the best for their organization—they play to feelings.

There is nothing wrong in selling sugared water; the question is, "What are you doing to make a difference in people's lives?" Think about the people you come in contact with in your work and in your personal life. What kind of experience do you create for them when they interact with you? Are you fully present and look them in the eye and make them feel valued and important? Are you really paying attention to what they're saying and receiving the message they're trying to communicate to you, or are you thinking of your answer or—even worse—your exist strategy?

It's easy to be preoccupied with your own thoughts and priorities, so you have to want to connect in a meaningful way with the other person, and make an extra effort.

Maya Angelou is right. People always remember how you made them feel.

*Source: Adapted from: E. Tan, The Inspirational Moment: 20 Power Thoughts that Will Make a Positive Impact in Your Life (e-book, 2013). (www. Theinspitationalmoment.com)

11.2. Earn the right to lead

11.2.1. Elizabeth Dole

"The key to successful leadership today is influence, not authority."
—Ken Blanchard

> **The Red Cross was built by volunteers. And our tradition of trust was built from Grassroots, in communities across the country. Our assistance is not delivered by strangers or faceless bureaucrats; rather, it's given by friends and neighbours. The Red Cross patch can be found on the arm of the merchant on Main Street or the retired teacher, two houses down . . . .**
>
> **I've thought a lot about that patch, and the over one million volunteers who wear it today. I've thought about how I wanted to get the message out that it is the volunteers who are the heart and soul of the Red Cross. And I decided that the best way I can let volunteers know of their importance is to be one of them—to earn the patch on my sleeve. Therefore, during my first year as president, I will accept no salary. I, too, will be a volunteer.***

The above quote by Elizabeth Dole (from her inaugural speech in 1991 as president of Red Cross) personifies the art of leadership—connecting to the people of the organization; teamwork; that there are no mundane tasks or unimportant people in the organization; and leading by example, to name a few. Nelson Mandela is another prime example of a person who personified great leadership qualities.

The above excerpt also highlights some important attributes of a leader: their strength of character and commitment, being part of the team, humility rather than arrogance, showing appreciation of its people, and upholding the vision of the entity.

I'm sure when you look at the list of attributes required to be a good leader, you will recognize one or two areas that may need room for improvement in your life. Perhaps now is the time to appreciate your shortcomings and to determine how you become more effective and influential as a leader.

Before you can do something, you must be something. You have to earn the right to lead.

*Source: Elizabeth Dole's salary as head of American Red Cross| Recordnet 2 April 1996 <http://www.recordnet.com/apps/pbcs.dll/article?AID=/19960402/A NEWS/...> accessed 19 May 2014

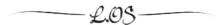

11.2.2. The Jeff King example

"A good leader inspires people to have confidence in their leader. A great leader inspires people to have confidence in themselves."

—anonymous

John Maxwell, in his book, The Right to Lead, relates a true story about a man, Jeff King, an infamous sled-dog racer who has won the 1,000-mile Iditarod race from Anchorage to Nome, Alaska, four times (1993, 1996, 1998, and 2006).

Jeff's modus operandi was to usually start the Iditarod race with sixteen dogs and then rotate the lead dog frequently, giving each dog a chance to lead until he found that natural leader—the one that was most persistent, able to lead, and motivate the other dogs.

When Jeff was congratulated for winning the 1998 Iditarod, he lifted up his lead dog and said, "Here is the leader who won the race for us."*

This method of selecting the natural leader of the pack proved successful to Jeff in that he won this gruelling race on four occasions. It's an interesting tactic to pit dog against dog and allow for the strength of character and those inherent and strong leadership qualities to come to the fore. There are a good number of businesses that adopt a similar method of promoting leaders and personnel.

Leadership is important no matter who you are or where you lead. Leaders earn the right to lead others. They became effective leaders not by making other people follow but by making themselves the kind of person people would want to follow.

Remember that a team or business takes its cue from its leadership, so there is a great deal of responsibility associated with leadership. Understand fully your requirements and obligations to lead others. You need to earn your right to lead.

*Source: Adapted from: J. C. Maxwell, The Right to Lead: Learning Leadership through Character and Courage (Edinburgh; Thomas Nelson, 2010).

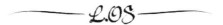

11.2.3. The elephant graveyard

"I make progress by having people around me who are smarter than I am and listening to them."

—Henry J. Kaiser

Elephants can live up to seventy years, but the key deciding factor to their life span revolves around their teeth. They go through six sets of molars, the last attained at the age of forty-seven. When the last set of molars gets whittled away the elephant can no longer sustain itself on its normal food requirements. It drops away from the herd to the softer foods found near dams or rivers.

This presents a twofold problem. The new diet causes severe stomach disorders, and, more importantly, there is insufficient food in this region to sustain the beast that requires eating approximately 500 kg per day, 10 per cent of its weight. The elephants soon become very frail and die; the riverbeds become the elephant's graveyards.

The good news is that businesses don't have to rely on just six sets of molars or a life span of only seventy years—businesses can outdistance generations, and there are examples where some have been around for centuries. Sadly, the converse is also true, and many businesses have disappeared into the annals of history.

Attention must be paid to the various stages of each business lifecycle. As long as the organization keeps evolving, changing with the times, or re-inventing itself, it will survive. It's the leader's obligation and responsibility to revisit its vision and working processes and determine what remains viable and what needs tweaking or further action. In many cases leaders are responsible for returns to shareholders, and their decisions affect the livelihood of hundreds or thousands of people. A great deal of trust and accountability rests on their shoulders. They have earned their stripes, the right to lead.

There are many ways and courses of action to keep the business from an early grave, so have the courage and conviction to do so. Perhaps we can take the advice offered by Henry Kaiser in the above quotation, and listen to other leaders and successful, experienced, and wise people.

11.2.4. Let us march

"Anyone who influences others is a leader."

—Chuck Swindoll

There is an ancient Greek myth about two generals trying to rally their troops for war. After the first general had spoken, the troops murmured among one another. "How well he speaks." However, no one moved. After the second general had spoken, the troops shouted in unison, "Let us march!"

The above anecdote has a couple of important messages for us. First, how you "sell" things to your "people"—be it employees, clients, or even your children—is very important. The tone, content, style, and sincerity of the message are vital. So appeal to their emotions, feelings, and passions.

It also has another fascinating, yet subtle meaning. People will follow a leader whom they trust and respect. They will soon see through any rhetoric or insincerity. They will follow a person who leads by example and does what he or she says they are going to do.

So how are you doing on this front? Is your communication with your "people" on a level that they are prepared to march with you, or are your words just passing over their heads? Make sure they buy into your message, vision, team, or concepts, and heed the call—"Let us march!"

11.3. Taking responsibility

11.3.1. The pilot, and the British and Irish Lions rugby supporters

"People need responsibility. They resist assuming it, but they cannot get along without it."

—John Steinbeck

A few years ago I was seated on a plane ready for take-off to Cape Town where I had accepted an invitation to be a keynote speaker at a conference. It was late at night, and there were very few passengers on this scheduled flight. Then, just before take-off, the captain received a call that the plane, chartered to transport the travelling fans of the British *and Irish* **Lions Rugby team in South Africa, had encountered technical problems and, accordingly, the passengers needed to be accommodated on all other flights bound for Cape Town.**

After an hour's delay, and while the plane was taxing to its position for take-off, the captain's voice came over the intercom, welcoming the British tourists to this country. He then announced that consequent of the last minute arrangements, the plane did not have time to "restock" and that, understandably, there wouldn't be sufficient food or drinks for everyone.

At first I was amazed that the captain would actually tell the passengers, who had been waiting around the airport for hours, that now their food and drink intake for the next two hours was limited or non-existent.

Then it struck me. The captain assumed responsibility for the situation and was upfront and honest with everyone. He didn't keep quiet and hope that many of the passengers would fall asleep or that they had eaten at the airport prior to boarding the plane. He also didn't leave the situation wholly to the air hostesses who would have to bear the brunt of the passengers' abuse and irritation.

He assumed responsibility. He did what captains should do. He did what everyone of us should do.

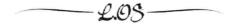

11.3.2. The culture of your business; theory x and y

"The best executive is one who has sense enough to pick good men to do what he wants done, and the self—restraint to keep from meddling with them while they do it."

—Theodore Roosevelt

The boards of the two fiercely competitive companies decided to organize a rowing match to challenge each other's organizational and sporting abilities. The first company was strongly "theory X": ruthless, autocratic, with zero staff empowerment. The second company was more "theory Y": a culture of developing people, devolved responsibility, and decision-making.

Race day arrived. The Y company's boat appeared from the boat-house first, with its crew: eight rowers and a helmsman (the cox). Next followed the X company boat and its crew—eight helmsmen and a single rower.

Not surprisingly the Y company's boat won an easy victory.

The next day the X company board of directors held an inquest with the crew, to review what had been learned

from the embarrassing defeat, which may be of benefit to the organization as a whole, and any future re-match.

After a long and wearing meeting, the X company board finally came to their decision. They concluded that the rower should be replaced immediately because clearly he had not listened well enough to the instructions he'd been given.*

There are a number of similar storylines to illustrate the two contrasting aspects of theory X and Y as advocated by Douglas McGregor.

In essence, both practices are used in business today, but the implications and results of the two are vastly different. Surely, as a leader, you don't want to have to "dangle the carrot" or use the big stick approach; there are so many more methods for growing, empowering, encouraging, and educating your employees.

The theory Y concept is the basis for a culture of happy employees. Happy employees will out-perform and out-service unhappy employees. Happy employees will create the right morale in the business place.

At the same time leaders, must not send out confusing instructions or blur the reporting lines of its personnel. They need to ensure that the chains of responsibility, lines of communication, and the delegation of tasks are clear, specific, and aligned to the success and vision of the organization.

It's the people that set the culture in the business, but the culture is influenced by the processes, rules, and styles of management as determined by its leaders. Creating the culture is not the sole responsibility of the management team; it rests on the shoulders of each and every member of the team or organization. You are all part of the "board" that determines your culture.

Consider the current culture in your organization, and if it's not to your liking, what can you do about it?

*Source: Stories, analogies and fables for business, training . . .—Businessballs <http://www.businessballs.com/stories.htm> accessed 20 May 2014

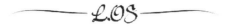

11.3.3. We are all leaders

"You can preach a better sermon with your life than with your lips."
—Oliver Goldsmith (Irish poet)

One of the newest world leaders to hit centre stage was President Obama. When one looks back at his campaigning days and the steps he took to succeed in taking up the highest appointment in the land, you will recognize that he displayed many leadership attributes. He excelled at earning trust, breaking down barriers, driving point's home, leaving strong lasting impressions, walking with a purpose, being confident and connecting with people.

He was also consistent (as was his policy) and made fun of himself. He referred to himself as a "skinny kid".*

There is a difference between leading and managing. Leadership in not telling people what to do; it's about getting people to follow you as opposed to pushing them in the direction you want them to go. It's a relationship, not a title.

As parents, siblings, teachers, preachers, managers, or employers we play an active part in leading and setting an example for others to follow. But the list doesn't end there; by default, it includes *you*.

You have a role to play in this world, and in some role in your life you are in a leadership position where you assume some form of control, guidance, experience, knowledge, skill, trust, and/or responsibility. So, lead by example. Leave a legacy. Be a great leader.

*Source: L. O'Sullivan, Client Service Excellence: The 10 Commandments (Johannesburg: Knowledge Resources, 2010).

11.3.4. A lesson in extraordinary leadership

"Reputation is made in a moment; character is built in a lifetime."

—James Leggett

> **"For me, this was about two babies lying alone in a New Delhi hospital. I was able to travel and wanted to do what I could. Sometimes life presents you with situations with few good solutions. This was one of those," the Crown Princess said in an official palace statement***

The above is an excerpt from the Norwegian Palace communiqué after the world learned that Norway's Crown Princess, Mette-Marit, had travelled in secret to India to care for the twins of a palace employee born to a surrogate mother there.

The employee was unable to get a visa from the Indian Government, so the future queen, armed with a diplomatic passport that granted her immediate access, hopped on to a plane and, without alerting Indian authorities, spent several days with the babies at the Manav Medicare Centre in New Delhi (where staff assumed she was a nanny) until the employee was given a visa to travel.

Great leaders sometimes have to take extraordinary decisions in support of their people when the opportunity arises. They need to take responsibility and be able to make immediate decisions.

When questioned at a later stage as to her motive, the Crown Princess promptly replied, **"It was the right thing to do."**

*Source: J. Glassman, Sales Guru Magazine, February 2012.

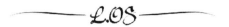

11.4. Lead by example

11.4.1. Turn around and see who is following!

"Before you can do something you must be something."

—Goethe

I love the story of a pregnant woman suing a construction company who was using a jack hammer near her home and claimed the noise and dust was disturbing the health of her unborn child . . . yet in the photo that appeared of her at the trial (in newspaper) she is seen with a cigarette in her hand.

Even more recently, the deputy traffic chief of a large city in South Africa was caught on camera driving without his seat belt buckled, speaking on a handheld cell phone/ mobile device.

Leadership is more about who we are than what we do. It's leading by example. Actions count more than words. There is also a big difference between what is said and what is done. Leading by example engenders trust, purpose, commitment, and respect. People will follow leaders they respect and trust.

It was Nelson Mandela that said, *"Be clear about your principles and never forget them. They should form the foundation for all you do."*

To determine what type of leader you are: Turn around, and see who is following.

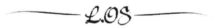

11.4.2. It all started with a piece of trash

"It is not fair to ask others what you are unwilling to do yourself."
—Eleanor Roosevelt

Matthew Emerzian, a successful music industry executive in Los Angeles, was walking back to his office with a co-worker one afternoon when he stopped to pick up a plastic fountain drink cover from the sidewalk and put it in a nearby garbage bin.

His co-worker was amazed and in fact blown away by such an act. To the co-worker, litter simply belonged to the litterer, not to the population as a whole. Emerzian explained to him that litter and pollution are everyone's

problem, not just the person who couldn't find the trash can. *

And the rest is history. Emerzian walked back to his office both angry and sad that people had such little respect for the world. He wondered what would happen if everyone in the country picked up one piece of litter on the same day . . . or perhaps ten pieces. The math was easy, yet so powerful. He then began to think of a few other easy things that a figure of approximately 300 million Americans could do to make a difference. This led to the birth of his book with co-author Kelly Bozza, *Every Day Matters—52 Ways to Make a Difference.*

It all started with one person leading by example and making a difference in the lives of society and the world at large. It just takes one person, or one act, or one piece of trash . . . and there is nothing stopping that person . . . being you.

*Source: Emerzn m & Bozza K, Every Day Matters—52 Ways to Make a Difference, (Edinburgh, Thomas Nelson, 2008)

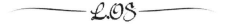

11.4.3. The scrutiny of leadership

"You are not responsible for what people think about you. But you are responsible for what you give them to think about you."

—anonymous

Linda Hudson had just been promoted to become the first female president at General Dynamics. While buying some new clothes for work, a lady at Nordstrom showed her how to tie a scarf in a very unusual kind of way that would complement her new suits.

She wore the scarf and suit to work and, on the following day, she ran into no fewer than a dozen women wearing scarves tied exactly like her.*

That's when Linda Hudson realized that life wouldn't be the same any more. As president of the company, she was not only thrust into the public eye of shareholders, analysts, and outsiders, but also, all of her employees. Everyone was watching her, and they noticed everything she did.

And, it wasn't just the way she dressed. It was about her behaviour, the example, and tone she set, the way she carried herself. As a leader, people will look at you in ways you never could have imagined.

With leadership comes intense scrutiny, the weight of responsibility, an extra workload, the challenge of managing new layers of people, and the way that employees assume the boss has both superhuman knowledge and power.

*Source: Adapted from: A. Bryant, The Corner Office: How Top CEOs Made It and How You Can Too, London, Harper Press, (2011).

11.4.4. Sermons we see

"Some of the greatest lessons in leadership are seen and not heard."

—Stan Toler

> **I'd rather see a sermon than hear one any day;**
> **I'd rather one walk with me than merely tell me the way.**
> **The eye's a better pupil and more willing than the ear . . . ,**
> **. . . I soon can learn to do it if you'll let me see it done.***

The above is a partial quote from Edgar Alan Guest's poem "Sermons We See", which epitomizes the importance of leading by example.

Every day we are being measured by others, either consciously or subconsciously. This could be in the workplace by clients, colleagues, and your bosses or in your personal life by family, friends, and members of the community. This examination entails various categories and includes one's strength of character or values, parental or family responsibilities, leadership and communication qualities, and whether you are a good example or not.

You can preach a better sermon by your action and example. Don't be a person that tells people to "do what I say" but rather be a person who tells them to "do what I do".

*Source: Sermons We See—Sofine's Poerty of Edgar Guest <http://www. sofinesjoyfulmoments.com/quotes/sermon.htm> accessed 20 May 2014

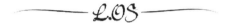

11.5. Make everyone feel important

11.5.1. The unsung heroes and heroines

"Leaders must be close enough to relate to others, but far enough ahead to motivate them."

—John Maxwell

> **"It is easy for us [as MPs] to praise ourselves for the work that we do, but 90% of the work [of Parliament] is made possible by you. You are the unsung heroes and heroines [of this institution] and this lunch comes nowhere near the value of what you do."**
>
> **She added: "I am what I am because of you. You men and women are the engines that keep us going."***

I came across the above quote in a local newspaper supplement. It's part of an address at a luncheon hosted by the National Assembly's speaker, Gwen Mahlangu Nkabinde, to her people in which she conveyed the most amazing words of appreciation and encouragement I have ever read. The guests were not dignitaries and power wigs in dark suits, but were Parliament's service officers, cleaners, administrative, and catering staff.

Here is a wonderful example of a person, a leader, who was able to show appreciation, even for the small and mundane tasks performed by members of her team.

*Source: L. O'Sullivan, Client Service Excellence: The 10 Commandments (Johannesburg; Knowledge Resources, 2010). (page 172)

11.5.2. The biscuit factory

"Conductor with baton leads an orchestra along. He never says a word, but his voice is loudly heard."

—Lex Sloop

Some years ago the following exchange was broadcast on an Open University sociology TV programme:

> **An interviewer was talking to a female production-line worker in a biscuit factory. The dialogue went like this:**
>
> **Interviewer: How long have you worked here?**
>
> **Production lady: Since I left school (probably about fifteen years).**
>
> **Interviewer: What do you do?**
>
> **Production lady: I take packets of biscuits off the conveyor belt and put them into cardboard boxes.**
>
> **Interviewer: Have you always done the same job?**
>
> **Production lady: Yes.**
>
> **Interviewer: Do you enjoy it?**
>
> **Production lady: Oooh, yes, it's great; everyone is so nice and friendly, and we have a good laugh.**
>
> **Interviewer (with a hint of disbelief): Really? Don't you find it a bit boring?**
>
> **Production lady: Oh no, sometimes they change the biscuits.***

The above certainly has lessons for us in both life and the workplace: the effects of a positive attitude, loyalty, pride in work, job satisfaction, that there are no mundane jobs, and belief in one's employer, to name a few. Leaders can also learn a great deal from the above.

But there is also a more profound message. Everybody has their own view on life and work, and one must accept that certain things (, for example, job status or career aspirations) that motivate you will not necessarily motivate someone else. People, especially your employees, have their own personal agenda; their specific needs, reasons, and sources of happiness in their life or career will differ widely from yours.

As a leader you need to recognize this fact, and ensure you don't impose your personal needs and ambitions on to other people who may not share them. You can't make assumptions. You need to know what makes people tick and appreciate issues from their perspective.

The trick is to make people feel important. Only then will you have the input and ability to lead, guide, and get their buy-in into the greater business goals and vision.

*Source: Stories, analogies and fables for business, training . . . -Businessballs, <http://www.businessballs.com/stories.htm> accessed 20 May 2014

11.5.3. The Susan Lowell story

"It's not what you take but what you leave behind that defines greatness."
—Edward Gardner

Susan Lowell had a desire to help troubled teenagers. One day, she quit her high-paying job and went to work as a school teacher in one of the roughest schools in California, a high school known for its drugs, gangs, and other serious problems. Not surprisingly, the school had one of the highest dropout rates in the state. The school board could hardly keep teachers because the students were unruly and rebellious. Nobody thought the new lady would last.

But Susan took a different approach. On the first day of school, she asked her students to write down their names and addresses and something interesting about themselves. While they were writing, she walked up and down the rows and secretly memorized each student's name. When they were finished she announced to the

class that they were about to have their first test. The students moaned and groaned.

She explained the test wasn't for the pupils but for her— that if she could call out each child's name correctly, then she would pass the test. If not, even if she missed just one name, the entire class would get an automatic "A" in their next test.*

And the rest of the story is history. Susan Lowell succeeded and passed her test 100 per cent. Not only were her students impressed and had her attention, they realized that this teacher was different. She was not there simply to get a pay cheque. This lady, they thought, believed in them and cared for them, no matter what their background or level of education. This lady believed they could become "somebody" one day.

Leaders understand that their team members or employees need to feel valued, recognized, and included. More importantly, leaders understand the importance of a name—that their team members and co-workers are not anonymous or just a number. Once people sense they belong, all things are possible.

The story of Susan Lowell also demonstrates a leader's greatness by the way they treat others and how to elicit their buy-in and willingness to support.

*Source: Adapted from: J. Osteen, Become a Better You: 7 Keys to Improving your Life Every Day (London; Simon & Schuster).

12 Change and innovation

12.1. Change what needs changing—not what's easy

12.1.1. Get rid of those old wineskins

"Not everything that is faced can be changed. But nothing can be changed until it's faced."

—Arthur Baldwin

In the biblical days wine was stored in leather wineskins that were animal skins dried and cured until the leather could be shaped into containers to hold the wine. Initially the wineskins were soft and pliable, but as they aged they often lost their purpose. They became hardened that the wine would leak and be lost. Accordingly, a policy was adopted that one should not put new wine in old wineskins.

In today's standards the same principles apply. You cannot simply advocate new passions or goals where there are well-set mindsets. You have to rid the mind of old habits and restrictions in order for new attitudes and change to take place. Change those mindsets that hinder your potential and are filled with barriers that hold you back.

New wine needs new wineskins. Get rid of those old wineskins.

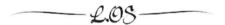

12.1.2. The wildebeest wisdom

"Change is not merely necessary in life—it is life."

—Alwin Toffler

The great wildebeest migration in the Serengeti, Tanzania, is certainly a sight to behold. The wildebeest, accompanied by large numbers of zebra and Grant's gazelle, Thomson's gazelle, eland, and impala start their annual pattern to seek favourable supplies of water and

grass. They travel hundreds of kilometres each year, beginning right after calving season on the Serengeti plains, moving north to the grasslands of the Maasai Mara.

They are persistent with their advance, and although many are injured or lost in the raging river crossing or eaten by crocodiles the wildebeest knows that for survival, change and adaption must occur.*

There are plenty other examples of this migration process in the animal and bird kingdoms. We can learn from nature and the instincts of these species. In life, we constantly face the barrage of "change"—so much so that it becomes part and parcel of our lives.

In general there are two groups of people when dealing with change: the "fighters" who will resist or challenge change and the "acceptors" who become conditioned to the fact that there will be changes, so they just go with the flow. Each style has its own set of implications, and one thing is for sure—change does not wait.

I can only hope that before the "fighters" pull out all of their "artillery" and the "acceptors" bury their heads in the sand, they have taken time to consider the following questions:

Is all change good or necessary, or is it change for the sake of change?

Have they (unemotionally) questioned the reasons, or do they clearly understand the motive for change?

Do they have a role or say in the matter?

How quick will they buy-in and adapt?

This is the key when dealing with change—the need to anticipate, understand, monitor, and adapt. Don't be afraid to change: follow the migratory pattern of the wildebeest. More importantly, don't be slow to embrace change. Have the wisdom to adapt to changing circumstances.

Change is necessary. Change is life.

12.1.3 The British Rail experiment

"Before we build a better mousetrap, we need to find out if there are any mice out there."

—Yogi Berra

There is a very interesting story with an even more interesting by-line concerning an experiment with British Rail. Over a number of years, British Rail experienced a real fall-off in business. To remedy the situation and to ensure that their marketing process was in order, they went searching for a new ad agency—one that could deliver an ad campaign that would bring their customers back.

When the British Rail executives went to the offices of a prominent London ad agency to discuss their needs, they were met by a very rude receptionist, who insisted that they wait.

Finally, an unkempt person led them to a conference room—a dirty, scruffy room cluttered with plates of stale food. The executives were again left to wait. A few agency people drifted in and out of the room, basically ignoring the executives who grew impatient by the minute. When the executives tried to ask what was going on, the agency people brushed them off and went about their work.

Eventually, the British Rail executives had had enough. As they angrily started to get up, completely disgusted with the way they'd been treated, one of the agency people finally showed up.

"Gentlemen," he said, "your treatment here at our agency is not typical of how we treat our clients—in fact, we've gone out of our way to stage this meeting for you. We've behaved this way to point out to you what it's like to be a customer of British Rail. Your real problem at British Rail isn't your advertising, it's your people. We suggest you let us address your employee attitude problem before we attempt to change your advertising."

The British Rail executives were shocked—but the agency got the account! The agency had the remarkable conviction to point out the problem because it knew exactly what needed to change.

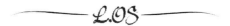

12.2. Change of strategy

12.2.1. The blind beggar

"Everyone thinks of changing the world, but no one thinks of changing himself."
—Leo Tolstoy

A man was standing outside a building with a sign that said: "I am Blind, Please Help".

A "creative publicist" was walking by him and stopped to observe. He saw that the man had only a few coins in his hat. He dropped in a few more coins and, without asking for permission, took the sign, turned it around, and wrote another announcement. He placed the sign at the blind man's feet, and then he left.

That afternoon the creative publicist returned to the place where the blind man sat and noticed that the hat was filled with notes and coins. The blind man recognized his footsteps and asked if it was he who had re-written the sign and what was now on it. The publicist responded, "Nothing that was not true. I just wrote your sign out a little differently." He smiled and went on his way.

The new sign read, "Today is a beautiful day, and I can't see it."*

Sometimes you need to change your strategy when something does not go your way, and you'll see it may just be for the best.

In the long run, however, sameness is the fast track to mediocrity—and mediocre companies, styles, or methods won't survive. Tuli Kupferberg said it best: "When patterns are broken, new worlds emerge." And that is your challenge—to convince your team or yourself for that matter that the "new world" you are trying to create is better than the one you're in.

But it's not that easy. It takes planning, self-discipline, patience, and courage and, of course, a creative spark, similar to the one we witnessed in the story above. Change can be a wonderful gift. It is the key that unlocks the doors to growth and excitement in any organization and provides an individual with a renewed zest for life.

Remember: If you always do what you've always done you'll always get what you always got.

*Source: Blind Beggar Inspirational Story-Share Divine Love—Blogger <http://sharedivinelove.blogspot.com/2008/10/blind-beggar-inspirational-story. html> posted 13 October 2008, accessed 20 May 2014

12.2.2. Two lions and an antelope

"Flexibility means you have bounce, any hardships in life you can trounce. With an attitude brilliant and strength that is resilient; you can win, I am pleased to announce."

—L. Sloot

There is a wonderful, fifteen-second snippet on YouTube, which pictures an antelope charging across the land, head bent and kicking up a cloud of dust in its wake. The scene unfolds whereby the antelope, keeping to its direct course, runs smack bang into a tree and falls stunned, at the feet of two lions—who will soon pounce on their feast.*

Sometimes in life or in the work environment we are like the antelope, hell bent on our daily or routine chores and processes, oblivious to the inroads made by technology, legislation, the needs of the community, or the competition. We don't look up and determine whether the road we are on is right and still viable.

Conversely, we may be like the two lions, waiting for things to happen and for business or other opportunities to fall into our laps. Perhaps we just stick to old tried and tested ways, using the formula of, "If it ain't broke, don't fix it."

In life, as in business, you must be able to deal with both change and unpredictability. The key is to remain flexible and open-minded in your dealings with people or situations; do not be rigid in your approach, and do not stereotype—a small change can make such a difference.

Determine if it is possible to break out of the old routines just to see that there are other options and to weigh these up with the "costs" of remaining resistant, stubborn, or inflexible. Look outside your boundaries, and consider the bigger picture; there is always a plan B or C, perhaps not that efficient—perhaps even more efficient. You will never know until you explore it . . .

*Source: Adapted from: www.youtube.com/watch?v=vgtlsosBujo Antelope runs into a tree—YouTube <http://www.youtube.com/watch?v=VGtLS0SBUJ0> posted 25 February 2011, date last accessed 18 May 2014.

12.2.3. Adapt and adopt . . . or die

"It is not the strongest of species that survive, or the most intelligent, but the one most responsive to change."

—Charles Darwin

In the old days, other than the real cricket lovers and purists, the five-day test matches were deemed a long, boring, and tedious sport. Most people did not appreciate the tests, skills, and endurance exhibited by the players— that it was a game within a game and that each session brought forth its own sets of drama, rewards, and demonstrations of teamwork.

Then entered the professional era, reduced games to first fifty overs and now twenty overs. Players are now dressed in bright-coloured gear. The white ball instead of the red is used. The game is played at night under floodlights. The games are fast-paced, exciting, and quick. Dancing girls, music, food, and beers have transformed cricket from a

dull sport to a family outing and entertainment. Woman and children are attending in their droves—screaming, clapping, and totally enthralled.

Wow, how the game of cricket has evolved. Note, I said evolved. The rules of the game are the same. There are still eleven players to each team; runs accumulate the same way; and batsmen still go out the same way. All that has happened is that the cricket authorities and sponsorship companies have transformed the game to appeal to the masses—to their market and to their clientele.

Business can take a leaf out of the book of cricket and ensure their people, processes, technologies, and most importantly, service offerings or products have evolved to meet their clients' wants, needs, and desires.

Business must not assume what the client wants or force it down their clients' throats. It works the other way around. Clients dictate the pace. Businesses must adapt and adopt . . . or die.

12.3. Be flexible

12.3.1. Have a plan B

"There are two primary choices in life: to accept conditions as they exist, or accept the responsibility for changing them."

—Denis Waitly

In the early 1900s farmers across the southern states of USA were facing a challenge. A tiny insect called the boll weevil had migrated from South America and was quickly destroying crops. They tried everything but could not get rid of this pestilence. There was nothing they could do but watch their crops being destroyed.

But then, as farmers were feeling defeated and down, scientist George Washington Carver came up with the idea to try something new—crop rotation. This eventually led to the harvesting of soya beans, sweet potatoes, and peanuts.

Peanuts proved to be the most successful crop with so many spin-offs and by-products. Peanut oil is used in hundreds of products—everything from cosmetics to paints, plastics to nitro-glycerine. Better still, it was discovered that the boll weevil did not like the taste of peanuts.

The peanut crops took off and flourished. The farmers enjoyed great success, better than cotton. Soon they were producing peanuts more than they required. Today the USA is the 3rd largest peanut producer of peanuts after China and India, in the world

What can be learned from the boll weevil saga?

- *Things will not always go according to the way you desire.*
- *It's OK to have a plan B, an alternative escape route.*
- *It's alright to change and try new things or ideas.*
- *Sometimes if you want to see things for the better, you have to take matters into your own hands. Action is fundamental.*

When it comes to change, get your people to understand that by taking personal responsibility and recognizing problems as opportunities, it will not only help the organization, but it will help them as individuals.

So the next time you are disappointed, feeling helpless or don't know the answer . . . don't give up: There is always a plan B. You may just find a solution better than cotton; you could find peanuts.

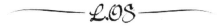 *L.O.S*

12.3.2. The lighthouse

"Be clear about your goal but flexible about the process in achieving it."
—B. Tracy

A ship was sailing on a dark, pitch-black night. The captain spotted a light in the distance and realized the foreign vessel was on a collision course with his ship. He immediately radioed a message, demanding that the vessel change its course ten degrees east.

"Cannot do it. Change your course ten degrees west," was the reply he received.

Annoyed, the captain despatched a harsher instruction. "I am a navy captain. I demand you change your course."

The captain was met with an immediate response. "I am a sea-man second class. Cannot do it. Change your course."

The captain was furious. He sent his final message. It said, "I'm a battleship, and I am not changing my course!"

He got a curt message in return. It said, "I'm a lighthouse. It's your choice, sir."*

There are a couple of important lessons we can learn from the lighthouse story. First, when it comes to leadership and the decision-making process, there is a fine line between being stubborn and firm on the one hand and flexible and adaptable on the other. While a leader should not be seen to be weak and rudderless, he or she should, at the same time, have the guts and strength of character to recognize that they are making an error of judgement, and alter course. They need to put their ego aside instead of running the ship into the rocks.

The other lesson pertains to embracing change and being adaptable. As a leader, deciding to make changes is the easy part. Effecting change and getting your people on board is much more difficult; it's an emotional and psychological process. Mostly, people are creatures of habit who usually resist change, and welcome routine. Uncharted waters are scary.

The lighthouse serves as a beacon of hope when it comes to selling or accepting change. It stands tall and strong, emits that comforting bright aura to dispel the sailor's fears, and it ensures that passing ships can safely alter their course and achieve their mission. As a leader you need to be like the lighthouse—to encourage and allay the fears and concerns of your people while at the same time guiding and steering them from the rock face of uncertainty or disaster to fulfilling their or the organization's vision and goals.

*Source: Adapted from: L. O'Sullivan, Client Service Excellence: The 10 Commandments (Johannesburg: Knowledge Resources, 2010).

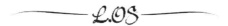

12.3.3. The Chinese washing machine

"Innovation distinguishes between a leader and a follower."

—Steve Jobs

A washing machine manufacturer received frequent complaints from their Chinese customer base that their washing machines were always blocking up. Perturbed at the frequency of these complaints, a team of experts was dispatched to China to identify the cause.

It was then discovered that the population were actually washing the sand off their crops of potatoes, which accounted for the blocking of the washing machines.

Instead of the senior executive of the washing machine company getting overly excited that they now had a valid excuse to repudiate any warranty claims consequent of the misuse of the item in question, they came up with a more ingenious plan.

They designed and built in a vegetable washing component to their washing machines and won the hearts and souls of the community.*

So easy and simple and yet so effective. It again reminds us that opportunities do in fact arise from problems or complaints. If business and front-line employees actually took the time to listen and talk to their clients or noticed their actions and quirks, so much mileage can be gained. So many ideas originate from end users; just be open and listen, really listen.

Often it's just a small tweak or adjustment to an existing product or service offering that is needed to revolutionize it into a "world beater". Be a leader not a follower.

*Source: L. O'Sullivan, Client Service Excellence: The 10 Commandments (Johannesburg: Knowledge Resources, 2010).

12.3.4. The cheeseburger

"It's hard to be 100% better than your competition, but you can be 1% better in 100 ways."

—Rich Melman

My children are very fond of burgers, but they don't always enjoy the garnishing placed on them. Invariably when they order a burger they politely ask the waiter to remove all the trimmings.

I recall an incident some years ago when, at a particular restaurant, the children noticed that a cheeseburger and chips was an option on the menu. There didn't seem to be the usual array of choices when it came to the burger. The children are not too fond of cheeseburgers, and, in reality, they just wanted a plain burger with their fries and cold drink. When placing the order for a plain burger the waiter related that he could not oblige, as it was not on the menu.

I was surprised by such a comment and asked him to please tell the chef not to add cheese to the order. It was such a simple thing to change but certainly a big thing in the life of this waiter. In fact I had to get someone more senior to intervene for us.

The above scenario begs a few questions to be asked. How flexible are you or your organization? How many times does this happen to you? How many gatekeepers do you need to get past to get a decision? And how many times do you have to complain to someone senior in a business or organization to get results?

You need to ensure your internal processes, systems, and rules are both "client friendly" and "employee friendly" and that your people are correctly empowered to act or engage on behalf of your organization.

Just think how much negative publicity your organization will receive or how much potential business it may lose for a layer of cheese.

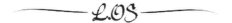

12. 4. Innovation need not come at a great cost

12.4.1. The tomato garden

"Imagination will often carry us to worlds that never were. But without it we go nowhere."

—Carl Sagan

An old Italian lived alone in New Jersey. He wanted to plant his annual tomato garden, but it was very difficult work, as the ground was hard. His only son, Vincent, who used to help him, was in prison. The old man wrote a letter to his son and described his predicament.

> **Dear Vincent,**
>
> **I am feeling pretty sad because it looks like I won't be able to plant my tomato garden this year. I'm just getting too old to be digging up a garden plot. I know that if you were here my troubles would be over. I know you would be happy to dig the plot for me—like in the old days.**
>
> **Love, Papa**

A few days later he received a letter from his son.

> **Dear Pop,**
>
> **Don't dig up that garden. That's where the bodies are buried.**
>
> **Love, Vinnie**

At 4.00 a.m. the next morning, FBI agents and local police arrived and dug up the entire area without finding any bodies. They apologized to the old man and left. That same day the old man received another letter from his son.

Dear Pop,

Go ahead, and plant the tomatoes now. That's the best I could do under the circumstances.

Love you, Vinnie*

This amusing story, an urban legend, has a strong message for us. Even from prison, Vinnie was able to make things happen. Our imagination, our ideas, and our creative spirit is alive and always there; it doesn't sleep, and it can't be locked away by anyone other than yourself. No matter where you are or what circumstances you find yourself in these innovative juices continue to flow throughout your being. Pay attention to them.

Perhaps we need to heed the example of Sam Walton, the founder of Wal-Mart Stores, Inc, who said, "I have always been driven to buck the system, to innovate, to take things beyond where they've been."

*Source: Helping Papa in the Garden—Urban Legendsonline.com <http://www. urbanlegendsonline.com/helpinh-papa-in-the-garden,> accessed 20 May 2014

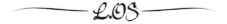

12.4.2. The Indian man

"If you are not willing to risk and do the unusual you will have to settle for the ordinary."

—J. Rohn

An Indian man walked into a bank and asked for a $5,000 loan for a two-week period. As security he tendered his $750,000 Ferrari car. The bank officials were amazed at this offer and gladly accepted the collateral for the loan.

Two weeks later the Indian returned to the bank and repaid $5,015.42, being his loan plus interest. Seeing this, the loan officer asked the Indian, "Sir, we are happy to do business like this with you, but while you were away we checked you out and determined you to be a millionaire. Why would you want to borrow $5,000?"

The Indian replied, "Where else in New York City can I park my car for two weeks and for only $15.42 and expect it to be there when I return?"

Talk about being innovative! The above is a true-life story, the Indian being Vijay Mallya, the flamboyant owner of United Breweries and Kingfisher Airlines who spotted an opportunity and took it to the next level.

Every innovation starts with an idea, but an idea is worthless until it is developed into an opportunity.

12.4.3. Maggi 2 minute noodles

"Nothing limits achievement like small thinking. Nothing equals possibilities like unleashed thinking."

—William Arthur Ward

Maggi 2 minute noodles—it's a simple, inexpensive, innovative, quick, and easy way to prepare a mini meal. All one has to do is to add water to a ready mix, and serve within 120 seconds.

Many mothers are pressed for time and want to give their children something that is not only convenient but also wholesome. Maggi takes the guilt away. Now it's evolved that teens, students, and workers use and eat them.

There are millions of ideas, inventions, and innovations that have changed the world and how we do things. Like Maggi, there are numerous that are simple, inexpensive, and easy to use.

An idea can be an enhancement of an existing product or work process; you don't have to start something from scratch, but you can build on it, and add real value. Innovation does not need to come at a high cost.

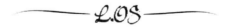

12.5. You can't accept change or be creative with old mindsets

12.5.1. The eagle

"A change in circumstances must be preceded by a change in behaviour."

—anonymous

> The eagle has the longest life span among birds. It can live up to seventy years, but to reach this age, the eagle must make a very difficult decision.
>
> In its forties its long and flexible talons can no longer grab prey, which serves as food. It's long and sharp beak becomes bent, and its aged and heavy wings, consequent of the thickness of the feathers, become stuck and stick to its chest and consequently make it difficult for the eagle to fly.
>
> Then, the eagle is left with two options: to die, or go through the painful process of change that lasts approximately 150 days. The process requires that the eagle fly to the mountain top and sit on its nest. There the eagle knocks its beak against a rock until it plucks it out. After plucking it out, the eagle will wait for a new beak to grow back, and then it will pluck out its talons.
>
> When its new talons grow back, the eagle starts plucking its old aged feathers and after five months the eagle takes its famous flight of rebirth and lives—for another thirty years.*

Just as the eagle in the above storyline, in order to accept change or be creative, we need to get out of our old and restrictive mindset. We need to get rid of those negative thoughts, habits, memories, and old traditions. Even toxic or abusive relationships will fit into this category.

Once freed from the past can we take advantage of the future; we can take on a new life.

*Source: unknown.

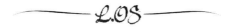

12.5.2. The fish-baking story

"Surf for opportunities daily—there will always be another wave."
—Larry O'Sullivan

A little girl was watching her mother prepare a fish for dinner. Her mother cut the head and tail off the fish and then placed it into a baking pan. The little girl asked her mother why she had cut the head and tail off the fish. Her mother thought for a while and then said, "I've always done it that way—that's how grandma did it."

Not satisfied with the answer, the little girl went to visit her grandma to find out why she cut the head and tail off the fish before baking it. Grandma thought for a while and replied, "I don't know. My mother always did it that way."

So the little girl and the grandma went to visit the little girl's great-grandma to ask if she knew the answer. Her great-grandma thought for a while, and then she said, "Because my baking pan was too small to fit in the whole fish."*

Just because your mum did it and even your grandma before it does not meant that you also have to do it. Times and circumstances are continuously changing and evolving. The world and its technological advances are moving faster and faster.

The Internet has made the world smaller and brought a great deal of transparency and competition to one's business models, pricing, warranties, policies, and business ethics. What worked five years ago may not be applicable today. What worked yesterday needs to be questioned today.

Don't fall back on old faithful systems and assumptions for the sake of not wanting to rock the boat. Don't be caught in the trap of pointless routines. Seek new ways, question old methods, and, on top of it all, embrace change.

*Source: Adapted from: Stories, analogies and fables for business training . . . —Businessballs <http://www.businessballs.com/stories.htm> accessed 20 May 2014

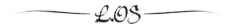

12.5.3. Are your dreams or ideas really impossible?

"You don't get $1million ideas from $1 vision. Think big, think differently, think creatively."

—anonymous

> "I can't believe that!" said Alice.
>
> "Can't you?" the queen asked in a pitying tone. "Try again, draw a long breadth, and shut your eyes."
>
> Alice laughed. "There's no use trying," she said. "One can't believe impossible things."
>
> "I dare say you haven't had much practice," said the queen. "When I was your age, I always did it for half an hour a day. Why, sometimes I've believed as many as six impossible things before breakfast."*

The above is an adaptation of a piece from Lewis Carroll, who wrote *Alice's Adventures in Wonderland* and the follow-up *Through the Looking-Glass, and What Alice Found There* and certainly gives us some food for thought.

We are encouraged to open our minds to the impossible—to get out of our comfort zones and negative patterns and old mindsets. If we don't, then how can we accept or embrace change on the one hand and be creative and innovative on the other?

Impossible things can happen. Miracles do occur. Have a bit of faith, and dream the impossible dream. If you can dream it, and if you can believe you can achieve it . . . then it can come to fruition.

*Source: Adapted from: Sales Guru Magazine, February 2013.

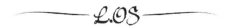

12.5.4. Change; parameters can make people secure

"The key to change . . . is to let go of fear."

—Rosanne Cash

There is an article I once read about children playing in a yard with no fencing. They all played around the teacher. Then, during the night, they erected fencing. The following day, those same children were now playing in the corners of the yard.*

The only change was the erection of the fence. There is a valuable lesson for us in this story. When changes are made, things can be uncomfortable and even scary (through fear of the unknown) for those affected. But the moment that parameters and fences are up, people start feeling more secure and at ease with the changes, and they are therefore more effective and buy-in more readily.

When it comes to implementing change, one has to appreciate the emotional and psychological aspects of the affected parties. A great deal will depend on how much information and notice is given, and if you can effectively allay fears and concerns.

Remember you can't get people to accept change or come up with creative ideas with old, fearful, or closed mindsets. Someone once said that if you focus on results, you will never change. If you focus on change, you will get results.

*Source: unknown.

——— *L.OS* ———

13 Service ethos

13.1. It's all about relationships

13.1.1. Deepen those relationships

"You can make more friends in two months by becoming interested in other people than you can in two years by trying to get people interested in you."
—Dale Carnegie

> **A bank wined and dined the new CEO of a long-standing client, treating him to a big steak dinner, cigars, and good brandy. Only afterwards did the banker learn that this CEO did not like that kind of evening—that he didn't enjoy meat, smoking, or drinking.**
>
> **Why had they assumed he would? Because that's what his predecessor liked. So what?**
>
> **So they just got the client thinking, "They don't really care about me. I certainly don't owe them my business. I have a better relationship with another bank—maybe I should talk to them."**

In essence, you need to become "the client expert" with extensive understanding of your client. You need to know your clients as well as they actually know themselves. You can use this knowledge to come up with the right solutions, to cross-sell, and provide value—added opportunities while at the same time showing the client that you and your organization are both working to the same agenda—for them, with them.

Taking a special interest in clients will guarantee that they will be more receptive to your service offering, and each interaction will be less stressful. It adds a unique flavour and consistency to the service you provide. There is real value in deepening those relationships.

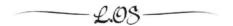

13.1.2. But what about me?

"Your most unhappy customers are your greatest source of learning."
—Bill Gates

In order to celebrate Mother's Day and our wedding anniversary one year I booked a weekend away to spoil my wife at a lovely hotel in the mountains of Swaziland. We have frequently visited this hotel in the past and have always been met with exceptional hospitality, great food, and loads of fun in the nearby casino. I did inform the hotel of the reason for our visit.

On our arrival, we were met with a series of disappointments. There was no immediate or available parking, as another event was being hosted. There was no warm welcome, no complimentary drink, or connection with us to acknowledge that we had arrived for a special, personal event. Instead, a form was flashed into my hands to sign, and I had to move our luggage to our room as soon as possible. After freshening up we went for their special buffet dinner, which again was a huge disappointment compared to previous visits. We gleaned that the special foods were being served at the gala function. It was then I learned that the king and prime minister of Swaziland were arriving at the hotel for an evening function.

During our meal the manager approached us to apologize and to see how we were getting on. To my surprise, my wife, so quietly and so profoundly, said to the manager, "Today there are three very important people at your hotel—your king, your prime minister, and me—but you forgot about me."

And do you know, my wife's statement is absolutely correct. We were paying guests, patrons, tourists, and good ambassadors to that hotel and country. But in one foul swoop, the level of service, in our opinion, had dropped from excellent to less than mediocre. Our needs and expectations were not met. Yes, we may not be as important as the king or prime minister in terms of status or money, but should status or wealth be the precursor to the type of service one receives from any organization?

You can't pick and choose in the service industry; you need to give 100 per cent attention and commitment. There is no "on or off" button.

Remember that every big client was once a small client. Clients' impressions last, and clients also think more from an emotional, rather than from a logical, point of view. So the next time you are serving a client, put yourself in the shoes of the client, and think of, "But what about me?"

13.1.3. The spirit of connection

"Deepen those relationships by making clients talk about themselves that they feel they are the centre of attraction."

—Plato

> **Part of my military training was spent at a newly established equestrian centre commonly referred to or known as "Horse School". There I learned many facets about horsemanship, from basic veterinarian symptoms to riding skills and mounted combat rules. The thing that really struck home was the spirit of connectivity between man and beast.**

> **I still to this day recall the sergeant's words, "When you groom your horse, make sure you have one hand on the horse and the other on the curry comb or body brush. Make sure the horse knows, feels, and gets your attention."**

Ask anyone in the equestrian field, and they will reiterate to you the importance of grooming horses. It's just as important as the exercising, training, or feeding for the simple reason that it shows you care; you are adding value, are accessible, and are bonding with the horse.

The selfsame principle applies in the business world. Clients—and employees for that matter—want that personal contact; they do not want to be treated as just a number or an inconvenience. Clients are the "heart" of your business. Your employees are the "soul" of the organization. They combine to be the "lifeblood" of the business. As a leader, ensure your people know, feel, and get your attention. Let them know they are valued and essential to the organization. In turn, ensure that your staff enjoy some form of connectivity with the clients of your organization and that these clients know and feel they are the centre of attraction.

The "spirit of connection" is a magnetic force that forges the start of a relationship.

13.2. We are all part of the value chain

13.2.1. There are no mundane jobs!

"Success in business requires discipline and hard work. Today's opportunities are just as great as they have ever been."

—David Rockefeller

A renowned violinist, Yehudi Menuhin, tells how he was once taken on a conducted tour of a restaurant kitchen, and he paused to watch the giant dish-washing machine in action. It was being attended by a kitchen employee who told him, "This is the most important job in the whole place. If we don't get the dishes real clean and keep the water hot enough to kill all the germs, folk will get sick."*

Do you know that he was absolutely correct. What seemed to be the most mundane, lowest in status, and least important job in so many other contexts, actually turned out to be the most vital of the lot.

It doesn't matter what your job is now. What does matter, however, is how you feel about it and whether you are happy doing it. There are no mundane jobs, just people who feel unimportant in their jobs. It's a state of mind.

Just like the law of nature, where animals, vegetation, fish, and so forth were created for a specific function, so, too, I believe that we, as humans, have a purpose and calling in life. Accept this, and get on with it. There will always be someone to lead, help, nurse, feed, or serve you. Conversely, there will always be someone for you to teach, guide, assist, feed, and serve.

There are no mundane jobs.

*Source: F. Gay, The Friendship Book of Francis Gay (Dundee UK; D.C. Thomson & Co Ltd, 1983).

13.2.2. Don't be afraid to get your hands dirty

"Leadership isn't about being liked but doing what you trust is right."
—Robin Sharma

My client related an amazing (true) story to me of an incident that happened on a plane during his return to South Africa following a week-long business trip abroad. It was one of those occasions when the body was exhausted, but the mind was playing games with my client—re-running the activities of the past few days and what could have been done to make the trip even more successful.

While he was engrossed in the "What if . . . ?" subconscious thought he noticed a fellow passenger, a few seats ahead of him, fully engrossed in a proposal he was working on. It was about 1.00 a.m., and it appeared that the rest of the people around them were in the "land of nod".

The next moment my client witnessed the most amazing scene. The man working on his proposal heard footsteps approaching him and, assuming it was one of the air hostesses on duty, and, without looking up, asked that person for a cup of coffee. "Certainly, sir!" came the reply.

A few minutes later the captain of the plane appeared before the astonished passenger, cup of coffee in hand.

Here was the captain of the plane attending to a mundane chore like making a cup of coffee. He didn't run off, expending energy, looking for someone to delegate the task. He led by example and put the client first.

He was humble enough to get his hands dirty and display to his staff that in the service field no one is bigger than the job at hand, and no one is bigger than the client.

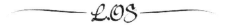

13.2.3. Forget rank

"All men are created equal, it is only men themselves who place themselves above equality."

—David Allan Coe

> **"I have been on a diet every day since I was nineteen, which basically means I have been hungry for a decade. I have had a series of not-nice boyfriends, one who actually hit me. And every time I get my heart broken, the newspaper slashes it about as though its entertainment. And it took two rather painful operations to look like this.**
>
> **"And one day not long from here my looks will go; they will discover I can't act, and I will become some sad, middle-aged woman who looks a bit like someone who was famous for a while."***

The above excerpt is taken from the movie *Notting Hill*. There is a part in this movie where a famous actress (played by Julia Roberts) accompanies a new boyfriend (played by Hugh Grant) to a dinner being held to celebrate his sister's birthday. At the end of the meal there is one chocolate brownie left, so it is agreed that each person at the gathering should tell a sad story from their life, and the one with the most sympathetic or saddest tale will get the brownie.

The man's sister and some close friends of the boyfriend, who are just ordinary citizens, each have a turn to relate their sorry tale. As they decide who has the honour of eating the brownie, the actress speaks up and says, "Hey, what about me?" Everyone is astounded, and their responses are varied, but in reality tend to say the same things we tend to say, and think the same things we tend to think—*No! You don't qualify. You are rich and famous; you are more important than us, and you can't possibly have problems like us.*

Don't be intimidated by the status, rank, or financial situations of clients. If you "drill down" to the core, you will realize that they are just human beings. They sleep, eat, and laugh like us. They also cry, get angry, and have feelings. Just treat them equally, fairly, and respectfully—and with 100 per cent commitment and passion.

The secret to success in sales and the service game is to treat every client on the "same level". You cannot adopt a policy of giving 100 per cent attention to one client and then 50 per cent, 60 per cent, and 70 per cent to the next three clients.

*Source: Notting Hill, dir. Roger Michell (1999).

£.OS

13.2.4. Every job fulfils a purpose

"No matter how insignificant the thing you have to do, do it as well as you can, give it as much of your care and attention as you would give the thing you regard as important."

—Mahatma Gandhi

The story is told of a cab driver who loved his job and took great pride in his work and reputation. His goal was to be the best cabbie in the world.

But to earn the title of "best cabbie in the world" this cabbie realized the importance of all aspects of his job, not just driving efficiently. First, he regarded the cleanliness of the vehicle and the appearance of the cabbie to be important—that vital first impression and sense of comfort to strangers. Next, he regarded as important the friendliness and open demur of the cabbie himself, exuding a sense of trust and open communication.

Then came integrity and add-on benefits of not over-charging fares, showing visitors the sights and places of

interest in the city, and fetching and taking them to their destination, at all hours of the day or night and in any circumstances. This cabbie displayed many of the above qualities and was certainly in demand for his service—no doubt being on the right path to being the best cabbie in the world.

The message above epitomizes the success formula in service and sales; to stand out in business you have to be different in some way. You have to offer unique products or services with a remarkable, special, and reliable "brand". The "brand" I am referring to in this instance is more powerful that your company's brand—it's your own personal brand.

No matter how elementary or routine your job, understand its purpose and the good that comes from your labours, from your personal brand. You have an important contribution to make to your business, to someone, or to society as a whole.

Do you know the biggest overhead of most businesses pertains to staff-related costs like salary, commission, and training expenses? If your job wasn't needed or important enough it would not be required, and the associated costs and energy could be allocated elsewhere in the business.

Don't let yourself down, and, more importantly, don't let others down. Remember, surgeons would not be successful without the efficiency and back-up of the theatre personnel. A world-class pianist would not be successful if the piano tuner did not apply himself to his trade. B.C. Forbes, the founder of *Forbes* magazine, once said, *"There is more credit and satisfaction in being a first rate truck driver than a tenth-rate executive."*

It's doesn't matter what job you do, you can make it a success, and you can stand out from others, just like the cabbie alluded to above. Every job has purpose, and we are all part of the value chain.

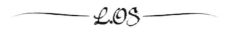

13.3. Four-star versus five-star

13.3.1. Now that's what I call great service—the Emily story

"If you are totally customer focused, you deliver the services your customers want and everything else follows."

—Roger Enrico (former president PepsiCo)

I recently noticed a slow puncture to my left-hand rear tyre and called in at one of those super quick vendors to get it sorted out. While I was waiting for the repair to the job, I noticed the shop adjacent to the tyre vendor was a biltong bar—my weak spot.

I quickly popped into this retailer and ordered R100 worth of their prime product. I wanted a soft drink to go with the biltong, but the selection on show was not to my liking. I enquired if they didn't by any chance have something more to my taste and was informed that the shop next door actually sold the items I desired.

I had just resigned myself to the fact that I had to walk next door to purchase my soft drink when the lady behind the counter said to me, "Just wait here a second; I'll quickly nip next door and purchase it for you."

How refreshing! How unusual in the fast foods industry! In my experience I reckon nine out of ten people would have told me, "Sorry, that's all we have" or alternatively referred me to the shop next door—end of conversation. But not Emily. Yes, that is her name.

Emily went the extra mile. Emily displayed the attitude, passion, and desire for client satisfaction. For a very simple, mundane task, probably 30 seconds of her time, and a cost of R10.00 Emily wowed me over.

Now Emily's name, act, and story is broadcast in all my talks and included in this book. That's what people want in the service industry—to be wowed, to feel most important, and to be the recipient of the most memorable experience, ever.

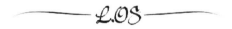

13.3.2. Make it the most memorable experience

"If you want to succeed you should strike out on new paths, rather than travel the worn paths of accepted success."

—John D. Rockefeller

In the early 1980s, Jan Carlzon had just been named the CEO of Scandinavian Airlines (SAS). His company was in trouble. They had 20,000 employees and had just been ranked by a consumer poll as one of the worst airlines in terms of service, profitability, and dependability in the world. Their service delivery was poor, they were in large financial difficulties, losing approximately $17 million per annum, and had an international reputation for always being late. Yet, one year later, in the same poll, they were ranked number one in all three categories. What happened?

Carlzon realized that they have "50,000 moments of truth every day", so he decided to focus on the most critical issue—serving the customer. He wanted to keep it simple: Identify every contact between the customer and the employee and treat that contact as "a moment of truth".

In addition to introducing the world's first separate cabin for business class, Carlzon adopted an ongoing training programme called "Putting People First", developed by Claus Moller of Time Manager International, which focused on delegating responsibility away from management and allowed customer-facing staff to resolve any issues on the spot. They were fully empowered and didn't need permission from the top.

The changes imposed by Carlzon saw a remarkable change in employee morale, and SAS was top performer in terms of service, punctuality, and profit.*

The concept adopted by Jan Carlzon was very simple and yet so rewarding. All it took was to build that buy-in—that sense of trust and empowerment in people—and the entire culture of the organization changed. People had responsibility and were able to give of themselves, and do their best. The value of a person resides in what, why, and how they give and not in what they are capable of receiving. If a person does their best, what else is there?

If Jan Carlzon could change the service level, mindset, attitude, and passion of thousands of employees as well as the profitability and dependability of the SAS business in such a short space of time, then surely his simple formula can work for you or your people or organization.

So, make it the most memorable experience ever—an experience they will never forget. Leave a legacy

*Source: Adapted from: L. O'Sullivan, Client Service Excellence: The 10 Commandments (Johannesburg: Knowledge Resources, 2010).

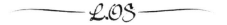

13.3.3. Ten important words

"We simply approach each client as if our living depended on it."
—Sydney Press

The ten most important words: "I apologize for our mistake. Let me make it right."

When something goes wrong, most people merely want to be heard and acknowledged. So listen, apologize, and then ask what you can do to make it right. To gain the edge in business, guarantee your clients a quick and efficient turnaround of complaints, and then take action steps to ensure there is no repetition of the same error.

The nine most important words: "Thank you for your business. Please come back again."

Repeat clients cost less than new clients, and they are often more loyal. As long as you are making sales you are still in the game (Guy Kawasaki).

The eight most important words: "I'm not sure, but I will find out."

It's all right if you don't know the answer; it's not right to make the client keep searching for it. That's your job. You need to show the client you care for their business.

The seven most important words: "What else can I do for you?"

Be prepared to go the extra mile: There is less competition there. It provides an opportunity to cross-sell other services and products and helps to "lock-in" the client.

The six most important words: "What is most convenient for you?"

Your customers will be pleasantly surprised when you ask what's convenient for them that you are actually thinking about them and their needs and other considerations.

The five most important words: "How may I serve you?"

This question reinforces your role in the relationship. Play that role the best you can. Reaching people isn't magic; it takes time and effort, but the rewards are great.

The four most important words: "How did we do?"

Feedback is critical! Your clients have a unique perspective, and they appreciate being asked. Many great ideas and suggestion have emanated from clients; so listen, really listen.

The three most important words: "Glad you're here!"

Customers who feel welcome spend more time and more money and are more likely to return. Loyal clients are like "royalty"; they become great brand ambassadors.

The two most important words: "Thank you."

This is basic manners and appreciation, but so many businesses neglect this concept—make the client feel 10 feet tall.

The most important word: "Yes."*

Become a yes-person. Determine what you can do, even if that represents a compromised solution. This is better than no solution. There is a big difference between can and cannot.

The ten important words dealt with above are an excerpt from the book entitled *Customer-love* by Mac Anderson. I have added my interpretation to the specific points for greater impact or to re-enforce a particular point.

These words are an illuminating reminder of how uncomplicated it is to make customers feel important and wanted. People don't care how much you know (or what you sell, or what type of service you provide) until they know how much you care. They are also the basis for five-star service and to maintain a model of consistency when it comes to people interaction.

*Source: Adapted from: M. Anderson, (2008) Customer-love: Great Stories about Great Service (Illinois USA (2008) Simple Truths).

13.4. The model of consistency

13.4.1. The Joe Girard story

"The most important single ingredient in the formula for success is knowing how to get along with people."

—Theodore Roosevelt

Joe Girard, who was inducted into the Automobile Hall of Fame in 2011, is recognized as the world's greatest salesman by The Guinness Book of World Records. He sold more than 13,000 cars in a career spanning fifteen years. Sometimes as many as 18 cars were sold in a day and 160 in a month.

Now that's what I call a model of consistency.

But the real success behind Joe's great achievement was personalized service—consistent and individualized service. He employed two people at his own expense, so he could send out up to 13,000 personalized (hand-written) cards and messages to clients each month. He wanted to show that he cared for them, and they were important to him. He also stayed on the "radars" of the clients, so when their cars were to be replaced, they would call no one else but Joe. When cars came in for a service, Joe played an active role with the mechanics to facilitate and ensure the client received great service.

Joe attributed his success to selling himself. One of his famous quotes is: *"I never sold a car in my life—I sold a Girard."*

There is another aspect to the story of Joe Girard that I want to share with you, something that is commonly known as the *"Law of 250"*.

> **In effect, he noticed** that **about 250 people attend most funerals or weddings. This told him that, generally, a person has an inner-circle of about 250 relations, family members, or friends, important enough to attend a life-cycle event. He concluded that each person he does business with represents 250 other people. So, if he did a great job, 250 more people are likely to get a recommendation to buy from him. If, however, he did a lousy job, he had just chased 250 people away. Joe tried to do a great job every time, and it paid off.***

Being a brand ambassador for one's organization is the hallmark for retaining clients and making it an experience the client won't forget. It's the formula that they will do business with you again and again.

*Source: Adapted from: L. O'Sullivan, Client Service Excellence: The 10 Commandments (Johannesburg SA: Knowledge Resources) and

Sandy Barris, 19 August 2013, Joe Girard's "Law" of 250| SandyBarris.com <http://www.sandybarris.com/2013/08/joe-girards-law-of-250> accessed 18 May 2014.

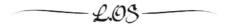

13.4.2. Consistency of service

"Success in neither magical nor mysterious. Success is the natural consequence of consistently applying the basic fundamentals."

—Jim Rohn

One morning in a posh hotel's dining room a guest calls the waiter over.

"Today, I would like to order two boiled eggs, one undercooked that it's runny and the other so overcooked that I can bounce it on the floor. Then I would like my bacon rubbery, toast burned with butter that's frozen that can't spread and extra-weak coffee, served at room temperature."

"Oh no, sir!" exclaimed the waiter. "We can't serve such a terrible meal like that."

"Why not?" asked the guest. "That's what I got yesterday."

Another humorous anecdote. Fortunately for the waiter and hotel, the client was able to correct the expectation of bad service previously experienced. Many other hotel guests would have packed up and gone on their way without the waiter or hotel even knowing of their fault.

Consistency of service, in this context, means doing the right things over and over again. Consistency must become a habit—a good habit. In business, it's the key to service excellence and customer trust and is a recipe for ensuring that your clients keep coming back. All that clients want is consistently good service, every day . . . every time.

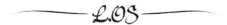

13.4.3. Silly service

"Being on par in terms of price and quality only gets you into the game . . . service wins the game."

—Tony Allessandro

After moving to a new town a man makes a list of people he has to notify of his change of address and starts phoning them, one by one.

Everything goes smoothly until he calls a company where he has an account. "I'm sorry," the assistant tells him,

"we can't do that over the phone—you'll have to fill in a change-of-address form."

"How do I get one of those?" asked the man.

"We'd be happy to provide you with one," the assistant says pleasantly. "May I have your new address so I can mail it to you?"

While the above joke is indeed amusing, it's not all that far-fetched. During the past six years of my writings, talks, and travels I have come across a host of silly but true examples of disservice, which I term "How not to do things".

Perhaps we can take solace in the wise words of Zig Ziglar: *"Your business is never really good or bad out there. Your business is either good or bad right between your own ears."* So pay attention, listen carefully, and apply a lot of common sense—don't become another statistic on "How not to do things".

Once you have mastered the way to do things right—do them consistently right.

13.5. First impressions, last impressions

13.5.1. The receptionist tells it all . . .

"The tongue weighs practically nothing, but so few people can hold it."

—anonymous

Recently I arranged to meet with a senior executive at his offices. I arrived a little earlier than the scheduled time and so was duly ushered and seated in the waiting area, which, incidentally, happened to be within ear shot of the four receptionists on duty. My waiting time proved to be an experience of note.

In those five to ten minutes that I sat in the waiting area I learned the names of several employees and/ or their personal assistants—who were on leave, off ill, at lunch, and, in fact, who never answered their phone

calls. I also gleaned much about the working culture and organizational structure of the organization.

The best was yet to come. One of the receptionists must have been "told off" by her superior and was really upset with what had transpired and, instead of doing her work, was relating the whole story, in her own sordid way, to her colleague. The language was "choice" and belittling, and the poor superior (whose name and managerial/leadership style became apparent) wasn't able to defend herself.

Yes, you may think this was a "one-off" situation, and I sincerely hope it was, but it could have a big impact on first impressions and lasting impressions to the hundreds of people who have called on that business and happen to spend some time in the reception area.

In reality, it happens with every interaction you have with a person, face to face, telephonically, email, or other. You are always being measured and "sussed out". People are always deciding whether they like you and trust you and whether they will deal with you. This rule applies to every person in your organization from the CEO right down to the messengers, drivers, and receptionists. It even applies to outsourced companies or agents who do work for your organization.

Everyone wears the badge of their organization on their sleeve. Each person has the responsibility to uphold the credibility and reputation of the business. Make sure everyone is on board.

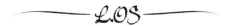

13.5.2. The greeting; first impressions

"All people smile in the same language."

—anonymous

The hands of those I meet are *dumbly* eloquent to me. I have met people so empty for joy that when I clasped their frosty fingertips it seemed as if I was shaking hands with a north—east storm. Others there are whose hands have sunbeams in them.*

Referring to the above quote by Helen Keller, I believe the impact of one's initial greeting and first impressions are not only restricted to a handshake . . . but also could a kiss, embrace, gesture, or greeting in any custom and include eye contact and facial expressions.

A smile is another form of greeting and indicative of the power of one's personality and confidence. People can tell whether a smile is genuine or forced. Nelson Mandela was a prime example of this; his charisma will be long remembered and so, too, will be his sincere, warm, and infectious smile.

It's all about connecting to another person, and this connection must happen within those first few seconds of personal or physical contact. It automatically demonstrates to a person a feeling of warmth or coldness, sincerity or falseness, joy or contempt, friendliness or disdain—or whether they are made to feel welcome or not. This simple, speechless gesture is the barometer or tone of the relationship and expression of the welcome.

Gary Zaltman (2003) points out that 80 per cent of communication is non-verbal. So step forward with a smile, and be eager to meet, greet, and welcome people. Ensure you make a great and lasting first impression.

Source: Quote by Helen Keller: "The hands of those I meet are dumbly <http://www.goodreads.com/ . . . /851969-the-hands-of-those-i-meet-are-dumbly—eloquent-to> accessed 20 May 2014

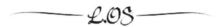

13.5.3. A lasting impression

"All lasting business is built on friendship."

—Alfred A. Montapert

I read of a lecturer, who, while on a speaking tour, needed to acquire some articles of a personal nature. Instead of taking his entire wallet with him, he withdrew a $100 note and proceeded to the nearest shop to make the intended purchases.

To his surprise the store clerk registered a bill for $105. All the lecturer had on him was this $100 note, $5 short to

pay for the goods desired. Embarrassed and while deciding which article he could hand back and have deducted off his bill, the manager of the store noticed the lecturer's predicament and quickly smoothed the way that enabled the man to keep all of his chosen articles for the fee of $100.

The next day, the lecturer needed a packet a cigarettes, and guess what?

Yes, he went to the selfsame store as the day before and, in fact, ended up purchasing some additional items for approximately $100. But it didn't end there; a bit later in the week, the man went to the selfsame store, and again the store benefited from his purchases.

So often we can lose a deal without even knowing it. The above example is one deal that didn't get away. For an initial loss of $5 that store benefited by some 300 to 400 per cent from the purchases made by the lecturer. In terms of the big picture, a $5 loss was easily absorbed within the gross profit of the initial $100 purchase made by the man.

Instead of worrying about an insignificant amount of money, embarrassing the client, or chasing the client away, that store reaped the benefit and, even today, people are still reading or hearing about his shopping experience.

How's that for a lasting impression?

———— *L.O$* ————

13.5.4. Do your homework

"Where focus goes, energy flows."

—L. O' Sullivan

An over-eager vacuum-cleaner salesman calls on a woman's house. He drops a handful of cigarettes butts and ash on the carpet and says to the woman, "If my vacuum cleaner doesn't pick up every last bit of this mess, I'll eat it."

"Get started," the woman says. "I don't have electricity."

Usually, the first step in sales or the service field is research; do your homework before meeting the client. In other instances, such as cold calls or walk-in business, the key is to find out what buyers want before you tell them what you can do for them.

Before delivering a sales pitch, try to build a profile of the client; the clearer the picture the easier it is to find value and opportunity. Ask a few questions, listen to what they say, and especially note what they don't say. Remember the old sales adage that *"the best sales people don't sell to their clients—they help them buy"*. Do your homework. Not only is it of crucial importance in sales, it's the ingredient to success in most things in life.

On the flip side, watch out for terms and conditions, con artists, and "special offers", and conclude your deals with your "eyes wide open". Research continuously. Be prepared and vigilant, and understand what you are doing.

When it comes to doing your homework, don't confuse planning with action. Abraham Lincoln famously once said that if he was given an axe and was told he had ten minutes to chop down a tree, he'd spend nine minutes sharpening the axe. Planning is important, but don't be caught up in the mindless humdrum of a "paralysis by analysis" or over-thinking. One can't sit on the fence indefinitely. So sooner than later, once you have weighed up the pros and cons, make that decision, or take the appropriate action.

13.6. The pitfalls of red tape

13.6.1. How bad policy encourages poor service

"Processes don't work, people do."

—John Seely Brown

The bank concerned had introduced a charge to be levied on transactions made by this bank for the credit of an account held by a different bank. The charge was 50 cents. A well-to-do, upper-class lady enters the bank and requests a transaction of $200 to her sister who banks at another bank in the same city.

> **The bank teller duly tells the lady that there will be a charge of 50 cents. Indignantly, the lady tells the teller, "I wasn't charged the last time."**

> **The teller immediately replies, "Well that will be $1 then."**

Coming from the banking field I couldn't resist relating this story. But I hasten to add, its moral applies to every business and every industry. Processes, red tape, and hidden costs can ruin the reputation of the brand or business. Don't let the rule book sacrifice your leadership style or creative thought processes.

Don't let bad policy drive your clients away or be the cause for poor service in your organization. Allow your employees to be flexible and adaptable and to have some discretion. Think about how you are adapting to serve your customers, not how you are forcing your customers to adopt your systems. In your clients eyes it's not always the cost but the principle involved.

Don't think red tape—think red carpet.

—————— *£.OS* ——————

13.6.2. Empowerment equals great service

"Wise are those who learn that the bottom line doesn't always have to be their top priority."

—William A. Ward

> **At the sporting day of one of my sons, I ordered a Boerewors roll (that is, a South African sausage roll with traditional farm-style sausage) from the tuck shop. When I got back to my seat, I soon discovered that they had instead given me a hot dog. Since I really wanted a Boerewors roll, I returned to the tuck shop with the intention of exchanging the purchase. When I explained to the counter person what had happened, the young lady's initial response was, "Let me talk to my supervisor."**

A more experienced worker next to her heard the conversation and said, "You don't have to ask the supervisor. This man did not get what he wanted, so give him is Boerewors roll. He is the client."

The above story highlights certain attributes like attitude, going the extra mile, and customer care. But none of these attributes would have resolved my dilemma to get my Boerewors roll if the experienced worker had not intervened. Empowerment is the key. Empowerment equates to great service.

To get the best out of your people you need to ensure that they are engaged, enabled (have the best tools for the job), but, most importantly, empowered. If you build organizations of high-trust, engagement, open participation, and empowerment, your employees will respond appropriately. Micro-management is the arch enemy to empowerment. It ruins trust, growth, and the confidence, energy, and passion of employees.

Yes, I am the first to concede that some employees don't accept their responsibility and need to be micro-managed to a degree. However, when employees find meaning from work, they collaborate more easily, innovate more insightfully, and are generally more productive. Give employees the tools and encouragement to first accept their responsibility and then to take charge of their tasks and circumstances so that they help you achieve the results you want.

Empowerment equals great service.

13.7. Add value to your job

13.7.1. Marty's personal brand

"Don't just let your business or your job make something for you, let it make something of you."

—Jim Rohn

The line I was standing in wasn't moving as quickly as I wanted, and I glanced towards the cashier. There stood an affable-looking man in his seventies. Slightly stooped

and of average build, he wore glasses and a nice smile. I thought, well, he's an old guy, and it probably takes him a little longer to get the chores done.

For the next few minutes I watched him. He greeted every customer before he began scanning the items they were purchasing. Sure, his words were the usual, "How's it going?", but he did something different to most checkout assistants: He actually listened to people's response. Then he would respond to what they had said and would engage them in a brief conversation.

I thought it was odd, reasoning that I had grown accustomed to people asking me how I was doing simply out of a robotic conversational habit. After a while, you don't give any thought to the question and just mumble something back. I could say, "I just found out that I have six months to live," and someone would reply, "Have a great day!"

This old cashier had my attention. He seemed genuine about wanting to know how people were feeling. Meanwhile, the high-tech cash register rang up their purchases, and he announced what they owed. Customers handed money to him, he punched the appropriate keys, the cash drawer popped open, and he counted out their change.

Then magic happened. He placed the change in his left hand, walked around the counter to the customer, and extended his right hand in an act of friendship. As their hands met, the old cashier looked the customers in the eyes. "I sure want to thank you for shopping here today," he told them. "You have a great day. Bye-bye."

The looks on the faces of the customers were priceless. There were smiles and some sheepish grins. Some customers would walk away, pause for a moment, and then look back at the old cashier; they couldn't quite comprehend what had just happened. *

This adapted excerpt from *The Richest Man in Town* by V.J. Smith, epitomizes what client service should be about. It's a sagacious message delivered by a very simple man, and it covers all the basics—attitude, passion, enthusiasm, pride in work, the most memorable experience, caring, sincerity, and treating others like you want to be treated.

I could go on and on . . .

Probably, what I believe to be the most significant attribute was the cashier's personal brand—it was unique, different, and special. If you don't see much value in what you do, you won't bring much value. The success of your job boils down to the "chemistry" emitted between you on the one hand and your business and clients on the other. A lot rests on how and why you promote the sale or service offered by your organization, and what you do to nurture it.

You are the difference—or certainly the perceived difference—that sets your service or product apart from those of your competitors. You are a precious asset to your business, so adapt your new personal brand—"YOU (Pty) Ltd" (substituting your name for "YOU", for example, LARRY (Pty) Ltd).**

The person who is most influential in making you successful is you. You have to sell yourself before you can sell your products and brand. Marty understood this.

Be a Marty today.

*Source: Adapted from: V.J. Smith, The Richest Man in Town (Sioux Falls, South Dakota; Pine Hill Press, 2005).

**Source: L. O'Sullivan, Client Service Excellence: The 10 Commandments (Johannesburg SA: Knowledge Resources, 2010).

13.7.2. Palchinsky philosophy

"Little remedies over time create complete solutions. Making progress is key."

—anonymous

Peter Palchinsky was a Russian engineer, commissioned by the Tsar to study some coal mines and projects in the old Russian Empire. He advocated three principles:

- *Variation—seek out new ideas, and try new things.*
- *Survival—when trying something new, do it on a scale where failure is survivable.*
- *Selection—seek out feedback, and learn from your mistakes.**

Palchinsky's principles, I believe, are still very relevant in current times, and certainly his philosophy, which covers several areas like innovation, risk management, and closed-loop learning to name a few, can be applied by businesses in today's environment.

There is a shrewd Jewish proverb that says, *"Ask advice from everyone, but act with your own mind."* It fits in well with Palchinsky's principle of obtaining feedback and input and using this information to continue with your zest for new ideas or things. Your innovative idea or proposed solution must be able to withstand the scrutiny and analysis from all parties and from all aspects of the business.

Don't let fear or the "risks" shut out the notion of a great idea. When incubating the new idea, find the balance between risk and reward. For creative ideas to work, you should look further than the micro-detail; see the big picture, and apply the principles of systems thinking—the ripple effects.

Many creative people, inventors, artists, and businesses have achieved success from Palchinsky's principles. Perhaps you can determine if these will work for you.

*Source: Harris C, Pritchard M and Rabins J (2013) Engineering Ethics; Concepts and Cases, USA, Google Books (2013)

13.7.3. Danny Flanagan

"When you capture the heart . . . you've captured the customer; get them to fall in love with your company."

—anonymous

Captain Danny Flanagan, a former navy pilot, with more than two decades of flying experience, individually welcomed aboard every passenger on his United Airlines plane. He went the extra mile and did things that no one else did, dreamt of doing, or even considered doing. Some of Captain Flanagan's exploits included:

- *Buying food for planeloads of passengers when their flights were delayed.*
- *Snapping photos of dogs in the cargo hold to show owners that their pets were safe.*
- *Calling parents of children travelling alone to comfort them.*
- *Standing at the door and greeting/welcoming each passenger on to the plane.*
- *Sending handwritten notes to frequent flyers.*
- *Raffling off bottles of wine.**

When asked why he did these things, Captain Flanagan replied, *"I want to treat them like I treat my family, and it works."* And guess what, his unique brand of hospitality rubbed off on the crew, and they, too, became great. Here was a person that put his rank and status aside and humbly went about instilling into his airline a special service ethos. He led by example, and he led well.

But Captain Flanagan did more than that. He added value to his job description, to his life, and, more importantly, to the lives of his passengers. He showed his passengers that he cared—that he regarded them to be important to him and his airline. He went the extra mile and cemented his own unique personal brand. He became a talking point within the industry—he was a walking, living advertisement for United Airlines and set the benchmark for other flight personnel in the industry.

He believed in the simple philosophy highlighted in the quote above: *"When you capture the heart . . . you've captured the customer; get them to fall in love with your company."*

That's just what you need in business—a legend who sets a contagious attitude and chain of service memories into motion. Why can't you be that person? Be a Captain Flanagan today.

*Source: M. Anderson, Customer-love: Great Stories about Great Service (Chicago USA; Sourcebooks, 2013).

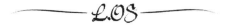

14 Communication

14.1. Be a world-class listener

14.1.1. Listen to advice

"Being a good listener means much more than simply hearing what people are saying. It means blocking out all distractions, giving the customer your undivided attention, and listening with your whole self."

—Michael LeBoeuf

> There is a memorable account told about a professional speaker who had an engagement in an out-of-town location. As he was getting dressed, he noticed that he had forgotten to bring his cufflinks with him, and his shirt had no sleeve buttons. Thinking it was a quick fix, he went down to the front desk at reception to enquire if they could assist him. Unfortunately, the reception didn't have any cufflinks, so they referred him to the small gift shop in the lobby. This proved fruitless, and the gift shop referred him to a shop down the road.
>
> Yes, you guessed it; the shop down the road didn't have any cufflinks; they referred him to another shop. And so it went on. As it was nearing time for his talk, he rushed back to his hotel and reported his failure to the woman at the front desk who coldly looked at him and said, "Sir, why don't you just buy another shirt?"

Sometimes we are too close to the problem that we can't see the proverbial "wood for the trees". We expend a great deal of time, money, and/or energy chasing a dead-end result. Sometimes it takes another person—a spouse, friend, colleague, or whoever—to help you see the folly of your ways or help you find an alternative solution.

You can't know everything, so don't be ashamed or afraid to get sound advice, but, more importantly, listen to that sound advice.

Be a world-class listener.

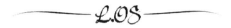

14.1.2. The horse whisperer

"A wise listener allows others to share their moods or feeling . . . and hears them."
—anonymous

Two teenage girls, while out horse riding, encountered a freak set of events that resulted in the death of one girl and the other (and her horse) being left critically injured, having been hit by a truck. To help her troubled and severely traumatized daughter and her equally injured horse (Pilgrim), the mother takes them to Montana to recuperate on the ranch of a "Horse Whisperer", that is, a horse healer of mystical talents.

The horse whisperer has a special gift for understanding horses and, as a result, he plays a vital role in improving the health and well-being of the injured teenager and her horse following the tragic accident.*

What makes this "horse whisperer" so special? What is this freak of nature—the unspoken language—that bonds human and horse into a spirit of mutual trust and understanding? The answer is simple—it's the essence of communication and trust and a must in all personal relationships and business dealings.

Pay particular attention to "what is not said". Research reveals that words only account to 7 per cent on the scale of importance in communication; tone makes up 38 per cent, and body language makes up the balance of 55 per cent.

Words can be professional and well-structured, and hence they can easily hide the true feelings or emotions of the issue at hand. Rely on tone and style of delivery. Don't talk . . . just listen. Listen to the voices, the tone, the body language, the suggestions, the ideas, and the problems of your employees, clients, family members, and friends.

*Source: The Horse Whisperer, dir. Robert Redford (1998), based on the 1995 novel The Horse Whisperer by Nicholas Evans.

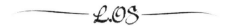

14.1.3. Listen intently to everyone

"Listen to others, even the dull and ignorant; they too have their story."
—Max Ehrmann

Can you recall the last time that you attended a live event like an opera or a musical show or witnessed the majestic rhythms and tunes of a live band or orchestra? If you can then you may recall the mastery of the performance, as the talented musicians, dancers, actors, or singers wowed you off your seat.

One thing that stands out for me is the synchronization of the acts and parties concerned—where every musician or member of the cast must, besides playing their part, be listening intently to everyone around them. This is vital, as otherwise the whole performance would be chaotic and a flop.

So, too, life would be chaotic if we only chose to listen to ourselves or a select few. We need to pay attention to the people, sounds, and circumstances around us. Someone once said that we have two ears and only one mouth, so use both ears!

Listening is a sure way to connect with others. When we listen with the intention of understanding others, rather than being content of our reply, we begin to engage in true communication and relationship-building. Stephen Covey best summarized this concept in one of his seven habits, *"Seek first to understand, then to be understood."*

We must become emphatic listeners—we mustn't listen only with our ears, but also our eyes, our mind, and our heart. Listen intently to everyone.

14.1.4. The brick

"Deep listening from the heart is one half of true communication. Speaking from the heart is the other half."

—Sara Paddison

A young and successful executive was travelling down a neighbourhood street, going a bit too fast in his new Jaguar when suddenly a brick smashed into the Jaguar's side door. He slammed on the brakes and backed the Jag back to the spot where the brick had been thrown. The angry driver then jumped out of the car, grabbed the young person who had thrown the brick, and demanded to know why he did it.

With tears dripping down his face, the youth who threw the brick pointed to a spot just around a parked car where his brother had rolled off the curb and fell out of his wheelchair. The brick thrower couldn't lift up his brother, so he resorted to the next best thing—to get someone's attention.*

I'm sure we can all recount those times when we tried to get help or someone's attention, and we failed. I recall an incident when I approached someone in the office to assist me to answer a question. I got an answer, but I wasn't sure if the answer was right. This person answered me but didn't look at me. His eyes were fixed on his computer screen, and he mumbled his reply out of the side of his mouth. I wasn't even sure if he had fully grasped the question I had posed, and he certainly wasn't certain that I had understood his response.

With this kind of attention to communication, it is no wonder that there is so much assumption and corridor talk in today's business culture.

On a bit of personal reflection, consider how you listen and communicate with your loved ones, colleagues, and customers. Are you attentive and empathetic? Do you demonstrate that you actually care and are listening? At times you may need to be intuitive, and read between the lines. You may need to work out what isn't being said in order to pick up on the real agenda.

Don't go through life so quickly or being so self-centred that someone has to throw a brick at you to get your attention!

*Source: Adapted from _The_Brick—Beliefnet.com <http//www.beliefnet.com/ Inspiration/2003/07/The-Brick.aspx> accessed 19 May 2014

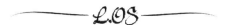

14.2. Don't be afraid to ask the question

14.2.1. Always ask

"Beware of the man who won't be bothered with details."

—William Feather

His request approved, a TV news photographer quickly used a cell phone to call the local airport to charter a flight. He was told that a twin-engine plane would be waiting for him at the airport.

Arriving at the airfield, he spotted a plane warming up outside a hanger. He jumped in with his bag, slammed the door shut, and shouted, "Let's go." The pilot taxied out, swung the plane into the wind, and took off.

Once in the air, the photographer instructed the pilot, "Fly over the valley, and make low passes, so I can take pictures of the fires on the hillsides."

"Why?" asked the pilot.

"Because I'm a photographer and need these pictures for my TV station," responded the photographer.

The pilot was strangely silent for a moment. Finally, he stammered, "So, what you're telling me, is . . . you're not my flight instructor?"*

One of the cardinal rules in sales or the service game is *asking*. Always ask! Ask questions, ask for clarification, and even ask for the sale or business opportunity. Ask questions and probe clients to open up their ultimate need to the key ingredient to a successful sale. Find out what buyers want before you tell them what you can do for them.

On the flip side I know a person who is always asking for favours, discounts, bargains, and reduced fees. At times I used to think that this person was quite arrogant and forthcoming. One day I asked him about his behaviour and his reasons for always pushing the boundaries. His answer was quite interesting, "If you don't ask, you will never get. I reckon I achieve 60 per cent of my targets."

My late dad always used to say, "Ask, never assume—for if you *assume*, you will be making an *ass* out of *u* and *me*." Asking is critical, not only in business but in life, and it covers some important categories like communication, leadership, negotiation, relationship-building, and self-development.

Always ask . . . what's the worst that can happen?

*Source: A J Bantac, Always Ask, Never Assume, Ajb {log} A JBatac <http://allanjosephbatac.com/blog/2010/10/always-ask-never-assume.html> date posted 27-10-2010, date of last access 19 May 2014

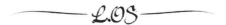

14.2.2. The blind men and the elephant

"In order to properly understand the big picture, everyone should fear becoming mentally clouded and obsessed with one small section of truth."

—Xun Zi

Six blind men were discussing exactly what they believed an elephant to be, since each had heard how strange the creature was, yet none had ever seen one before. So the blind men agreed to find an elephant and discover what the animal was really like.

It didn't take the blind men long to find an elephant at a nearby market. The first blind man approached the beast and felt the animal's firm flat side. "It seems to me that the elephant is just like a wall," he said to his friends.

The second blind man reached out and touched one of the elephant's tusks. "No, this is round and smooth and sharp—the elephant is like a spear."

Intrigued, the third blind man stepped up to the elephant and touched its trunk. "Well, I can't agree with either of you; I feel a squirming writhing thing—surely the elephant is just like a snake."

The fourth blind man was of course by now quite puzzled. So he reached out and felt the elephant's leg. "You are all talking complete nonsense," he said, "because clearly the elephant is just like a tree."

Utterly confused, the fifth blind man stepped forward and grabbed one of the elephant's ears. "You must all be mad—an elephant is exactly like a fan."

Duly, the sixth man approached, and, holding the beast's tail, disagreed again. "It's nothing like any of your descriptions—the elephant is just like a rope."*

And all six blind men continued to argue, based on their own particular experiences, as to what they thought an elephant was like. It was an argument that they were never able to resolve. Each of them was concerned only with their own idea. None of them had the full picture, and none could see any of the points of view of the others. Each man saw the elephant as something quite different, and while in part each blind man was right, none was wholly correct.

The lesson is simple. When it comes to communication or problem solving, ensure that you see, appreciate, and understand the "big picture"—the whole elephant and not just the tail or ear. There is never just one way to look at something or to say something—there are always different perspectives, meanings, and perceptions, depending on who is looking or who is listening.

Maybe you need to ask questions to establish the other person's perspective or to find the common ground or mutual understanding. At least then you will know if you are reading from the same hymn sheet or if your ideas, concepts, or thinking are poles apart.

*Source: <u>Andre Koen</u>, 'Diversity Workbook—Google Book Results <http//books.google.co.za/books?isbn=0578020890> accessed 19 May 2014

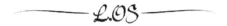

14.2.3. Ask the right question

"By asking the right questions you will get the right answers and right results. You will also unearth a host of opportunities."

—anonymous

For months a man was trying to summon the courage to ask his pretty girlfriend to marry him. Eventually, he found the right opportunity when they were all alone, and he began his request as follows: "There are quite a lot of advantages in being a bachelor, but there comes a time when one longs for companionship, someone kind and faithful and who listens to me and who shares my joys and sorrows."

To his delight he saw a sympathetic gleam in his girlfriend's eyes and that she was nodding in agreement. Then she said, "So, you are thinking of buying a dog?"

The above tale is quite laughable, but sadly it's also true. How many times do we try to say something, and it comes out all wrong or at least not in a way that was understood by others as we intended? How many times are the words, messages, or instructions of others, our superiors or clients, for example, misinterpreted or mistaken because we are too scared, shy, or embarrassed to ask for clarification? How many opportunities have we missed for fear of speaking up?

Remember, if you ask the wrong question then you will get the wrong answer. So frame your question carefully. Use a bit of psychology. The manner, the tone, and the words used can count for and against you. If you ask in a threatening, aggressive, or demanding manner you usually get a person's back up. While you may still get the outcome you sought, the nature of the communication would have been far from satisfactory. It could jeopardize future interactions.

I always try asking for a favour in a polite, humble, and respectable manner. Invariably they look at my sad eyes and take pity on this old man and oblige. Find an approach that will work for you. And if you get what you want be gracious and thankful.

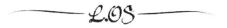

14.3. Psychology in communication

14.3.1. Harsh words break relationships

"If you propose to speak, always ask yourself, is it true, is it necessary, is it kind."
—Buddha

> **A woman and her millionaire husband visited their construction site. A worker who wore a helmet saw her and shouted, "Hi, Emily! Remember me? We used to date in the secondary school."**
>
> **On the way home, her millionaire husband teased her, "It's a good job that you married me. Otherwise you would now be the wife of a construction worker."**
>
> **She answered, "You should appreciate that you married me. Otherwise, he would be the millionaire and not you."***

Many personal relationships break off because of communication—mainly the words expressed, whether in jest or anger. Words can be encouraging, or they can be like a "dagger in the heart". As in the case of the above narration, when a couple is too close or too comfortable with each other, they tend to forget mutual respect and courtesy. Frequent exchange of remarks like the ones above plants the seed for a bad relationship. It's like a broken egg; it cannot be reversed.

The same principle applies in the workplace and in your dealings with employees and clients. It's not only what you say or how you say it, but tone of voice and the style in which you express yourself are also considered. People need to feel the sincerity, trust, and warmth emanating from you. Be accountable for the words you speak—for others will take them to heart. Many words expressed in jest or intended as a joke actually have an element of underlying truth to them. Beware of the "psychology" behind the message.

Remember the wise message from Mother Teresa: *"Kind words can be short and easy to speak, but their echoes are truly endless."*

*Source: anonymous.

14.3.2. What makes people "tick"?

"You cannot teach a man anything; you can only help him find it within himself."
—Galileo

I love the story told by author, Francis Gay, about the missionary, new in his job, who found that the workers in the fields carried their loads on their heads, and not understanding the culture and thinking he was relieving their hardship, made arrangements for each of the workers to be supplied a wheelbarrow.

The next time he saw them they were carrying the loaded wheelbarrows on their heads!

The above story illustrates the importance of understanding others—their business, culture, traditions, and habits. It's central to one's success in life, in business, in negotiation, or in outwitting the competition or opposition. What makes people "tick" is the core psychological ingredient needed by any leader in any business, team, sport, club, or organization. It is also the key in sales and service.

This is where communication and listening skills come into the equation. They play such a big part in collating, understanding, identifying, and learning about the needs, wants, and desires of one's clients or the people you interact with. Don't take people just at face value. Each person has a story to tell, and each person's outlook on life is shaped by some event in their lives or something they learned or experienced.

Everybody is wired differently. The trick is for you to know what makes them "tick".

14.3.3. It's how you ask or say it

"A little experience often upsets a lot of theory."

—Samuel Parkes Cadman

> **Jack and Max are walking to a religious service. Jack wonders whether it would be all right to smoke while praying.**
>
> **Max replies, "Why don't you ask the priest?" So Jack goes up to the priest and asks, "Father, may I smoke while I pray?"**
>
> **The priest says, "No, my son, you may not. That's disrespectful to our religion."**
>
> **Jack goes back to his friend and tells him what the good priest told him. Max says, "I'm not surprised. You asked the wrong question. Let me try."**
>
> **Max goes up to the priest and asks, "Father, may I pray while I smoke?"**
>
> **The priest eagerly replies, "By all means, my son. By all means."**

The moral: The reply you get depends on the question you ask.

There is no doubt that one must apply the principles of psychology when dealing with people. Just as there are different categories of people when it comes to personalities, characteristics, ideologies, education, experiences, and behaviours, each with their own needs, priorities, expectations, and vision, so, too, there are different ways of interacting with different people.

You don't need a degree in psychology to be able to do this—but you do need to unearth or establish what makes that person "tick" and then match your own style, charm, communication techniques, skills, and so forth to achieve what you want from the situation. Someone once said, *"One must learn to think like your customer before you can close every sale."*

When you find yourself trapped in a cage with a tiger, you quickly learn in which direction to stroke its fur. Apply psychology in communication. Remember it's how you ask or say it.

14.3.4. Understanding cultures and traditions

"Never mistake knowledge for wisdom. One helps you to make a living; the other helps you make a life."

—Sandra Carey

> **A disappointed salesman of Coca-Cola returns from his Middle East assignment. A friend asked, "Why weren't you successful with the Arabs?"**
>
> **The salesman explained, "When I got posted in the Middle East, I was very confident that I would make a good sales pitch, as Cola is virtually unknown there. But I had a problem: I didn't know how to speak Arabic. So, I planned to convey the message through three posters, pasted all over the place.**
>
> **First poster: A man lying in the hot desert sand . . . totally exhausted and fainting.**
>
> **Second poster: The man is drinking our Cola.**
>
> **Third poster: Our man is now totally refreshed.**
>
> **"If they were pasted all over the place, then surely you should have achieved great results!" said the friend. "The hell it should have!" said the salesman. "I didn't realize that Arabs read from right to left."***

To succeed in business, leaders and management have to continually bridge the great divide—bringing education, culture, poverty, and socio-economic conditions into play. This is where communication is tested and, sadly, this is where communication falters and breaks down. So often there is a lack of willingness to close this gap and openly communicate in the spirit of mutual understanding and diversity.

Take a stand today, and let's learn about one another, and appreciate the untold customs, beliefs, and behavioural traits. Let's rebuild the essentials in open communication.

*Source: Adapted from: an email—author unknown.

14.3.5. What are you hiding behind that mask?

"The cave you fear to enter holds the treasure you seek."

—Campbell

In the movie Mask, Rocky, a young boy whose face is disfigured by a congenital ailment, struggles to live a normal life. He, as expected, is teased consequent of his looks.

After being goaded about his face and being told to take off his "mask" he responds to his abuser in a strong manner. "I'll take my mask off if you take your mask off."*

How many of us wear an invisible mask and hide our true feelings, emotions, and hurts? We tend to put on a big brave front to the world, yet, deep inside, we are insecure and afraid. There also seems to be many different "facades" that we will use at different times of the day, dependent on whom we meet or the circumstances we find ourselves in.

It may somehow surprise you to know that others may have an inkling of what's behind your mask and that they also have hidden similar or even worse secrets.

Perhaps, for businesses or people to grow and for success to be obtained, we need to become more open and trusting, similar to little children playing a game, and we need to take some risks—"I'll take my mask off if you take your mask off."

*Source: based on: Mask, dir. Peter Bogdanovich (1985), based on the life and early death of Roy L. "Rocky" Dennis.

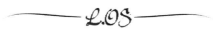

14.4. Make sure the other party understands

14.4.1. Why do you want a divorce?

"Hearing is one of the body's five senses. But listening is an art."
—Frank Tyger

> **A judge interviewing a woman about her pending divorce, asks, "What are the grounds for your divorce?"**
>
> **"About two hectares with a pool and tennis court," replied the woman.**
>
> **"No," said the judge, "I mean what is the foundation of this case?"**
>
> **"Oh," said the woman, "it consists of bricks and mortar."**
>
> **"No," said the judge with a sigh. "I mean what are the relations like?"**
>
> **"I still get on well with my mother-in law," responded the woman.**
>
> **Pulling his hair out, the judge asks the woman, "Does your husband ever beat you up?"**
>
> **"Oh yes," she replied. "Every Tuesday and Thursday he's up before me, as he goes to the gym."**
>
> **In utter frustration, the judge blurts out, "Madam, why do you want a divorce?"**
>
> **"Oh, I don't want a divorce," she replies. "I've never wanted a divorce. My husband does. He says he can't communicate with me."**

This joke appeared in the local *You* magazine a few years ago and certainly confirms Frank Tyger's quote that listening is an art. However, listening is only one part of the equation. Understanding makes up the balance to good communication.

With differing levels of education, experience, and culture, and differing levels of knowledge of jargon, terminology, and technology, it is no wonder that there is so much miscommunication these days. In order to be understood, everyone must first understand the basis of their relationship, message, or intent. Don't assume. Check, and re-explain.

14.4.2. Boy giving blood

"Risk comes from knowing what you are doing."

—Warren Buffett

A little girl named Liza was suffering from a disease and needed blood from her five-year-old brother who had miraculously survived the same disease, as he had developed the antibodies needed to combat the illness. The doctor explained the situation to her little brother and then asked the boy if he would be willing to give his blood to his sister. The boy hesitated only for a moment before agreeing to help his sister.

As the transfusion progressed, he lay in bed next to his sister and smiled as the colour returned to Liza's cheeks. Then the boy's face grew pale, and his smile faded. He looked up at the doctor and asked with a trembling voice, "Will I start to die right away?"*

Being young, the boy had misunderstood the doctor; he thought he was going to have to give her all of his blood.

The key to communication is to explain things in a clear and concise manner. In turn, ensure that the recipient has understood the message or what was required. Ask them, and gain clarification or confirmation.

*Source: Lee Ryan Miller, Inspirational Story—Four Short Stories—Spiritual Endeavors <http://www.spiritual-endeavors.org/inspirational-stories/4-short-stories.htm> date posted, unknown, last date accessed 19 May 2014

14.4.3. The new hotel employee

"The greatest gift we can give each other is the quality of our attention."
—Richard Moss

> **A new hotel employee was asked to clean the lifts and report back to the supervisor when the task was completed. When the employee failed to appear at the end of the day the supervisor assumed that like many others he had simply not liked the job and left.**
>
> **However, after four days the supervisor bumped into the new employee. He was cleaning in one of the lifts. "You surely haven't been cleaning these lifts for four days, have you?" asked the supervisor, accusingly.**
>
> **"Yes sir," said the employee. "This is a big job, and I've not finished yet. Do you realize that there are more than forty of them, two on each floor, and sometimes they are not even there?"***

I'm not sure who is the author of the above excerpt, but its message is certainly an important one and reminds the communicator (whether in the workplace or other) of how vital it is to ensure that the message they are delivering is clear, concise, understood, and, most importantly, not ambiguous.

Just because the communicator understands the intent or message it doesn't mean the receiver is on the same wavelength as the communicator. The trick here is to ensure the message is aligned or attuned between communicator and receiver.

*Source: Adapted from: Stories, analogies and Fables for business, training and Public, <http://www.businessballs.com/stories.htm> date lasted accessed 19 May 2014

14.4.4. No exit strategy

"Take the trouble to stop and think of the other person's feelings, his viewpoints, his desires and needs. Think more of what the other fellow wants, and how he must feel".
—Maxwell Maltz

A man checked into a hotel for the first time in his life and goes up to his room. Five minutes later he called the reception desk and said, "You've given me a room with no exit. How do I leave?"

The desk clerk said, "Sir, that's absurd. Have you looked for the door?"

The man said, "Well, there's one door that leads to the bathroom. There's a second door that goes into the closet. And there's a door I haven't tried, but it has a 'do not disturb' sign on it."

South Africa, with its population of approximately 55 million people, is a microcosm of the world with its inhabitants numbering in the region of 7 billion. It's a country made up of many different races, cultures, ethnic groups, and professions. It has eleven official languages, and like other countries, it trades, invests, and deals with the free world in many fields, financial and other.

Communication is the international language at play here. South Africa and her people need to understand, respect, and appreciate the differing perspectives, viewpoints, cultures, and rules of the people and countries it deals with. A certain gesture or word in one culture can be deemed as an offence in another. A certain word or phrase could be misinterpreted with significant consequences.

In order to achieve success and cement good relations, businesses and their employees need to have a full appreciation of these factors and at the same time must ensure that their messages and communiqués are done with the right decorum, respect, and care.

These same subtleties and nuances apply in our life exchanges on a daily basis. Everybody we come into contact with will have a different viewpoint, need, or level of education. We need to appreciate these differences and ensure that we bridge the gaps in our communication interactions.

15 Support and mentorship

15.1. You have to play your part

15.1.1. Are you performing to the ability others see in you?

"We can't all be winners, but we can be champions in our own right."

—Natalie du Toit

Zig Ziglar began selling aluminium cookware door to door for the WearEver aluminium company. For the first few years he was a less than successful salesperson (a nobody) until one day, after a regional sales meeting, a company executive pulled him aside and told him he had *real ability*.*

Those words inspired him to become one of the best salespersons in a giant of a company. He went from zero to hero. Isn't it amazing what you can achieve with the right inspiration, motivation, or few words of encouragement from someone who recognizes the true potential in you as a person? But that's not good enough—you also have to come to the party. You need to have the self-belief, determination, and commitment to achieve, and you need to take action.

There is a biblical saying that goes, *"If you walk with wise men, then you become wise."* To become successful you must mix with the successful. So establish your network and your support base. Find a mentor, and let their enthusiasm and vision rub off on you.

To realize the potential others see in you, you have to also play your part. Don't let yourself down. Don't let your believers down.

*Source: Adapted from: Robert Cummings, MWP: Zig Ziglar-University of Mississippi <http://www.olemiss.edu/mup/dir/ziglar-zign>date posted 19 October 2007, date last accessed 19 May 2014

15.1.2. You are worthwhile

"You get the best effort from others not by lighting a fire beneath them, but by building a fire within."

—Bob Nelson

Bob Danzig was in five foster homes during his youth and spent his childhood trying to find someone to love and appreciate him. When he was nine years old, he had a new social worker.

One day, after she had done all the paperwork to move him to yet another foster home, she sat him down, looked him directly in the eyes, and said, "Bobby, I want you to always remember these words: You are worthwhile."

Bob says that no one had ever said anything like that to him, and each time they met, she repeated those words. They became an affirmation of appreciation that he heard over and over again in his head.

Many years later, Bob took a job at the "Albany New York Times" as a copy boy, and his very first boss was a woman named Margaret. After he had worked there about six months, Margaret called him into her office one day and asked him to sit down. He thought for sure he was going to be fired!

She looked him right in the eyes and said to him, "I have been the office manager for fifteen years—I have been observing you—and I believe you are full of promise."*

Those two positive messages of appreciation and hope played over and over again in his head and ultimately gave him the courage to be the very best he could be. Sixteen years later, Bob became the publisher of the "Albany New York Times", and seven years after that, he became CEO of "Hearst Corporation" (Hearst Newspapers"), one of the largest newspaper companies in the world.

Bob credits his success and change of circumstances all to those simple words of support and love. What a wonderful example of how little gifts of appreciation can make such a difference in a life.

A little bit of encouragement can be a game changer. Let's practise the concept as advocated by Bob Nelson; you get the best effort from others not by lighting a fire beneath a person but by building a fire within them. Let's play our part to ignite the fires in another.

*Source: Adapted from B. Glanz, The Simple Truths of Appreciation: How Each of Us Can Choose to Make a Difference (Illinois, Simple Truths 2007).

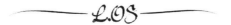

15.1.3. The winner's circle

"Nobody knows what you are capable of. Put your fingers on your wrist and feel the beat of your own heart."

—Dotty Walters

I recently visited a couple I know who are racehorse breeders and who have their stud farm in one of the most picturesque areas of the country—the Franchhoek area in the Cape. I actually arrived on the day when there was great excitement in the stable, as a foal had been born only a few hours earlier.

This couple and their personnel looked on with glee and satisfaction, almost like grandparents at their first sighting of their new grandchild. They weren't too perturbed what colour it was or what it looked like.

The foal was healthy and ahead of it lay its bright future. It was a thoroughbred, with all the genes and attributes to be a champion one day. All it needed was the time, belief and effort to be expended to make it one.

In like manner, our employees and subordinates—and even our children and loved ones—are at times like this foal. They have the right attributes, talents, and ambitions; with a bright future ahead of them. Over time, and with the right handling, support, and education, they will maximize their potential and manifest into a true champion.

Like it or not, you as a leader, manager, parent, friend, counsellor, or mentor will have a role to play to guide and unleash that inherent ability and get them into the winner's circle.

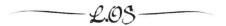

15.1.4. Appreciation: a form of encouragement

"Appreciation; Babies cry for it, grown men die for it."

—John Maxwell

According to author Gary Chapman and co-author Paul White in their book The 5 Languages of Appreciation in the Workplace: Empowering Organisations by Encouraging People, there are five methods of appreciation generally used in the workplace:

1. **Words of affirmation—words expressed to communicate thanks or appreciation.**
2. **Quality time—giving a person some undivided attention.**
3. **Acts of service—providing assistance or support.**
4. **Tangible gifts—a thoughtful and valued gift.**
5. **Physical touch—Handshakes, high-fives, and so forth.***

In the humdrum of everyday life, it's so easy to forget about ordinary courtesy. So often people forget that a word or two of appreciation can change the recipient's day; from merely a sense of duty to a value-added proposition. A simple word of thanks can enrich a person's life and, amazingly, it costs very little to express it. If you don't believe me, then just consider how you felt when someone heaped the praises on to you.

This is where the psychology and emotional aspects of leadership, coaching, and parenting come into play. The secret is to understand your people in order to know which "language" of appreciation to use. For some people it may be a combination of the above, but there will always be an optimum factor or preference.

And now for the hard part: Consider what makes your employees, friends, and family members feel appreciated and valued, and then look for ways to express these is a more meaningful manner. Sincerity is a prerequisite.

Play your part to support, encourage, and appreciate your fellow employees and people in your life.

*Source: Adapted from: G. Chapman and P. White, The 5 Languages of Appreciation in the Workplace: Empowering Organisations by Encouraging People (Chicago; Northfield Publishing, unknown date).

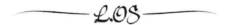

15.2. The importance of people to any organization or community

15.2.1. The ice-cream stand analogy

"If you want to put your customer first—put the person serving the customer first, first."

—Peter Drucker

A man went into the ice-cream business, selling his product from a second-hand, converted caravan on a vacant lot. As you can imagine, he spent a great deal of time deliberating about his business and where to place his portable ice-cream stand. A great deal of consideration was given to its look, location, name, competition, furniture, and fitting as well as an advertising and marketing campaign.

Now I have not mentioned a few very important aspects that he overlooked: the price and quality of the ice cream, the service ethos of the business, and the approach to ensuring a steady stream of patrons. You see, an ice-cream stand without ice cream or people purchasing the product is not an ice-cream stand.

In any business the same principle applies—the importance of people to making it a success. A bank, for example, is not a bank without people, that is, employees and clients. It could have all the gold and money in the world sitting in its vault, but it's the people who are responsible for the day-to-day trading of the concern.

Appreciate and recognize the importance of your people (clients and employees), and ensure your employees have the tools, products, services, and accountability to take care of your clientele.

Treat your clients (and staff) with your best "soft serves" and ice-cream desert dishes that they so richly deserve; without them, there will be no ice-cream stand.

15.2.2. A teacher's kindness

"If someone is going down the wrong road, he doesn't need motivation to speed him up. What he needs is education to turn him around."

—J. Rohn

In his book Become a Better You: 7 Keys to Improving Your Life Every Day, Joel Osteen relates a lovely story about a school teacher who got word that one of her pupils—the roughest student in her class—owed one of the street gangs a hundred dollars.

The teacher knew this child had no money, and the non-payment of the debt to the gang could even result in the death of the student, so she loaned him the funds but under one condition—that the pupil would promise to re-pay the teacher on the day he graduated.

The pupil became the first person in his family ever to earn a high school diploma.

This teacher's act of kindness touched this pupil's heart. Nobody had ever shown him that kind of love. Nobody had ever believed in him enough to think that he could actually graduate. This teacher believed in him and believed in all her students—so much so that they began to believe in themselves.

Many of us are like this pupil. We simply need somebody to spark a bit of hope and encouragement into our lives and for somebody to say, "Yes, you can do it. You've got what it takes!"

Like the teacher in the above story, do you see the potential in people—members of your family, friends, or even colleagues at work? Do you inspire and motivate them and help bring out the best in them? As Joel Osteen says, "Don't focus on what they are right now; focus on what they can become."

When you believe the best in people, you help to bring the best out of them.

15.2.3. It takes a village to raise a child

"It takes a village to raise a child."

—African proverb

> **I chose that old African proverb to title my book It Takes a Village because it offers a timeless reminder that children will thrive only if their families thrive and if the whole of society cares enough to provide for them.***
>
> **And we have learned that to raise a happy, healthy and hopeful child, it takes a family, it takes teachers, it takes clergy, it takes business people, it takes community leaders, it takes those who protect our health and safety, it takes all of us. Yes, it takes a village.****

There is a profound truth in the above statements by Hillary Clinton, then as America's First Lady. One cannot achieve success acting in isolation (personal, in business, or in your career). Even the Lone Ranger had Tonto as an accomplice. Look behind every winner, and you will find a great coach. Look out in front of every superstar or great achiever, and you will find caring people offering encouragement, support, and able assistance.

And so it's also applicable in your life. You need a mentor, partner, team, or other person to encourage, teach, and guide you, but make sure you have the right support structure—someone who has your vested interests at heart.

There is a phrase "success by association" where people who strive for personal excellence or development will find ways to be associated with other positive, successful, and inspiring people. They listen, watch, and copy them. It takes a village to make a child.

Who inspires you the most and why? How can you be like this person? What about you? What role do you play in mentoring or helping others? Remember that you are part of the village, so play your role.

*Source: remarks made by First Lady Hillary Rodham Clinton at launch of her book. Hilary Clinton's Speech On—It Takes A Village To <http://ww.happinessonline.org/LoveAndHelpChildren/p12.htm> date last accessed 19 May 2014

**Source: Hilary Clinton-1996 Democratic Convention Speech, http://storiesofusa.com/hillary-clinton-1996-democratic-convention-speech> date last accessed 19 May 2014

——— *L.OS* ———

15.2.4. The scorpion and the frog

"Be careful the environment you choose for it will shape you; be careful the friends you choose for you will become like them."

—W. Clement Stone

The scorpion asked a frog to carry him across the river because he couldn't swim. The frog wanted assurances that the scorpion wouldn't sting him, and his fears were allayed when the scorpion said, "If I do, we'll both drown."

So the scorpion hopped on, and half way across the river the scorpion stung the frog. As they were drowning the frog asked, "Why?"

The scorpion replied, "I can't help it; it's my nature to sting."*

The scorpion's words send out a strong message. Your growth, development, and, in some cases, your healing, can only take place when you walk with the right people. Learn to recognize toxic relationships, and walk away from them before they take you down with them.

A toxic relationship is like a body part with gangrene; if you do not amputate, the infection will spread. Unless you have the courage to cut off what will not heal, you will end up losing much more. You cannot partner successfully with someone who does not share your goals. You can't dance the foxtrot with someone who only wants to waltz. You picked the wrong dance partner.

While mentors are important to any organization or community make sure they are working with and for you and not back-stabbing or belittling you. When you enter into an arrangement or look for the help and support of someone, make sure that you do so with your eyes wide open. Ensure that they have your vested interests at heart.

*Source: The Scorpion and the Frog-Wikipedia, The Free Encyclopedia <http:// www.en.wikipedia.org/wiki/The_Scorpion_and_the_Frog> date last accessed 19 May 2014

15.3. Don't underestimate the power of encouragement

15.3.1. The piano story

"You need to be aware of what others are doing, applaud their efforts, acknowledge their successes, and encourage them in their pursuits. When we all help one another, everybody wins."

Jim Stovall

A mother wished to encourage her small girl's interest in the piano and so took her to a local concert featuring an excellent pianist. In the entrance foyer the mother met an old friend and while they were talking, the little girl wandered off, which went unnoticed by her mother. The staff were notified, and an announcement was made, asking the audience to look out for the little lost girl. With

the concert due to start, the little girl had still not been found.

In preparation for the pianist's entrance, the curtains drew aside, to reveal the little girl sitting at the great piano, focused in concentration, quietly picking out the notes of "Twinkle, Twinkle, Little Star". The audience's amusement turned to curiosity when the famous pianist entered the stage, walked up to the little girl, and said, "Keep playing."

The pianist sat down beside her, listened for a few seconds, and whispered some more words of encouragement. He then began quietly to play a bass accompaniment, and then a few bars later he reached around the little girl to add more accompaniments. At the end of the impromptu performance the audience applauded loudly as the pianist took the little girl back to her seat to be reunited with her mother.*

It takes just a few moments to make somebody's day, to help someone with their own personal aims and dreams—especially someone who looks up to you for encouragement and support.

Like the pianist in the above story, we, too, can play a very important role in unearthing the gold or diamonds in a person. All we need to do is bring it to the surface, and then let it develop into the finest of jewellery.

Johan Von Goethe said it best, *"Treat people as if they were what they ought to be, and you help them to become what they are capable of being."*

*Source: Stories, analogies and Fables for business, training and Public <http://www.businessballs.com/stories.htm> date last accessed 19 May 2014

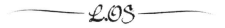

15.3.2. The push

"If you want to learn to swim, jump into the water. On dry land no frame of mind is going to help you."

—Bruce Lee

The eagle gently coaxed her offspring to the edge of the nest. Her heart quivered with conflicting emotions as she felt their resistance to her persistent nudging. "Why does the thrill of soaring have to begin with the fear of falling," she thought. The ageless question was still unanswered for her.

As with the tradition for her species, her nest was located high on the shelf of sheer rock face. Below was nothing but air to support the wings of each child. Despite her fears the eagle knew it was time. Her parental mission was all but complete. There remained one last task—the push.

The eagle grew courage from innate wisdom. Until her children discovered their wings there was no purpose for their lives. Until they learned to soar, they would fail to understand the privilege it was to have been born an eagle.

The Push was the greatest gift the Eagle could offer her offspring; it was her supreme act of love. And so, one by one she pushed them . . . and they flew.*

What a wonderful illustration of the eagle's love and encouragement and the growth and development of her offspring. It's a remarkable story about the gift of independence that helps her offspring find their purpose in life.

We can learn a great deal from the courage and innate wisdom of the eagle. Sometimes we need a push to get us going in our lives. Sometimes we need to take that plunge, spread our wings, and fly.

There is another aspect to the Push. Sometimes we need to be the eagle. We need to do the pushing—motivating and encouraging a person, be it a family member, friend, or employee.

*Source: Even Eagles need a Push movie—You Tube <http://www.youtube.com/watch?v=_ap8u-xD8xc> date of post 12 August 2009, date last accessed 19 May 2014.

15.3.3. Dame Elisabeth Schwarzkopf

"Begin to appreciate each other's gifts and you begin to appreciate your own limitations".

—M. Scot Peck

Elisabeth Schwarzkopf was a renowned soprano who spent her later years teaching pupils all over the world. When interviewed about this activity she responded in the most humble and profound manner, "There is so much talent about, and I feel so privileged that I am able to pass on what lessons I have learned."*

Consider the role you play or could play in helping others . . .

Yes, you probably won't have talents or skills that will make you as famous as Elisabeth Schwarzkopf, but take heart that you, in your own special way, are gifted with your own unique set of skills and talents. You are not a copy. You may be blessed with gifts in physical form like a great athlete or in mental form, such as those of an inventor or entrepreneur, or in spiritual form, where you inspire other people.

Don't underestimate the power of encouragement.

*Source: Adapted from: F. Gay, The Friendship Book of Francis Gay (Dundee UK; D.C. Thomson & Co Ltd, 1983).

15.3.4. Master eagle

"You never know when one act or one word of encouragement can change a life forever."

—Zig Ziglar

"How far can I travel?" asked one of the eaglets.

"How far can you see?" responded the master eagle.

"How high can I fly?" quizzed the young eaglet.

"How far can you stretch your wings?" asked the old eagle.

"How long can I fly?" the eaglet persisted.

"How far is the horizon?" the mentor rebounded.

"How much should I dream?" asked the eaglet.

"How much can you dream?" asked the older, wiser eagle with a smile.

"How much can I achieve?" the young eagle continued.

"How much can you believe?" the old eagle challenged.*

The above is a wonderful fable about a nest of young eagles seeking the wisdom and advice from their role model, their master eagle. This was an important day for the eaglets, as they were preparing for their first solo flight from the nest.

The eaglets were nervous and inquisitive—the world lay at their feet. What could they expect out in the blue yonder? They were about to take a step into the great unknown. The conversation was in reality a confidence-builder as they prepared to embark on their destiny.

I'm sure we can identify with these eaglets. There are many times in our lives that we need the sage advice and words of encouragement from the master eagles in our community and life.

The fable does continue, and the banter was persistent with the little eagles demanding answers to many questions. Eventually in response to the obvious frustration of the eaglets the master eagle gave them the soundest of advice any mentor can give to its protégé:

> *"No one can tell you how high to fly or how much to dream. It's different for each eagle. Only God and you know how far you'll go. No one on this earth knows your potential or what's in your heart. You alone will answer that. The only thing that limits you is the edge of your imagination. . . . Look to the horizon, spread your wings, and fly."*

*Source: Adapted from: M. Anderson, The Power of Attitude (Edinburgh; Thomas Nelson). (Based on the story "Look to the Horizon, Spread Your Wings, and Fly.") by Tom Reilly,

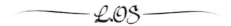

15.4. Be a good mentor, a leading example

15.4.1. Augusto "Goose" Perez

"Making the kids feel better, even if it's just for a moment, is worth more than all of my medals."

—Augusto "Goose" Perez

Augusto "Goose" Perez was diagnosed with cancer in 2000 and after a long battle lost his leg in 2003. He then decided to put his efforts into adaptive sports, and a couple of years later he was selected to be a part of the US Paralympic Wheelchair Curling Team.

He subsequently represented his country in two Paralympics Games, was selected to the US national team for six straight years, won gold at two US Open events, won a sportsmanship award, and was even named the "US Curling Male Athlete of the Year" in 2008. In addition, he participated in Adaptive Outrigger Canoe events at the international level where he enjoyed success at the highest level and was inducted into the International Canoe Hall of Fame in 2009.

Not only was he a world-class athlete, but he also gave back to the community and became the ambassador for the Hartford Paralympics Athlete Program, which enables Paralympic athletes around the country to be able to train at the highest possible level.

Goose also got involved with the US Anti-Doping Agency and the US Olympic Committee's "Team for Tomorrow Humanitarian Fund". He now travels around the country, visiting paediatric centres, bringing hope to all of the children.*

According to Goose, there is not a worse disability than the lack of seeing ability in people. Perhaps we can take a leaf out of his book, and apply the following lessons in our daily lives:

a) Look for the potential in others, particularly our employees and children.
b) Encourage, grow, and develop your people and loved ones.
c) Have a strong, open, and positive mindset.
d) Have the "drive" to achieve one's goals, despite any setbacks.
e) Do not have the mindset of a victim, but that of a victor.
f) Work hard, and adopt a never-give-up attitude in order to achieve success.
g) Shoot for the moon, if you can't reach for the stars.

Goose understood that despite his handicap and disability he had a role to play in society, including to help and encourage others. He became a role model, a leading example for the entire world to see.

If Goose can do it, then so can you. Life isn't only about having—it's also about giving.

*Source: Andrew Collins, Goose's Story; Livestrong Blog <http://blog. livestrong.org/2010/11/23/gooses-story> date of post 23 November 2010, date last posted 19 May 2014

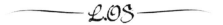

15.4.2. The starfish

"We must not, in trying to think about how we can make a big difference, ignore the small daily differences we can make which, over time, add up to big differences that we often cannot foresee."
—Marian Wright Edelman

There is an ageless story whereby a person walking on a beach notices a kid stooping to pick up something and hurling it into the sea. As this person nears he notices this boy picking up a starfish from the thousands that have been washed up on the beach and returns it to the ocean.

The person looks around at the carnage and says to the little one, "You are wasting your time; there are thousands of these starfish stranded on the beach."

"Yes," said the boy again, stooping and picking up a single starfish and hurling it back into the seas. He then exclaimed, "But to this one I have made a difference."*

But to this one I have made a difference . . . It doesn't matter how huge the task, or how futile the effort, start with the first step. If you don't start you can never end, or make a difference. History is strewn with examples where someone started a campaign, a cause, or charity association, and leading by example and momentum, the events have prospered. In this instance, I'm always reminded of the infamous words uttered by Neil Armstrong when he landed on the moon, "One small step for man, one giant leap for mankind."

In like manner, so often a small act of kindness, no matter how insignificant, can be of substantial benefit to another person. We don't really know what's in the hearts and minds of others and what inner distress and turmoil they are experiencing. I always try to subscribe to these famous words of Paul Spear, "To the world you may be one person, but to that person you may be the world."

Be a good mentor. Lead by example

*Source: The Star Fish-Roger Knapp <http://www.rogerknapp.com/inspire/starfish.htm> date last accessed 19 May 2014

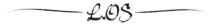

15.4.3. The value of a second opinion

"You can tell whether a man is clever by his questions. You can tell whether a man is wise by his answers."

—anonymous

The boy left school and the world "lay at his feet". He told his parents his elaborate plans that he was going to enrol on a cruise liner, and see the world. After a few years he

would return, wiser and older, buy a car and house, find a "real job", get married, and have children.

The father, with a smile on his face, calmly said, "Son, come down from 'cloud 9', and let me tell you how things work in the real world." The father went on to burst this young man's bubble, so much so that the youngster got upset and angry and stormed out the house.

So often we think we know all the answers. Many times our ideas or thought processes are impulsive or ill-advised or lack substance. We tend to get upset when people try to intervene or warn us of the folly of our ways, and despite their protests, we hurtle forward into the world of hurt, despair, and failure.

Getting a second opinion from a valued, experienced "campaigner" doesn't mean that you are weak; it may save you a lot of money, energy, or time and help you figure out your priorities and responsibilities in life.

Don't be too quick to disregard a wise, experienced, and knowledgeable person, particularly when they don't have "an agenda"; they only have your best interests at heart.

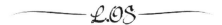

15.4.4. The butterfly story

"The task of the leader is not to put greatness into people, but to elicit it, for greatness is there already."

—John Buchan

A man found a cocoon of a butterfly. One day as a small opening appeared, he sat and watched the butterfly for several hours as it struggled to force its body through the little hole. Then it seemed to stop making any progress. It appeared stuck.

The man decided to help the butterfly, and with a pair of scissors he cut open the cocoon. The butterfly then emerged easily. Something was strange. The butterfly had a swollen body and shrivelled wings. The man watched the

butterfly, expecting it to take on its correct proportions. But nothing changed. The butterfly stayed the same. It was never able to fly.*

In the man's kindness and haste, he did not realize that the butterfly's struggle to get through the small opening of the cocoon is nature's way of forcing fluid from the body of the butterfly into its wings so that it would be ready for flight.

When we coach and support others we need to do so in a balanced way, not like the man in the above story, who, despite the best intentions in the world, did more harm than good. Everyone learns at a different pace, and everyone has different attributes and talents, and everyone has a different will to learn and achieve.

Some leaders believe in throwing people into the deep end to see if they can swim. The results are not always successful: some "swim", but many "drown", with dire consequences to their confidence and self-esteem. On the other hand, being too slow to let go of the reins can equally undermine a person's aspirations or independence levels. Coaching, teaching, enabling, facilitating, or parenting is a skill that requires a great deal of discernment, honesty, patience, and, above all, responsibility—all the attributes of a great leader.

The butterfly analogy is a wonderful guide for you in these circumstances. Hold the butterfly too tightly, and you will squash its wings and stifle its flight and growth. Hold it too loosely, and it will fly away before it is mature enough to do so.

*Source: The Butterfly Story-Greatest Inspirational quotes (Happiness-Inspiration-wisdom <http://www.greatest-inspirational-quotes.com/butterfly-story.htm> accessed 17 May 2014

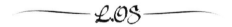

16 Balance in life

16.1. Make good use of your time

16.1.1 Eat that frog

"Procrastination is attitude's natural assassin. There is nothing so fatiguing as an uncompleted task."

—William James

> Your "frog" must be the most difficult task on your things-to-do list; it's that task or thing you are most likely to "put off" for some reason or other. Author Brian Tracey, in his book, Eat that Frog, advocates a wonderful concept—you "eat" and finish that task first, and then you will have the energy and momentum for the rest of the day to tackle those other chores.

> But if you don't . . . you let the frog sit there on a plate while you do a hundred unimportant things that will drain your energy, and you won't even know it.*

The "Eat that Frog" concept encourages you to immediately tackle that daunting task, chore, or project that has been worrying, irritating and gnawing at you—yes, possibly that one that's sitting on the edge of your desk, gathering dust, or covered in moss. We are world champions at finding reasons as to why that job cannot be done *now*—the "why do it today when it can be done tomorrow" kind of thinking. The problem with this approach is that it ultimately affects our psyche and works on our subconscious.

Can you appreciate how much time you actually waste just thinking about what must be done instead of doing it? Time is your ally when you take action, but time is a two-sided coin. If you procrastinate or hesitate, time becomes your enemy. Use your time wisely. So get your priorities right. Make a to-do list, and divide it up into areas of importance and urgency. Do the most important or most pressing items first. Also, ensure the list is not too long and cumbersome; you do not want to feel stressed out just looking at it.

Set a time line to complete the task/s, or you will never get them finished. Work a system to eliminate distractions (from children, colleagues, emails, and so on), and try doing those difficult or demanding tasks when your "body clock" is functioning at its optimum. Use the latest technologies, or, where possible, enlist the help of others. Learn to say "no"; if you are overwhelmed with work then you will be doing yourself and your team or business a disservice by taking on more.

Make good use of your time.

*Source: Adapted from: L. O'Sullivan, Client Service Excellence: The 10 Commandments (Johannesburg: Knowledge Resources, 2010).

Adapted from: B. Tracey, Eat that frog! 21 Ways to Stop Procrastinating and Get More Done in Less Time (San Francisco; Brett-Koehler Publishers, 2007).

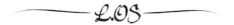

16.1.2. Time is like a river

"Time is like a river; you cannot touch the same water twice because the flow that has passed will never pass again. Enjoy every moment of life!"

—anonymous

Imagine there is a bank that credits your account each morning with $86,400. It carries over no balance from day to day. Every evening the account deletes whatever part of the balance you failed to use during the day. What would you do? Draw out every cent, of course!

Each of us has such a bank. Its name is time cc. Every morning, it credits you with 86,400 seconds. Every night it writes off, as lost, whatever of this you have failed to invest to good purpose. It carries over no balance. It allows no overdraft. Each day it opens a new account for you. Each night it burns the remains of the day. If you fail to use the day's deposits, the loss is yours.*

Wow! A scary thought. I don't know who wrote these lines, but they are spot on. Time waits for no man. To realize the value of *one year*, ask a student who failed a grade. To realize the value of *one month*, ask a mother who gave birth to a premature baby. To realize the value of *one week*, ask the editor of a weekly newspaper. To realize the value of *one hour*, ask the lovers who are waiting to meet. To realize the value of *one minute*, ask a person who missed the train. To realize the value of *one second*, ask a person who just avoided an accident.

Time is free, but time is priceless. You can't own time; you can only use it. Treasure every moment you have. And treasure it more because you shared it with someone special, special enough to spend your time. Yesterday is history. Tomorrow is a mystery. Today is a gift. That's why it's called the present.

Time is like a river; don't let it pass you by.

*Source: unknown.

————— *£.O$* —————

16.1.3. The multiplier effect

"All problems become smaller if you don't dodge them, but confront them."
—William F. Halsey

> **"It's the old story about the frog in a pan of cold water. If you throw a frog into a pan of hot water it will jump around, suffer greatly, and die. Yet, if you put the frog in the pan of cold water, put it on a stove, and heat it to boiling point, the frog doesn't stir, doesn't feel it, doesn't notice it. At the end the frog is dead."***

The moral is simple enough: Things happen incrementally that one doesn't notice until it is too late.

Be aware of the small things that you neglect, put off, or don't pay attention to because these small things will multiply, grow, and fester. The day will come when these small things will turn into one big monster. It could affect many areas of your life: stress or drugs dependency that affects your health, lack of savings that affects your retirement, or lack of knowledge that affects your career.

Heed the signs, and don't be caught off guard. Don't procrastinate or put off for tomorrow what should be done today. Time doesn't wait for you, and everything will catch up with you over time. Don't be caught out like the frog in the story above.

*Source: excerpt from: Bob Roberts, dir. Tim Robbins (1992).

16.1.4. What would you do if you knew that you would die today?

"Life is like a ten-speed bike. Most of us have gears we never use."

—anonymous

There is a scene in the movie Another Day that centres on one's belief in destiny and death. The following question is posed, "What will you do if you knew you will die today?"

The answer given is rather profound and refreshing: "I don't give a damn what I miss when I die. It's what I miss if I live that I worry about."

Let's not get caught in that trap that when old age or a dreaded disease strikes we live in regret of the things we did not do—that we were afraid to do or did not feel we had the time or resources to do.

The late Steve Jobs understood the importance of making the best of his short time on Earth, making his life worth living and now being remembered for the greatness he achieved. Take note of one of his quotes, a testimony to his philosophy of life:

"Remembering that I'll be dead soon is the most important tool I've ever encountered to help me make the big choices in life. Because almost everything—all external expectations, all pride, all fear of embarrassment or failure—these things just fall away in the face of death, leaving only what is truly important."

The graveyards are full of people who have lived unfulfilled or unhappy lives—don't become another statistic. Live for today; live your dreams, and your life!

*Source: Another Day, dir. Jeff Reiner (2001).

--- *£.OS* ---

16.2.1. Beating stress

16.2.2. Choose how you use your day

"If you are stressing over something, you are not doing so in solo, in a vacuum. You are leaking stress onto everyone with whom you come in contact—your colleagues, your friends, and your family."

—Liisa Kyle

A lecturer, when explaining stress management to an audience, raised a glass of water and asked, "How heavy is this glass of water?"

Answers called out ranged from 20 g to 500 g.

The lecturer replied, "The absolute weight doesn't matter. It depends on how long you try to hold it. If I hold it for a minute, it's not a problem. If I hold it for an hour, I'll have an ache in my right arm. If I hold it for a day, you'll have to call an ambulance. In each case, it's the same weight, but the longer I hold it, the heavier it becomes."

He continued, "And that's the way it is with stress management. If we carry our burdens all the time, sooner or later, the burden will become increasingly heavy: and we won't be able to carry on."

"As with the glass of water, you have to put it down for a while, and rest before holding it again.

When we're refreshed, we can carry on with the burden. So, before you return home tonight, put the burden of work down: Don't carry it home. You can pick it up tomorrow. Whatever burdens you're carrying now, let them down for a moment if you can."*

We all experience stress, sometimes every day. Stress can be disguised in many forms, whether its worries about work, family, relationships, or friendships. Stress has become part of our everyday living.

The good news is that you don't have to just live with being "stressed out". Experts these days tell us there are some ways to conquer or at least reduce this "animal", and live a more relaxed lifestyle. Breathing, diet, exercise, and rest are all forms of stress relievers.

You may not be able to control stressful situations that happen around you or to you, but you can change the way you react to those events. Monitor yourself for signs of stress, fear, anxiety, and pessimism. Notice when you judge yourself or others. Realize when you are trying to control the situation or others. Observe your effect on others. This will give you a clue as to how you are managing or dealing with stress.

Remember that when you are stressed it not only affects you but everyone around you.

*Source: Adapted from: Stress Management—Gannett Health Services—Cornell University<http://www.gannett.cornell.edu/topics/stress> author unknown, last accessed 12 May 2014

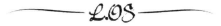

16.2.2. Choose how you use your day

"Be yourself, everyone else is already taken."

—Oscar Wilde

"Choose how you use." These words by Linda Ellis are her daily affirmation and "decision maker". The 16 hours or 960 minutes that she is awake each day is her time—and she alone has the choice with whom she will share those moments as well as what situations or emotions are or

aren't worthy of taking up her precious time. It's all down to personal choice*

Linda even takes it a bit further. In her book, *Simple Truths of Life*, she makes a very interesting comparison to a person's deliberation in making a purchase. For example, "How much thought do you put into a decision to buy a dress or shirt for R960-00?" Quite a bit, I fancy. In comparison, "How much thought goes into how you spend your 960 minutes each day?"

Whether you use your "full active" quota of sixteen hours per day or not (assuming you sleep for eight hours per day), it's vital you choose how you use each day. Choose what is important to you. Reflect on your life-work balance, and bear in mind those things that will stress you out, or give you rest or pleasure.

As you contemplate how you will use your time, consider these words from the poem "24 Hours" author unknown:

> *I am rich. I have 24 hours to spend.*
> *Like golden coins they shine for me.*
> *Let me not waste them; neither let me feverishly*
> *spend them in hectic, nerve-shattering activity . . .*
> *When I wake tomorrow, my purse will be filled with 24 coins*
> *all shining and new! And I shall be 24 hours older and wiser.***

Choose how you will use your day.

*Source: Adapted from: L. Ellis, **Simple Truths of Life: A Collection of Lessons Learned** (Illinois; Simple Truths, 2009).

**Source: excerpt from the poem, "24 Hours". Author unknown

16.2.3 You don't have to catch other people's paper clips

"You either walk inside your story and own it or you stand outside your story and hustle for your worthiness."
—Brené Brown

During a psychological session, a young male patient was relating to the psychologist how much other people

affected him in his life. He (the patient) didn't care much for these people, but he was "too nice" to say no or stand up to them. The psychologist tried to reason with the young man and spoke about the concept of him giving his power away to other people.

The young man didn't grasp the point, so the psychologist picked up a paper clip and threw it at the young man, asking him to catch it. The young man duly caught the paper clip, at which instance, the psychologist asked the patient why he had caught it. *"Because you asked me to catch it," was the reply.*

The psychologist continued to look at the man. Without saying a word, and about 30 seconds into the silence, the patient suddenly got it. With a big smile on his face he said, *"Ah! So I am doing things other people want me to do, but not what I want to do?"*

This is a lovely story with an equally "catchy" message; you don't have to catch other people's paper clips. I don't know the source of this story, but its message is quite profound, so I sincerely hope that person won't have any objection to me sharing this with you.

You don't have to follow the route that other people have mapped out for you. You don't have to always be at their beck and call, and you certainly don't have to give your power, your dreams, and/or your happiness away.

Trying to do what other people want you to do or live the way other people want you to live can be very demanding, stressful, intimidating, and overwhelming. The worse part of any of the above scenarios is that it erodes your self-confidence and free will and passion for life—your own life.

Consider, "Are you always catching other people's paper clips?" If so, it may be high time you get off the "poor me" train and take back your power and life.

Leo Buscaglia, an author and motivational speaker once said, "The easiest thing to be in the world is you. The most difficult thing to be is what other people want you to be. Don't let them put you in that position."

16.3. Measuring your lifestyle

16.3.1. Balancing five balls in the air

"Value has a value only if its value is valued."

—anonymous

> **"Imagine life as a game in which you are juggling some five balls in the air. They are Work, Family, Friends, Health and Spirit and you are keeping all of these in the air.**
>
> **You will soon understand that work is a rubber ball. If you drop it, it will bounce back. But the other four balls— Family, Health, Friends and Spirit—are made of glass. If you drop one of these; they will be irrevocably scuffed, marked, nicked, damaged or even shattered. They will never be the same. You must understand that and strive for it."***

The above is an extract from the infamous 30 second speech by Bryon Dyson (the former CEO of Coca-Cola). His message to his employees was to work efficiently during office hours, leave on time, and give the required amount of energy and quality time to your family and friends and, more importantly—yourself.

And so how are you doing in this game of life? How many balls are you juggling in the air?

Balance in life is a decision. Take care of your body for it's the only place you have to live. How you spend your days is, of course, how you spend your life. John Maxwell, an author and leadership/ motivational speaker advises that one can measure the success or lifestyle of a person merely by how they spend their day.

Do not forget about the most important things in life, and don't forget about your family, friends, and spirit. Find that "work versus play" or "family versus self" balance.

Which balls are you juggling in the air right now?

*Source: extract from: B. Dyson, speech, email circulation, date 26 November 2009. [Bryon Dyson was the former CEO of Coca-Cola.]

16.3.2. The butterfly point

"To help others develop, start with yourself."

—Marshall Goldsmith

Michael Neill, author of You Can Have What You Want; *Proven Strategies for Inner and Outer Success (2006),* **refers to the "butterfly point" concept. "Imagine what you want is like a butterfly. Hold it too tight and you will squash it, hold it too loosely, it will fly away."**

This quote really resonates with me. One has to find the right balance in life, be it in your job, relationships, goals, eating, drinking, or even exercising.

One who exerts too much power or control over a loved one or subordinate, for example, will soon witness rebellion, anger, or other serious traumas. Too little control has its own set of nasty consequences. One can't be overly competitive or domineering.

So, find the right mixture: Hold that "butterfly" in a trusting, empowering, caring, and evenly balanced manner.

16.3.3. "Mummy, may I please borrow $25?"

"In this world it's not what we take up, but what we give up, that makes us rich."
—Henry Ward Beecher

A woman came home from work late, tired and irritated, to find her five year-old son waiting for her at the door. Her son asked his mum a question, "Mummy, how much do you make an hour?" The mother was taken aback and demanded to know the reason for the question.

"I just want to know. Please tell me, how much do you make an hour?" The mother then confided in him that she earned $50 per hour. At this, the son asked if he could borrow $25 from his mum.

The mother was furious. "If you want money to buy a silly toy or some other nonsense, then you march yourself straight to your room and go to bed. Think about why you are being so selfish. I don't work hard every day for such childish frivolities."

The little boy quietly went to his room and shut the door while the woman sat down and began to wonder why her son wanted the money.

After a while she went to her son's room to confront him and gave him $25. The little boy sat straight up, smiling. "Oh, thank you Mummy!" he yelled. Then, reaching under his pillow he pulled out some crumpled up bills. The woman, seeing that the boy already had money, got angry again.

The little boy slowly counted out his money, and then he looked up at his mother. "Why do you want more money if you already have some?" the mother grumbled.

"Because I didn't have enough, but now I do," the little boy replied. "Mummy, I have $50 now. Can I buy an hour of your time? Please come home early tomorrow. I would like to have dinner with you."*

This story is an adaptation of one that was emailed to me a number of years ago when I was writing my first book, *Client Service Excellence: The 10 Commandments*, and it fitted right into a particular theme I was working on: "Balance work and pleasure". The above story is a sharp reminder that we must *not* make our career our life; there is something happening outside the four walls of the office.

We should not let time slip through our fingers without having spent some of it with those who really matter to us, those close to our hearts.

Do remember to share that fifty dollars' worth of time with someone in your life today.

*Source: Adapted from: L. O'Sullivan, Client Service Excellence: The 10 Commandments (Johannesburg SA: Knowledge Resources 2010).

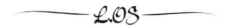

16.3.4. The night watchman story

"Either you run the day or the day runs you."

—Jim Rohn

Someone once related a story to me that I think has a very profound message for all of us. I'm not sure of its source but it pertains to a factory night watchman who had the responsibility to alter all the clocks in the factory by one hour. This event obviously coincided with British Summer Time (BST) when all the clocks in the United Kingdom are altered forward by one hour.

The following day, as he arrived at church, he found to his amazement that the congregation were on their way home. He didn't adjust his own clock . . .

Consider: Are we like this night watchman? Are we better giving advice than heeding our own advice? Are we so busy meddling in the affairs of others that we are neglecting to take taking care of our own issues, problems, or life decisions?

The secret in life is that if you want to help others you have to first help yourself. You need to first ensure that your life is in order and is a leading example to others. It's the case of those who live in glass houses shouldn't throw stones; how will people listen to or respect you if your life is a contradiction?

The night watchman story also reminds me of a couple of clients I had who both held very senior jobs in different listed companies. These parties were termed work-a-holics, working more than eighty hours per week. They did an amazing job for their company and received many accolades and great bonuses. Sadly, they didn't attend to their personal/family affairs with the same gusto; when they died their last will and testaments weren't up to date. One left a sizeable estate to his ex-wife, and the other died intestate.

Don't let this happen to you. Don't only be a night watchman, but also be a day watchman. Watch over your personal affairs, health, and family with the same passion and responsibility as you watch over your work functions. Find that balance.

—————— *L.OS* ——————

16.4. Don't sweat the small stuff

16.4.1. Rocks and sand

"You can escape the world, but you cannot escape life, which is what you are."
—Alan Cohen

A philosophy professor stood before his class and had some items in front of him. When class began, wordlessly he picked up a large empty mayonnaise jar and proceeded to fill it with rocks, rocks that were about 2 inches in diameter.

He then asked the students if the jar was full. They agreed that it was. So the professor then picked up a box of pebbles and poured them into the jar. He shook the jar lightly. The pebbles, of course, rolled into the open areas between the rocks.

He then asked the students again if the jar was full. They agreed it was.

The students laughed.

The professor picked up a box of sand and poured it into the jar. Of course, the sand filled up the space.*

The professor went on to explain the parable of the rocks, pebbles, and sand and to associate it to life. The rocks are the important things—our family, our partners, our health, and our children—anything that is so important to us that if it were lost, we would be nearly destroyed.

The pebbles are the other things that matter like our job, our house, our car.

The sand is everything else. The small stuff.

If we put the sand into the jar first, there is no room for the pebbles or the rocks. The same goes for your life. If you spend all of your energy and time on the small stuff, then you will never have room for the things that are important to you.

Take care of the rocks first—the things that really matter. Set your priorities. The rest is just sand.

*Source: Rocks and sand—Roger Knapp <http://www.rogerknapp.com/inspire/ rockssand.htm> date last accessed 11 May 2014

16.4.2. Broaden your focus!

"Rowing harder doesn't help if the boat is headed in the wrong direction."
—Kenichi Ohmae

While on holiday at Port Alfred in the Eastern Cape province of South Africa I noticed two young children, about five or six years of age, enjoying themselves on the edge of the ocean. They each had a bodyboard and were watching the waves intently, presumably hoping to pick the right one to wash them up the beach. It was a hit-and-miss event: Sometimes they got dunked; at other times, their faces gleamed as they were washed ashore.

It was then that a freak side-wash came and swept them completely out of the controlled swimming area and into the rocks and turbulent sea that caused panic among bystanders and required action by the lifeguards to rescue them.

This story is a clear example of what happens to you when you focus solely on your aspect or goal in your life; you don't see that "side-current" (divorce, burn out, health issues) that can change your lifestyle in one foul sweep and can turn the sweetness of achievement into regret and unhappiness.

The same principle applies in the business world. You cannot operate in a cocoon. You need to be abreast of changes in the industry, in legislation, in your clients' behaviours, and, of course, your competitors. Failure to do so will be at your peril.

As you live or work in the present, take note of all the other factors in your life that you may be neglecting. While you have your eye on your future, broaden your focus so that you don't get tripped up with something from left field. Ensure that your life is rotating on the correct axis.

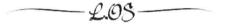

16.4.3. The troubles tree

"If you are too afraid to bring your best to work you will never do your best work."
—Robin Sharma

The carpenter I hired to help me restore an old farmhouse had just finished a rough first day on the job. A flat tire had made him lose an hour of work, his electric saw had quit, and now his ancient pickup truck was refusing to start. While I drove him home, he sat in stony silence.

On arriving at his house, he invited me in to meet his family. As we walked towards the front door, he paused briefly at a small tree, touching the tips of the branches with both hands. After opening the door, he underwent an amazing transformation. His tanned face was wreathed in smiles, and he hugged his two small children and gave his wife a kiss.

Afterwards, he walked me to my car. We passed the tree, and my curiosity got the better of me. I asked him about what I had seen him do earlier. "Oh, that's my trouble tree," he replied. "I know I can't help having troubles on the job, but one thing for sure, troubles don't belong in the house with my wife and the children. So I just hang

them up on the tree every night when I come home. Then in the morning, I pick them up again." "Funny thing is," he said with a smile, "when I come out in the morning to pick them up, there aren't nearly as many as I remember hanging up the night before."*

Yes, we all have a bad day at the office, but the "troubles tree" analogy encourages us not to take our problems home with us. It's certainly not fair to take the issues you are experiencing with your boss or that irritant client home and to also make it the problem of your wife and children. In similar vein, it's also a reminder to us not to take our personal problems to work for these will eventually manifest in your standard of work and possibly affect those around you.

Leave the "office at the office", and leave the "home at home." Don't take work home where you spend your personal, social, and family time, and, conversely, respect your employer's time and stipend by devoting most of your working day to matters of the job.

Find your own "troubles tree", and let it become a habit, a place where you can park these events or circumstances for another day. Perhaps they won't seem too big an issue in the morning.

*Source: The troubles tree-Motivation-Academic tips. <http://academictips. org/blogs/the-trouble-tree> date last accessed 17 May 2014

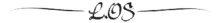

16.5. Listen to that internal voice

16.5.1. What good shall I do today?

"As one person I cannot change the world-; but I can change the world for one person."

—Paul Spear

Benjamin Franklin began and ended every day with the following questions: "What good shall I do this day?" and "What good have I done today?" He started every day by getting clear about what action steps he would take that day to fulfil his intention of doing good and

ended the day with a little performance review and being self-accountable.*

Life these days is so hectic, and time is scarcer than before. Connectivity, economic upheaval, globalization, technological advancements, pressure, and deadlines at the workplace all have huge effects in terms of our daily routines and personal lives. Family life has also been rearranged; takeaway or fast foods are the norm, and there is greater dependency on drugs, alcohol, and even social media. When will we find the time for our spiritual or personal considerations?

Take "time out" of your busy schedule, and consider these two basic and yet profound questions—"What good shall I do this day?" and "What good have I done today?"

*Source: Adapted from: Marci Shimoff <http://www. marcishimoffblog.com-Happy for no reason> date last accessed 19 May 2014

16.5.2. Get to know the real you

"Always be yourself, express yourself, have faith in yourself, do not go out and look for a successful personality and duplicate it."

—Bruce Lee

Myles W. Miller has a motto, "If I know who and what I am, no one can tell me who and what I am not."

Very interesting. Despite what the world thinks of him, he only thinks great thoughts about himself. Can we learn from this? Decide who and what you are right now, and don't be overly swayed by what others think of you. Create and maintain a positive, upbeat outlook and image of yourself . . . love yourself.

As I mentioned elsewhere in this book, self-awareness is key to your ability to understand yourself, and, in so doing, you will appreciate the various stages of your existence—your physical, spiritual, emotional, and mental sides. You will soon realize your strengths, weaknesses, needs, desires, love, passions, and attitudes and why you are at peace . . . or not.

Remember there is nobody like you in this whole world. You are special and will always remain so. Accept yourself, love yourself, respect yourself, and appreciate your good qualities. Be at ease with yourself.

As you live your days, so you live your life. A great life is nothing more than a series of great, well-lived days strung together like a beautiful necklace of pearls. Don't die with the music still in you. Every day counts, and every day contributes to the quality of your life.

Get to know the real you. Establish the motto or credo that you live by each day—all day, every day.

16.5.3. Limitless

"It is confidence in our bodies, minds and spirits that allows us to keep looking for new adventures."

—Oprah

In the movie *Limitless*, Eddie Morra, a down-on-his-luck writer with the same bad luck with relationships, is by chance introduced to a "wonder drug" by his ex-brother-in-law. This drug makes one smarter with super-human mental abilities and clarity.

With the drug, he is able to stimulate his brain power, allowing him to write books, learn new languages, learn the piano, and even decipher stock-trading algorithms to significant success. All of his fears and shyness was gone. This new Eddie creates great fame and wealth, but then . . . he soon discovers that the drug has detrimental side effects.*

This leads to some interesting points to consider. What is the best version of yourself? What would you do to access this version in order to accomplish great things? Would you take performance-enhancing drugs to make you limitless? Would you use your new skill in an ethical, productive, creative, or meaningful purpose?

In today's world there are so many people looking for such "wonder drug". Just take note of how many use forms of alcohol, caffeine, nicotine, and all sorts of soft or hard pharmaceutical components. Many lives and families and careers have been ruined by substance abuse.

Yet, one doesn't need a drug to enhance one's energy and motivation levels or to find one's purpose or happiness in life. The secret is in defining what's important to one and then living one's life within those clearly defined morals, values, and vision. Everyone has the potential and power to be "limitless" without any crutches and chemical aids; one just needs the right passion, attitude, focus, and mind-power.

*Source: Adapted from: Limitless, dir. Neil Burger (2011), based on the 2001 novel The Dark Fields by Alan Glynn.

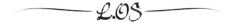

The finale

Having read this book or even parts of this book, I hope it has stirred the "juices" within you and helped to inspire or motivate you to improve, change, or alter certain aspects of your life—be it in the personal, family, or work environment.

As I implied in the introduction, you are the "driver"—the CEO—of your attitude, passion, success, leadership qualities, service ethos, and career. Nobody, but nobody, can dictate these matters to you—not your parents, spouse, colleagues, or bosses. You alone are behind the wheel, and you alone are the "driver" of your own journey and destination.

So, "How is your driving?" What does your dashboard say? What lies in the road ahead of you or around the next bend, and how will you steer past those "potholes" and "traffic jams" that await you? Are you looking with hope through the windscreen, or are you still focused on the rear-view mirror, that is, on past events and circumstances?

To conclude, therefore, I have found it fitting to include some excerpts of the work of Steve Maraboli, entitled, "Why not you?". The words will speak to your heart, mind, and soul, and they will be the catalyst for making a difference in your life, thereby touching the lives of others.

*Today, many will awaken with a fresh sense of inspiration. Why not you?

*Today, many will break through the barriers of the past by looking at the blessings of the present. Why not you?

*Today, for many, the burden of self-doubt and insecurity will be lifted by the security and confidence of empowerment. Why not you?

*Today, many will rise above their believed limitations and make contact with their powerful innate strength. Why not you?

*Today, many will choose to live in such a manner that they will be a positive role model for their children. Why not you?

*Today is a new day! Many will seize this day. Many will live it to the fullest. Why not you?

Larry O'Sullivan

Bibliography and Recommended Reading

Anderson, M. *The Power of Attitude* (Edinburgh; Thomas Nelson, 2004).

Anderson, M. *You Can't Take a Duck to Eagle School* (Illinois; Simple Truths, 2007).

Anderson, M., *Charging the Human Battery* (Illinois; Simple Truths, 2008).

Anderson, M. *Customer-love: Great Stories about Great Service* (Chicago; Sourcebooks, 2013).

Anderson, M. and Feltenstein, T., *Change for the Good: You Go First; 21 Ways to Inspire Change* (Illinois; Simple Truths, 2007).

Bayles, D. and Orland, T. *Art and Fear: Observations on the Perils (and Rewards) of Artmaking* (Oregon; Image Continuum Press, 2001).

Bryant, A. *The Corner Office: How Top CEOs Made It and How You Can Too* (London; Harper Press, 2011).

Cavanaugh, B., *The Sower's Seeds: 120 Inspiring Stories for Preaching, Teaching and Public Speaking* (Mahwah; Paulist Press, 2004).

Crow, R. *Rock Solid Leadership: How Great Leaders Exceed Expectations* (Illinois; Simple Truths, 2006).

Ellis, L., *Simple Truths of Life: A Collection of Lessons Learned* (Illinois, Simple Truths, 2009).

Emerzian, M. and Bozza, K., *Every Monday Matters: 52 Ways to Make a Difference* (Edinburgh; Thomas Nelson, 2008).

Fried, J. and Hansson, D., *Rework* (London; Vermillion (Random House), 2010).

Gay, F., *The Friendship Book of Francis Gay* (Dundee UK; D.C. Thomson & Co Ltd, 1983).

Glanz, B., *The Simple Truths of Appreciation: How Each of Us Can Choose to Make a Difference* (Illinois; Simple Truths, unknown date).

Goldsmith, M. and Reiter, M. *What Got You Here Won't Get You There: How Successful People Become Even More Successful* (New York; Hyperion, 2007).

Hamilton, B., *Soul Surfer: A True Story of Faith, Family and Fighting to Get Back on the Board* (New York; MTV Books, 2004).

Hansen, M.V. and Canfield, J., *Chicken Soup for the Soul* (Florida: HCI, unknown date).

Harford, T., *Adapt: Why Success Always Starts with Failure* (New York; Farrar, Straus and Giroux, 2011).

Hattingh, L. and Claasen, H. *African Wisdom* (unknown publisher, unknown date).

Larson, C.B., *Illustrations for Preaching & Teaching; from Leadership Journal* (Michigan; Baker Pub Group, 1984).

Lenehan, A., *The Best of Bits and Pieces* (Fairfield, USA; The Economic Press, 1994).

Lombard, V. and Lombardi Jnr, *What It Takes to Be # 1* (gift edition) (Edinburgh; Thomas Nelson, 2012).

Maxwell. J.C., *The Right to Lead: Learning Leadership through Character and Courage* (Edinburgh; Thomas Nelson, 2010).

Miller, A., *Death of a Salesman: Play in Two Acts*, USA, Dramatists Play Service, 1952

Neal, D.T., Quinn, M. and Wood, W., *Habits; A Repeat Performance* (New Jersey; Wiley Blackwell, 2006).

Ortberg, J., *If You Want to Walk on Water, You've Got to Get Out of the Boat* (Michigan; Zondervan Publishing Company, 2003).

Osteen, J., *Become a Better You: 7 Keys to Improving Your Life Every Day* (London; Simon and Schuster, 2007).

O'Sullivan, L., *Client Service Excellence: The 10 Commandments* ((Johannesburg): Knowledge Resources).

Parker, S.L. with M. Anderson, 212; *The Extra Degree* (Illinois; Simple Truths, 2005).

Richmond, G., *A View from the Zoo* (Edinburgh; W Pub Group, 1987).

Robbins, A., *Unlimited Power* (London; Simon & Schuster 1988).

Sharma, R., *The Secret Letters of the Monk Who Sold his Ferrari* (London; Harper Element, 2011).

Smith, S.B., *In All his Glory:. The Life of William S. Paley the Legendary Tycoon and his Brilliant Circle* (New York; Random House Inc, 2003).

Smith, V.J., *The Richest Man in Town* Sioux Falls, South Dakota (Pine Hill Press, 2005).

Thomas, I., *Power of the Pride: How Lessons from a Pride of Lions Can Teach You to Create Powerful Business Teams* (Johannesburg; Ian Thomas, 1992).

Toler, S, *Minute Motivators for Leaders—Quick Inspiration for the Time of your Life* (Massachusetts; Dust Jacket Press, 2011).

Towery, T.L., *Wisdom of Wolves: Nature's Way to Organisational Success* (New Mexico: Walnut Grove, 2010).

Tracey, B., *Eat that Frog! 21 Ways to Stop Procrastinating and Get More Done in Less Time* (San Francisco; Brett-Koehler Publishers, 2007).

Waldman, R. Lt Col, *Never Fly Solo: Lead with Courage, Build Trusting Partnerships, and Reach New Heights in Business* (New York; McGraw Hill, 2009).

About the Author

Larry O'Sullivan

Larry O'Sullivan is currently a private banker with a leading financial institution in South Africa with forty years of experience in general, international, corporate, and private banking fields. He is passionate about customer service and about helping and "uplifting" people. He is a published author of a book, *Client Service Excellence: The 10 Commandments.* (Knowledge Resources, 2010)

Larry believes that one can't get people to serve or, in fact, to give of their best in the workplace or in life unless they are motivated and happy. He has cunningly devised a way of combining both his and other well-known stories into various themes of inspirational and service related matters that will help you the reader to achieve success in both business and life.

Larry has been speaking at conferences and team-builds for six years on a wide range of topics, blending inspiration and themes of motivation with service-related matters and can be followed on Facebook (Larry O'Sullivan) or Twitter (ClientServiceEx).

About the Book

How Is My Driving? is a wonderful concept that brings the responsibility back to you the reader. By substituting the word "DRIVING" with words like . . . Service, listening, leadership, attitude, relationships, goals or lifestyle, you will be able to map your coordinates on the journey to success in life, sport, sales, service or business.

Lightning Source UK Ltd.
Milton Keynes UK
UKOW04f0414080714

234720UK00002B/49/P